D1314860

ADVANCED ACTING

ADVANCED ACTING
Style, Character, and Performance

ROBERT COHEN
UNIVERSITY OF CALIFORNIA, IRVINE

Boston   Burr Ridge, IL   Dubuque, IA   Madison, WI   New York
San Francisco   St. Louis   Bangkok   Bogotá   Caracas   Kuala Lumpur
Lisbon   London   Madrid   Mexico City   Milan   Montreal   New Delhi
Santiago   Seoul   Singapore   Sydney   Taipei   Toronto

McGraw-Hill Higher Education

*A Division of The **McGraw-Hill** Companies*

1 2 3 4 5 6 7 8 9 0 DOC/DOC 0 9 8 7 6 5 4 3 2 1

Library of Congress Cataloging-in-Publication Data
Cohen, Robert
    Advanced acting : style, character, and performance / Robert Cohen.
      p. cm.
    Includes index.
    ISBN 0-7674-2542-1
    1. Acting. I. Title.

PN2061 .C582 2001
792'.028—dc21

2001030847

Sponsoring editor, Janet M. Beatty; *production editor,* Jennifer Mills; *manuscript editor,* Anne Montague; *design manager and text/cover designer,* Susan Breitbard; *art manager,* Robin Mouat; *manufacturing manager,* Randy Hurst. This text was set in 10/12 Sabon by Thompson Type and printed on 50# Finch Opaque by R. R. Donnelley & Sons Company.

Page 86 George Altman, Ralph Freud, Kenneth Macgowan, and William Melnitz, *Theater Pictorial: A History of World Theater as Recorded in Drawings, Paintings, Engravings, and Photographs.* Copyright © 1953 Regents of the University of California, © renewed 1981 Felicia Gilbert, William Melnitz. Used with permission of the publisher. **Page 115** © Biblioteca Apostolica Vaticana. 3878, 85v. *Phormio* IV, 3. Used with permission. BN lat. 7899, 58v. *Eunuchus* V, 2. Bibliotheque Nationale de France. Used with permission. **Page 173** Brissart and Suave Engraving from *Tartuffe,* The Harvard Theatre Collection, the Houghton Library. Used with permission. **Page 216** Boyd, A. S., "The Battle of the Sexes," *Punch.* Used with permission. **Pages 234–236** Reprinted with permission from *Angels in America, Part One* copyright © 1992, 1993 by Tony Kushner. Published by Theatre Communications Group. **Pages 244–246** From *The Piano Lesson* by August Wilson, copyright © 1988, 1990 by August Wilson. Reprinted by permission of Dutton Signet, a division of Penguin Putnam Inc. **Pages 250–254** Excerpts from *Wit* by Margaret Edson. Copyright © 1993, 1999 by Margaret Edson. Reprinted by permission of Faber and Faber, Inc., an affiliate of Farrar, Straus, and Giroux, LLC.

www.mhhe.com

To my past, present,
and future colleagues
at UC Irvine

⤳ Contents ⤳

⇁ Preface ↼

Nearly twenty years ago, I wrote a textbook called *Acting One,* which was designed to provide the syllabus for a beginning course in stage acting. Such a course, in my view, is best limited to the performance of basic (that is, realistic) stage interactions between relatively ordinary and present-day human characters. I would hope that the work in such a course would be followed by extended acting experience in realistic scenes and plays, both from dramas of our own day and from the classic realistic repertory of modern American and European theatre.

Such roles, however, do not remotely include everything that actors might be called on to do. During the last three millennia, actors have been asked to play gods, demons, animals, ghosts, machines, kings, queens, fairies, elves. They have been challenged to appear as mutes, amputees, transsexuals; to be twice or half their age or more—and sometimes both within the same play; and to play as if differently gendered, or with a sexual orientation different from their own. Actors must be seen to live in centuries different from their own, and to practice professions different from those for which they have been trained; they must credibly seem to worship deities and spirits different from those they personally believe in, and to adhere to philosophies different from those they personally practice; finally, they must perform acts, and feel emotions, radically different from those they have ever done or felt in their entire "real-world" lives.

Moreover, they have to do this in front of public audiences—and often in front of professional critics. And they have to perform unselfconsciously, all the while aware they will probably be judged on their credibility, clarity, charisma, appearance, and seeming appropriateness for their role.

None of this is easy. Moreover, these "extensions" of the actor's own personality have, during many ages in the past, often been considered immoral, if not criminally blasphemous: Actors were excommunicated from the medieval church, and regularly banned from public office or religious burial during many periods up to recent times, for performing roles at a distance from themselves, or from accepted forms of moral behavior. Even today, actors are often identified—usually to their detriment—with roles they perform.

Even internal extensions of the actor's own feelings may be considered grounds for attack. Shakespeare's Hamlet muses that actors pretending to feel things they only imagine are in fact monsters:

Is it not monstrous that this Player here,
But in a fiction, in a dream of passion,
Could force his soul so to his own conceit
That from her working all his visage wanned,
Tears in his eyes, distraction in's aspect . . . ?

Hamlet is speaking of the Player (actor) who has just managed to grow pale and cry real tears during the performance of a mere dramatic monologue; "faking" tears, Hamlet says, may be considered a monstrous act. And when Nick Bottom, in Shakespeare's *A Midsummer Night's Dream*, offers to play a female part in an upcoming play, he says he will do so in "a monstrous little voice." Even today, the actor is often considered a monster—as in the French term, *monstre sacré* (sacred monster), used to designate the most celebrated Parisian stage performers.

But even if it is not monstrous or immoral, extending yourself in any of these directions is certainly difficult, at least if you seek to convey the human authenticity and truthfulness that are the foundations of basic acting—as described in *Acting One* and in virtually all other basic acting texts. Yet making these extensions is important, not only for the enlargement of your own art, but for the creation of truly vital theatre: dramatic works that reach beyond the mundane dimensions of daily life, and carry us—participants and audiences alike—into the realms of history, myth, and archetype.

How to approach these tasks is the basic subject of this book, which might have the subtitle "Extensions of Yourself." And the goal of the book is easily described: to show you how to extend yourself into a different century, a different way of speaking, a different profession, a different age or gender or philosophy or religious belief, *and still be yourself*. Both sides of this "extensions of yourself" challenge are crucial: *extensions* are those aspects of the script that are beyond your current daily behavior and belief, and *yourself* is the core of your being that encompasses your body and soul (or, if you prefer, your physiology and psychology).

When we talk of these extensions, we are really talking of only three things: *style, character*, and *performance*. All three words are well known in theatre discourse; none, however, have an entirely settled definition. And since a great many words, including deliberately vague if provocative aphorisms, such as Georges de Buffon's "Style is the man himself" and Jean Giraudoux's "Without style nothing lives, nothing survives: everything is in *le style*," have been bandied about in efforts to explain them, in this book we will try to use these words in a simple and clear manner; to wit:

Style will refer to the ways a specific *group* of characters—and sometimes *all* the characters—behave and think within a play. The ways they *behave* could include, for example, that they speak in blank verse, or wear Greek tunics, or wail loudly when they grieve, or eat with chopsticks, or kneel to superiors, or fly like angels, or the men show off their calf muscles to attract women, or the women pad their bosoms to attract men. And the ways they *think* could include, for example, that they worship the moon, prize human sacrifice, reward witticisms, love danger, eat snakes, or fear Satan. A play may contain more than one style within it, of course. In *A Midsummer Night's Dream,* there are three groups of characters: aristocratic lovers, lower-class workingmen, and fantastical fairies. Each of these groups comprises a sort of separate world, whose members generally behave and think in similar ways, so that the aggregation of their behaviors and thoughts constitutes an individual *style,* as reflected in their speech, dress, actions, and expressed desires.

Character is the opposite of style. Character is how each *individual* behaves and thinks, as distinct from the general style of his or her group. If, among the lower-class workingmen in *A Midsummer Night's Dream,* Nick Bottom is louder, fatter, and more explosive than the rest, and Snout is meeker, slighter, and more soft-spoken, that is a function of each man's individual character. If, in Act 1, Scene 2 of *Hamlet,* the title character wears basic black while everyone else is wearing colorful royal garb, and his tone is sarcastic while the others express themselves in courtly phrases (and both of these are indicated by the text), these are functions of Hamlet's individual character. And if, in the world of *Henry IV,* Hotspur is contentious and outspoken in a world otherwise favoring diplomacy and tact, that is a function of his character, as it is a function of the characters of Molière's Alceste (in *The Misanthrope*), Ibsen's Hedda Gabler, Shaw's Jack Tanner (in *Man and Superman*), and Tony Kushner's Roy Cohn (in *Angels in America*).

Style makes for environments, character makes for drama, and both emerge only in regard to (and in contrast with) each other. Character is thus a measure of differentness: how each individual stands apart from the surrounding crowd. And plays are great when, among other things, they create rich worlds of collective behavior—which is to say, styles—and striking characters who stand both in and apart from them.

Performance is the way we act in order to inform, or impress our personality upon, persons outside our immediate field of vision, people whom we expect (or hope) to overhear us. It is also how we sometimes act, in certain stylized plays (by Aristophanes, Shakespeare, Molière, and Bertolt Brecht, among many examples), to directly inform, or impress our personality upon, a theatre audience. A *performative act,* or an act of performing, also describes deliberate "theatricalized" behaviors—such as singing, dancing, miming, or adopting a "theatrical voice"—onstage or in everyday life.

Since style is where a dramatic world begins, creating the context for both character differentiation and performative elaboration, this book begins with the subject of style.

A Word About the Book's Structure

This book is divided into two parts. The first is a series of exercises and discussions that lead to an understanding of the fundamental nature of style and character in acting, without regard to identifying any individual style, historical or otherwise. Where dialogue used in this portion comes from dramatic works, and not all does, the works are mostly from early English drama—medieval and Shakespeare—and a little Chekhov. Such exercises (two of which are brief scenes) are self-contained, and no further knowledge of the scripts or the period is required to engage with them.

Part Two is a series of substantial scenes and discussions of those scenes. The dramatic material here is drawn from different eras of Western theatre history, arranged chronologically and represented by specific authors: Greek tragedy (Sophocles), Italian *commedia* (Machiavelli), English Renaissance drama (Shakespeare), French neoclassic comedy (Molière), English Restoration comedy (Behn), European drama of the Belle Epoque (late nineteenth-early twentieth century: Shaw, Chekhov), and contemporary American drama (Tony Kushner, August Wilson, Margaret Edson). These scenes are presented intact (some with slight editing), and then divided into smaller units with specific acting challenges posed. The scenes are broken down and approached in different ways, some emphasizing poetic structure, some subtext, some stylistic movement, and some rhetorical ploys: All of these approaches, of course, would be combined in the ultimate performance of any role, but singling out what I feel is the dominant approach for each scene is, I believe, an effective strategy for teaching—and learning—a great variety of acting methodologies. My suggested way for handling the material in this part would be for an entire class to work on the scenes presented, and then for students to prepare, under the instructor's guidance, other scenes from the same era or genre. Naturally this could take anywhere from a semester to a year or two, depending on how many eras or genres are attempted.

The scenes in Part Two are self-contained, but naturally it would be useful for students to eventually study the entire plays these brief excerpts come from, and to learn about the corresponding historical/literary periods as well.

Discussion accompanies and follows the practical work in every case, but rarely precedes it. It is my view that acting, at least past the beginning level, is best learned by getting it up first, and then shaping it through coaching, discussion, and direction. Theory plays a role too—it can be very helpful in clarifying and regularizing a process—but the process must be learned, or at least acquired, first; virtually all *useful* dramatic theory, from Aristotle and Shakespeare to Stanislavsky and Grotowski, originates in the *experience* of theatre, not from isolated musings on art. Theory is invaluable in helping an actor intensify and expand on the skills acquired in practice, but neither theory nor criticism alone governs or creates artistic work.

Finally, while *Acting One* had virtually no footnotes, *Advanced Acting* has quite a few. This book, unlike its predecessor, deals with dramas from a wide variety of periods, bringing archaic and unfamiliar words, now-obscure references, literary structures, and a few topics of scholarly dispute or qualification into the picture. To keep the text actor-centered and forward-moving, I relegated most of this historical and literary material to footnotes, which can be passed over—at least on an initial reading—by students not wishing to become distracted by secondary threads or qualifications.

A Word About Gender

While each selected scene was initially written to be performed by one man and one woman, all the roles can be played—in acting class, anyway—by students of any gender. But even in professional theatre, cross-gender casting has been, throughout world history, more a rule than an exception, with men playing all the roles in Greek and Roman theatre, much medieval theatre, and all of Shakespeare's, and with both all-male and all-female companies dominating Asian theatre throughout history and even in the present day. Japanese *kabuki,* for example, which began in the seventeenth century with exclusively women actors, has been all-male now for more than three hundred years; traditional forms of Japanese *noh,* Korean *kamyonguk,* and Thai *khon* are also all-male, while the popular Japanese Takarazuka company is all-female, as is the Xiaobaihua Shaoxing Opera of China. A recent spate of cross-gender casting in professional European and American theatres, particularly in classical plays, which has seen female actors scoring tremendous successes in the roles of Hamlet, King Lear, and Richard II, and male actors earning plaudits as Cleopatra, Rosalind, and Lady Bracknell, only extends this history.

A Word About Race

All exercises and scenes may be performed by students of any race. But of course students performing across racial lines must immerse themselves in the culture of the role they are portraying, so that their efforts do not rest on crude stereotyping or caricature. And students coming from the majority culture (in the United States, this basically means Eurocentric, Christian, white cultures) normally have to work harder at this, since persons from minority cultures are usually well informed, from their earliest school years, in the history and values of the cultural majority. But this immersion in another culture is a challenge to embrace, not avoid: Theatre in general, and acting in particular, are exceptionally socializing arts, providing a living, breathing access—one that is not merely intellectual, but emotional and physical as well—to persons across a cultural divide. Acting that crosses these boundaries can bridge the gaps between ourselves and those we think of as "others," and can make the strange familiar. The actor's challenge, then, is to investigate and experience, as deeply as possible, what it would be like to live in the cultures he or she portrays.

This is not easy, of course, and efforts in this direction are often controversial: August Wilson, among others, argues persuasively that his plays should be staged only by African American directors, and presumably would so argue for the actors in black roles to be African Americans as well, but he has so far indicated this only for professional productions, not classroom activities. Naturally African Americans will, in general, have a stronger immediate familiarity with the themes, expressions, and language tropes in an August Wilson play than will others (just as Russians may have a deeper instinct for the subtleties of Anton Chekhov, and gay men the complexities of Tony Kushner), but this book, after all, is about seeking extensions of ourselves—and discovering ourselves—through the process of acting in plays written by people with widely varying histories and cultures. Every exercise and scene in this book, therefore, should be considered a worthy challenge for every student who reads it, as long as the students rigorously investigate the cultural worlds—including such common aspirations, histories, beliefs, and inclinations as may be understood—of the characters they seek to portray.

A Word About Class Procedure

Most of the exercises and all of the scenes in this book require lines to be learned in advance of class. Generally, this means exercise and scene assignments for each lesson should be given at least two days before the lesson takes place, and, for scenes, preferably four to seven days. And since precision of language characterizes all of the dramatic material herein, it is absolutely essential for all lines to be learned *exactly* as they appear on the page. While the actor should be free to improvise movement, gesture, vocal and facial expression, tone of voice, tactics, goals, inner actions, and timing within the moments of performance, the author's words must be delivered as written (or translated). To paraphrase the text, no matter how innocuously, is not merely to diminish (if not destroy) the dramatic impact of the work, it is to avoid the very challenge of this book, which is to channel the actor's own energy and personal sense of truth into an environment unlike our own. To make the present and the immediate real for an audience is a big challenge, but to make the past and the unfamiliar real is an even larger one—and that's the task I want to put to you on these occasions.

A Word About the Drawings and Photographs

This book includes a number of historical drawings and engravings, plus modern costume sketches and production photographs that illustrate visual aspects of plays from different periods. None of these visual materials should be considered "definitive" illustrations of historical production styles, however. The engravings and drawings reflect the styles of their various illustrators and can be presumed to be only impressions of their subjects, particularly the famous *commedia* engravings by Callot and Fossart. Some were clearly executed from imperfect memory (the *Titus Andronicus* drawing of 1594, for example, differs from the script in details of the scene, showing two sons rather than one). Thomas Hope's drawings of Greek and Roman costumes were copied from classic statuary, not from life, and therefore reflect the style of the sculptors; they were first published in 1812. Other historical drawings are at least partly incomplete in at least some details (the Swan Theatre drawing shows spectators on one side of the theatre, and none on the other), or were done by unskilled draftsmen. And, of the modern work, the expert drawings by Iris Brooke are composites of period dress, drawn from her lifetime of research on this subject, rather than specific illustrations of actual garments, while the photographs reflect, as they must, individual productions that present period plays and styles within the artistic conceptions of their modern designers and directors.

Nonetheless, the historical drawings and engravings are the best, and in some cases the only, visual representations we have of earlier eras; most of them are famous among theatre historians. And the more modern drawings and photographs are persuasively suggestive of costumes, stagings, and acting styles that reflect the original theatre aesthetics of the dramatists represented in this book.

Acknowledgments

My thanks extend first to my students at the University of California, Irvine, who, in their work in my classes, have inspired and shaped virtually every sentence in this book. I am also enormously grateful to Libby Appel and Amy Richard at the Oregon Shakespeare Festival, Richard Devin at the Colorado Shakespeare Festival, Cam Harvey and Bruce Lee at the Utah Shakespearean Festival, Cris Gross at the South Coast Repertory Theatre, Bil Schroeder at the Yale Repertory Theatre, Charlotte Webb at the London Performing Arts Library, Scottie Hinkey and Phil Channing at the Irvine Focused Research Program in Medieval Theatre, and, in previous decades, press officers of the American Conservatory Theatre, Stratford Theatre Festival, Royal Shakespeare Company, and Guthrie Theatre for their assistance in selecting and acquiring the production photographs appearing in the following pages.

I am particularly happy to extend my profound personal gratitude, and enduring professional admiration, to the staff of Mayfield Publishing Company—now part of the McGraw-Hill family—who have nurtured this book at every step since its inception, particularly sponsoring editor Jan Beatty, production editor Jen Mills, and manuscript editor Anne Montague.

Finally, I'd particularly like to thank the following reviewers for their thoughtful comments about the manuscript: Ron Gural, Tulane University; Dale McFadden, Indiana University; Tom Mitchell, University of Illinois; and Deana Thomas, University of Louisville.

I

The Exercises

IN PART I, A NUMBER OF EXERCISES AND, TOWARD THE END, THREE short scenes introduce fundamental principles in nine acting lessons that pay increasing attention to style, then character, and finally performance before an audience.

The exercises and short scenes in this section should be considered as simple études, or practice pieces. There is no attempt in Part I (though there is in Part II) to seriously describe, much less analyze, individual plays, historical periods, or styles of individual dramatists.

Consequently, the études in this section can be fully explored simply as what they are and without reference to play or period. In Part I, basic principles of acting in style and character are the entire subject, and discussions of verse structure, period deportment, and the author's larger intent are presented only to the extent they serve to encourage the student to learn these principles from a guided practicing of the étude.

Where dramatic material is used in Part I, it is drawn from two main sources. Medieval theatre is the principal one, chosen because it is the earliest theatre we have in English and because the stories are relatively familiar. Also, this was a theatre written to be performed by amateurs, townspeople who would gather once a year, usually on Corpus Christi Day in the springtime, to re-enact in public the Bible stories with which they and their audience were familiar.

The secondary source for material is Shakespeare, presented in very brief fragments because this is useful in understanding fundamental principles of character. Shakespeare's sense of character, as we shall see much further in Part II, is comprehensive and extraordinary, and a good start may be made in the two-line exchanges and short speech fragments that appear in Part I.

Two scenes in Part I are from Sophocles and Chekhov. They anticipate longer scenes from these authors, and more complex discussions of their styles, in Part II.

Style

◆ EXERCISE 1-1

Baby Talk

Sit in a chair. Imagine that you have suddenly experienced total paralysis from the neck down—you cannot control any part of your body except your head. Terrified that you will soon experience paralysis in these muscles as well, you want to call for help. Fortunately, you have full use of your voice, and there is a cell phone in the room. But there is no one within earshot, and you cannot reach the phone!

Suddenly, you become aware that there is in fact *one* person nearby, a little girl about two or three years old, and, though curious, she is also very frightened. If you could get her to bring you the phone and hold it up to your face, you could probably dial 911 with your tongue.

So speak to the imaginary girl in words of your choosing, asking her to pick up the phone and bring it to you.

But *watch out*! If you appear too frightened, or speak too loudly, or do anything the little girl thinks is scary, she will almost certainly run away and never come back.

In a class situation, everyone in the class should try this exercise, one at a time.

After the first go-round, have one class member play the role of the adult and another—squatting or kneeling—the child, and then switch parts.

Measure your success in this exercise by how tempted the child was to pick up the phone.

How did you approach this problem? Before discussing it, try this variation on the same exercise.

◆ EXERCISE 1-2

Baby Moves

You're in a situation similar to 1-1, but this time you are standing near a wall. You are not paralyzed, but for reasons you don't understand, every time you move more than one foot from the wall you experience incapacitating pain. You need help, fast. And there's the little girl again—with the phone—across from you as before. You cannot go over to her, for you'll collapse in agony if you move away from the wall. Once again, try to talk the imaginary girl into bringing you the phone so you can summon help.

This time you can move, kneel, squat, sit, or lie down—as long as you stay within one foot of the wall.

But *watch out! Don't frighten her!*

In a class situation, everyone may try this, one at a time.

Afterward, try 1-2 as a group exercise: With all the actors having their backs to as many walls of the room as are available, and with an imaginary child located in the middle of the room. Or have one actor, or the instructor, play the role of the child.

Now that you've tried both of these exercises, what did you find yourself doing? Did you use your regular everyday voice in 1-1, or did you use a different one? In 1-2, did you remain standing, or did you lower yourself in some way?

If you are like most people, you began to "baby talk," adopting a baby vocabulary and a baby voice to get what you wanted. Your voice went a bit higher, a bit softer, and a bit more musical; you chose the simplest and friendliest possible words, such as "sweetie" and "honey"; you may even have invented words or expressions, like "tickle tickle!" or "hoppy here!" And you probably changed your facial expression as well, smiling rather than frowning. Maybe you also winked your eyes, waggled your eyebrows, or made funny faces. In general, you probably coaxed rather than explained and did your best to entertain the child while persuading her to do what you needed done.

In Exercise 1-2 you probably did all this but also made yourself appear smaller: perhaps by kneeling, squatting, bending over, or lying down. This would be quite natural, of course—you were trying to make the little girl less afraid and were seeking to win her trust by becoming more little-girl-like yourself.

In all this you were performing "in style," for this is what style is in real life: *a behavior you adopt to assimilate with a particular person or group of persons.* And assimilating with other people is often a useful, even essential, means of getting what you want, or need, from those persons.

Style, therefore, is not so much what you *are* as what you *do* to gain the trust (or the admiration, or the confidence) of other people in a given situation. It is an *action*, not an affectation. It has a purpose and is used to achieve goals. Speaking baby talk in this exercise does not mean that you're a baby, or that you're a smiley, eyebrow-waggling sort of person; it only means that you have *adopted these behaviors* for a few moments in order to get what you need.

What is significant about this? Four things.

1. *Style is not primarily decorative; rather, it is useful—sometimes it is necessary.* Talk baby talk, and a baby will gain confidence and approach you. Talk adult talk, and you'll scare the child away (and, in this exercise, starve—or worse).

2. *Style is not automatic behavior, it is chosen behavior.* You have a choice to make here: talk baby talk and live, or talk adult talk and die. You choose to talk baby talk in order to get help, not because you're a babylike person.

3. *Style is a function of the person addressed as much as or more than the person who is doing the addressing.* You don't talk baby talk because *you're* a baby but because *the person you're talking to* is and will respond to you better if you speak her language.

4. *Style is something we learn, not something we intrinsically are.* Baby talk may not come naturally or immediately to you; you may have to improvise and practice it a bit before you get good at it.

The first style we learn is our family's: how to get along with our parents and how to compete successfully with our siblings. When we go to school, we learn, much more problematically, how to be popular within what we see as a social set: how to fit in, how to wear the right clothes and use the right expressions, how to be "cool."

Of course, we may not succeed in fitting in. This may be the result of external factors—our race, religion, dialect, social or economic class, physical or intellectual defects (as we perceive them)—or it may be because of an incompatibility, as we see it, between our now-ingrained family style and the perceived school style. But if, in our early school years, we fail to fit in to what we see as an "in" group, we then almost certainly seek to fit in to an "out" group; the pressure to conform to *some* group is all but overwhelming in those years.

And later, as we start to differentiate ourselves as adults, we may assimilate the styles of many groups. We develop a way of speaking and a set of behaviors suitable for interacting with family, friends, colleagues, and hoped-for romantic partners. We develop professional styles: the attorney's deferential courtroom decorum ("May it please the court" rather than "Listen here, Judge"), or the new car salesperson's hearty greeting with a right hand briskly extended ("Hey, how ya doin' today?" rather than "May I help you?"). Doctors, morticians, teaching assistants, building contractors, rock singers each have (and continually refine) their distinctive on-the-job styles—which include their dress, posture, grooming, language, and manners of both speaking and moving—and each of these styles might be quite different from the ones they use with friends, family, or romantic partners.

Furthermore, all these styles are essentially *learned;* they are not simply intrinsic to the individual who sports them. No one is born "cool," or a lawyer, or a rock singer; one learns the style of various subcultures or professions—both consciously, by instruction from mentors, and, more commonly, unconsciously, by aping desired role models. We aggressively acquire the styles by which we dress, move, and frame our discourse and appearance.

So, to quote T.S. Eliot, you "prepare a face to meet the faces that you meet." We are *all* stylized actors, and good ones, too.

Mastering a *dramatic* style is roughly the same process—though it ordinarily must happen much more quickly and much more as a result of imagination and research than actual real-world experience.

Think back to Exercises 1-1 and 1-2. Did you feel that some people in the room were better at baby talk than you were? Maybe they have had more little children to practice on over the past few years. Maybe they have bolder imaginations or fewer inhibitions than you do. And maybe you were too worried about looking foolish, or about showing your classmates a less serious side of yourself or your personality. All of these factors are important in the art of developing an acting style: the *experience* to prepare you for employing a style easily and with confidence, the *imagination* to allow you to be creative (and in this case infectious) in languages and manners not normally your own, and the *playfulness* that permits you to express yourself fully, enthusiastically, and (by common standards) outrageously. No one can master style without taking the chance of looking like a fool.

Master these exercises, and you have taken the first—but giant—step toward playing in style. You have left your own style behind and adopted another, not because you found it prettier or cleverer (or just because you were told to) but because you found it *useful*.

Summary

Style is not only something one performs in the theatre, it is something we all do in life; it is a behavior we purposefully adopt to address different sorts of people. Style is, therefore, something we do, not something we are: It is something we can both learn and choose as suits our purposes.

Caveat: We mustn't ignore the fact that in real life, styles originally employed for a purpose may simply become habitual, in which cases they become hollow. A child continually rewarded by indulgent parents for "cute" baby talk may continue to employ infantile speech well into adolescence, or even into adult life. While this may prove occasionally appealing (it was a trademark of Marilyn Monroe and has become a hallmark of the "bimbo" stereotype), it more often is seen as irritating. This sort of hollow style may become an aspect of character, as we shall see in a later chapter, but it is not a useful approach to acting in style.

LESSON

2

Stylized Exchanges

♦ EXERCISE 2-1

Pig Latin

With a partner, memorize the following "scene." Make up your own situation (for example: B has asked her roommate A to turn off the music so she can study, while A has just come to the best part of the CD and wants to hear it to the end), and play the scene as truthfully as possible.

A: No.

B: Yes.

A: No!

B: Yes!

A: NO!

B: YES!

We will assume that the argument naturally escalates in intensity—in volume as well as in precision—as it goes through the three paired exchanges, as indicated by the use of exclamation points and capital letters.

Now, assume that your partner does not speak English, only pig Latin! *You* can speak either language, but in order for your partner to understand you, you must speak in his or her language.

Now, employing the same situation, play the scene just as truthfully as you did before—if not more so. But speak in pig Latin instead of English so that you can be understood. (Your partner follows the identical instructions.) Thus:

A: Ohnay.

B: Essyay.

A: Ohnay!

B: Essyay!

A: OHNAY!

B: ESSYAY!

One might expect that this dialog escalates in intensity as well—even in nonsense syllables!

Do you feel a bit silly doing this? That wouldn't be surprising—but if you do, it's only because you're not yet acting truthfully. Do the scene again, and do it *entirely seriously; you really* want her to turn off the music, or, in the other part, you really want to hear to the end of the CD, but can only make her understand this by speaking pig Latin to her.

What you and your partner are doing in this exercise is, just as in Lesson 1, *creating a style.* You are acting truthfully—trying to achieve a real goal with and through another person—and you are wholly "in the moment" as you perform this, but you are speaking in an invented, artificial language, not the one you use in your daily life. And that is what acting style is all about.

So do whatever you can, short of physical contact, to get what you want in this exchange. (Understand that removing physical contact from the list of possibilities allows you and your partner to throw everything else you've got—voice, gesture, and emotion—into the exercise without having to be concerned with causing or receiving physical harm. So by avoiding the physical contact, and knowing your partner will as well, you can really let yourselves go with everything else in your behavioral repertoire!)

Repeat the exchange, but make up a more intense argument this time. Suppose you are each trying to get your hands on the lottery ticket you believe to be the million-dollar winner. Or to be the one let into an invitation-only audition for an upcoming feature film. Repeat two or three times, letting the argument escalate further each time.

◆ E X E R C I S E 2-2

Speaking in (Foreign) Tongues

Now vary the exercise by using *real* languages; for example:

Spanish (or Italian)

A: No.

B: Si. *(pronounced "see")*

A: No!

B: Si!

A: NO!

B: SI!

German

A: Nein. *(pronounced "nine")*

B: Ja. *(pronounced "ya")*

A: Nein!

B: Ja!

A: NEIN!

B: JA!

Russian

A: Nyet. *(pronounced "nee-YET")*

B: Da. *(pronounced "da")*

A: Nyet!

B: Da!

A: NYET!

B: DA!

French

A: Non. *(pronounced something like "nawhh")*

B: Oui. *(pronounced something like "weehh")*

A: Non!

B: Oui!

A: NON!

B: OUI!

Hungarian

A: Nem. *(pronounced "nehm")*

B: Igen. *(pronounced "EE-gehn")*

A: Nem!

B: Igen!

A: NEM!

B: IGEN!

Japanese

A: Hai *(pronounced "HAH-ee")*

B: Ie. *(pronounced "ee-EH")*

A: Hai!

B: Ie!

A: HAI!

B: IE!

Turkish

A: Evet. *(pronounced "eh-vet")*

B: Hayir. *(pronounced "hah-yurh")*

A: Evet!

B: Hayir!

A: EVET!

B: HAYIR!

If you can, get someone in your group who speaks the language—or even better, a native speaker—to help you with the exact pronunciation, and try to use this as precisely as you can.

Remember your acting assumption: that *you* speak both English and the second language with equal fluency, but *the person you are speaking to* speaks only the second language. You are not using the second language in order to be pretty, or fancy, or clever, or "dramatic," but only to achieve your goal: to get the other person out of the room—or whatever other goal your situation creates for you.

Again, with this exercise you are creating a style, in this case not with an artificial language but a real one. And you are speaking it not because you *want* to, but because you *have* to: because it's the only way you can communicate effectively.

Once again, we see that style is not decoration or elaboration or aesthetically "heightened language"; it is, rather, a communication born out of necessity. We adopt "stylized" speech, therefore, for only one reason: to be understood. Thus, in these cases, stylized speech is also a *winning strategy.*

Style, of course, is not merely a matter of language—baby talk, pig Latin, or foreign tongues—but of a wide range of vocal, physical, emotional, and associational factors, including body language, gesture, proxemics (how close you get to people), vocal tone, and facial expressions. Indeed, without thinking about it, you and your partner probably introduced some of these stylistic factors into your performance of the Spanish, German, Russian, French, Hungarian, Japanese, and Turkish versions of these exercises, just from whatever unconscious associations with these cultures you may have developed over the years. It is almost automatic, for example, for some people to become a little more bombastic when speaking German, or more unctuous when speaking French, or more whimsical (particularly after watching Roberto Benigni!) when speaking Italian—even if they don't know half a dozen words of those languages. That these characteristics often seem to be stereotypes doesn't mean natives don't exhibit them, and foreigners often pick them up when they are immersed in the culture where they're commonly practiced.

Now repeat Exercise 2-2 in pig Latin. Do you find that you have added a little body language and vocal expression to this as well—something more than you did when you just exchanged "yes" and "no" in English? Perhaps these additions come from your early associations of pig Latin: speaking it in elementary school, for example, or speaking it to your little sister, or to children in the neighborhood. Something in the language kicks off a slightly different "you" from the one you "play" at other times. Or perhaps it is just an extra oomph you use to make yourself understood in a second language.

Or, even more interesting, perhaps you are unconsciously trying to beat your acting partner (and, in this case, your adversary—the one you want to win your goal from) by *speaking pig Latin better* and more forcefully than he or she does.

The fact is that speaking to achieve a goal carries with it the desire not merely to adopt a style but to *excel* at it. You not only want to speak pig Latin, you want to speak *great* pig Latin (or great Spanish, German, Russian,

French, Hungarian, Japanese, or Turkish), even if it's your second or third language. You want to speak great pig Latin not because it's an inherently better language than English but simply because you want to beat your opponent—through your greater eloquence and intimidating forcefulness. And in order to be forceful, to be compelling, to be eloquent, you must master the style that the situation requires.

In speaking pig Latin, of course, you are creating a wholly *literary* (which is to say imaginary) style. For unlike baby talk, French, or German, pig Latin is not and has never been a natural spoken language anywhere in the world. Rather, it is a way of speaking that has been consciously made up by human beings; it is contrived, just like the more poetic and theatrical formulations of blank verse, rhyming couplets, and Italian sonnets.

But all styles are literary—and in part imaginary, and in part interpretive. The "German style," or the "French style," as seen, say, by an American, describes a set of observed behaviors as well as a set of generalized perceptions of those behaviors. This is because we observe all behaviors through our own filters of interpretation, and sometimes even our prejudices. Say "Zulu style" to an American white supremacist and you will provoke a radically different image than you would if speaking to a black South African. And a true Zulu would probably have little idea of what you mean: We rarely think of the behavior of our own group as a "style," any more than we think of our own way of speaking as an "accent"—although we know others may so call it. (In our unconscious minds, Americans speak "normally"; it's the English and Scots and Australians who have "accents." And we believe that we *behave* "normally" as well—it's in those *other* countries where folks drive on the "wrong" side of the road.)

Thus style in speaking is entirely natural to the person who has grown up with it. And if you grew up speaking pig Latin, it would be natural to you as well. By making pig Latin the only way to communicate, as in Exercise 2-1, you are making style real for yourself; it becomes the only way you can achieve your goal, and, therefore, you must really employ it. And get good at it. And, indeed, *excel* at it.

♦ E X E R C I S E 2-3

Contemporary Greetings

With a partner, come together as if with a friend on the street and shake hands, saying:

A: Hey, how ya doin'?

B: Fine, how're you?

How did you shake hands? In the conventional fashion, with hands extended thumbs-up, straight from the body's midsection? Or the 1960s "hippie shake," with hands extended fingers-up, grasping around your partner's thumb? Or the athlete's high-five slap? And, if conventional, was your (or your partner's) handshake firm, like a politician's, or painfully aggressive, like an enraged rival's, or limp, like a reluctant accomplice's? And is it correct to associate personality traits with different styles of handshake?

With the same or another partner, cast yourselves as a doctor and a patient. Come together as if in the doctor's office and shake hands, saying (and using your partner's actual name):

PATIENT: Good morning, Doctor [last name].

DOCTOR: Good to see you, [first name].

Or as a student and professor, saying:

STUDENT: Professor [last name]!

PROFESSOR: [first name]?

Or as a cheerleader and a basketball player, saying:

CHEERLEADER: Great game, [first name].

PLAYER: Thanks, [first name].

Make up other greetings appropriate to persons known to you and your partner, and rehearse these with appropriate handshakes and language.

Varied Salutations

But of course there are dozens of different kinds of greetings. Besides the conventional and thumb-lock handshakes and the high-five, there are the knuckle-rap, the cheek kiss, the air kiss, the bear hug, the sudden ("surprised") head-cock and grin, and the outstretched, splayed arms.

Handshakes of any sort, as a common form of greeting, date only to the first part of the nineteenth century—and even then only in Western, or Westernized, cultures.*

---

* Desmond Morris, *Bodytalk: A World Guide to Gestures* (Jonathan Cape, 1994), p. 124. While most greetings today propose little more than pleasure at meeting others, there are times we see the ancient roots of such practices of

What is common to all eras, however, are conventionalized greetings, which we may call salutations. People have "saluted" each other in some recognized fashion since the beginning of human civilization. And "recognized fashion" is a vital ingredient of this salutation because it assures that the greetee will recognize that the greeter's intentions are, at minimum, peaceful. The modern handshake, for example, evolved from the greeter's desire to show that his fighting (right) hand was not holding a dagger; it was, therefore, not merely a courteous gesture but a survival tactic.

Beyond survival, greetings are used to show (or perhaps to feign) respect, appreciation, or subservience. Lowering the body implies fealty, a medieval term acknowledging the obedience required of those of lower social rank. In a society that believed in the divine right of kings, such self-lowering even suggests a greater distance from God. And the actor's deep bow or curtsy at play's end originally signaled, to a royal patron, "If I failed to amuse you, please feel free to chop off my head immediately!"

And such salutations vary enormously by culture and period. In Japan, for example, the handshake is never employed (except in Western or international business contexts); rather, the bow is universal, with the depth of the bow dependent on the status of its user. In China, the *kowtow*—a full-body prostration—was current through many dynasties, and in Ottoman cultures a nine-point kneel (feet, knees, elbows, hands, forehead touching the ground) was mandatory before the sultan and remains the primary submissive pose during Islamic prayer. Kisses are common in American and European society, often between men and women, or women and women, and sometimes, particularly on the European continent, between men and men. In America and England, this is usually a peck on the cheek, or an "air kiss" that doesn't actually touch flesh to flesh, while in France, kisses on both cheeks are mandatory, and in Poland, three kisses—first on one cheek, then the other, then the first again—are routinely expected, particularly between men who adhere to this custom. And in military cultures around the world, a variety of crisp salutes serve the purposes of both greeting and rank recognition.

This great variety of greetings existed as well in former times. There is, therefore, no single "Elizabethan bow" or "Restoration curtsy" but, rather,

---

greeting and obeisance. The handclasps between Menachem Begin and Anwar Sadat in 1979, and Yitzak Rabin and Yassar Arafat in 1993, both brokered by U.S. presidents during formal ceremonies, were long-sought and hard-won representations of peace efforts between bitter Middle Eastern enemies; in neither case was anyone certain until the last second if the rival leaders would actually press flesh. And the kneeling and curtsying (sometimes resisted) of actors and state officers before the English queen at public receptions or knighting ceremonies is a reminder of the social authority—at least symbolic— retained by hereditary monarchs in class-conscious societies.

A Renaissance bow   Wearing his traditional multicolored costume and black eye-mask, Arlecchino, a rascally character from the Italian *commedia dell'arte*, takes a bow in the sixteenth century. Arlecchino's right hand proffers his hat, while his left hand holds at the ready a traditional "slapstick"—a trick baton that makes a comically loud slapping sound when hitting a victim on the buttocks.

a wide menu of dips and bobs that have been used in every period and every culture. Few of these are standardized by formal law, and all would have varied according to the personality and athleticism of the individuals employing them; nonetheless, there are some basic patterns of such salutations that are characteristic of most periods. Some of these are outlined and described in the box below and elsewhere in this book.*

 ## MEDIEVAL AND ELIZABETHAN SALUTATIONS

There are hundreds of different salutations and acknowledgments of deference known to have existed during the late medieval and succeeding Elizabethan and Jacobean eras.

Kneeling, ordinarily on one knee, was universal for servants before their masters or superiors. And petitioners to royalty or high officers (as well as convicted criminals or captured warriors) knelt on both knees: "Lend me your knees," says the kneeling Mariana, employing the plural, to Isabella in Shakespeare's *Measure for Measure* when urging her friend to kneel beside her before the duke. A 1594 drawing of a production of *Titus Andronicus* shows Tamara and two of her captured sons down on both knees before the victorious Titus.

While modern handshake didn't exist in these times, most researchers believe that military men, from the Roman era forward, grasped each other right hand to right wrist, with the greeter's left hand following to grasp the other's left forearm just below the elbow, thereby signaling that neither had warlike intentions.

Bowing and curtsying were the standard greetings and shows of deference among most cultured and courtly persons (those about whom most plays of the time were written) in this period. These salutations could be anything from a simple bending of the knees and tipping of the head, for persons of either sex, to the more elaborate bows (for men) and curtsies (for women) described below. Mastering these salutations is one of the basic tasks of actors in any traditionally staged play of medieval or Shakespearean times.

Male Bows

By a courtier: With the feet comfortably apart and at right angles or a bit more (the dancer's fourth position), the left leg is drawn directly

---

* Much more can be found on this subject in Isabel Chisman and Hester E. Raven-Hart, *Manners and Movements in Costume Plays* (Kenyon-Deane, 1934), and Bari Rolfe, *Movement for Period Plays* (Personabooks, 1985).

Kneeling in supplication   The crowned Queen Tamara kneels before the victorious Titus, begging him to spare her two sons—also kneeling—in what is believed to be the only existing sketch of an actual Shakespearean performance (of *Titus Andronicus*) during the dramatist's lifetime. Titus, wearing somewhat of a mini-toga, is backed by two guards dressed in standard Elizabethan attire and wielding Elizabethan halberds, indicating that stage props and costuming in Shakespeare's day did not rigidly adhere to historical consistency. Aaron the Moor is shown on the right, delivering the victims. From a manuscript of c. 1594.

back in a sweeping motion, with the left foot landing anywhere from fifteen to twenty-four inches directly behind the right one. At the same time, the upper body angles forward, while the right hand sweeps upward in a large circle, removing the hat and sweeping it toward the person greeted, before circling back down to a resting place at the front of the left hip, with the hat dangling below, its inner lining facing the body. The left hand, meanwhile, rests on the back of the left hip (at the sword hilt) or is swept to that position by a more modest circle in the opposite direction of the right hand—a move helpful for balance.

The same bow may be used by a hatless courtier, but the right hand sweeps by the person greeted in a gesture of pleasantry before landing, palm inward, on the left hipbone, sometimes joining the left hand in a tight clasp.

By a country servant: A quick bend of both knees and a downward tip of the head, while the right hand removes the cap and brings it to the chest, where it is held by both hands. (The hatless servant may keep the hands to the sides or bring them to the chest.)

(continued)

(continued)

A messenger's obeisance   A messenger or servant bows before two ladies, one standing and one seated, in a detail of the famous drawing of London's Swan Theatre, originally made about 1596 by one Johannes de Witt and subsequently redrawn by one of his friends. While the drawing is best known for its uniquely detailed view of a Shakespearean-era theatre interior, it also shows three actors of that time in what appears to be a realistic depiction of a stage action, either in performance or dress rehearsal.

By a court messenger or officious servant: The courtier's bow, but much deeper and often reversed. In the famous Johannes de Witt drawing dating from 1596 of what seems to be a rehearsal, or perhaps a performance, in London's Swan Theatre, a servant, holding an angled staff in his left hand, is shown executing such a bow.

Rising from all such bows is basically a matter of simply reversing the movements.

Whereas the petitioner "lends a knee" in ancient parlance, the bow, in an Elizabethan court or manor, was called "making a leg," and the point of making an especially good leg was to show off the fine flex and contour of one's calf, as well as the expensive silk hose dressing it. That is why the feet are always turned out (at approximately right angles) in such bows. In addition, a confident pursed smile, cock of the head, and gaze of the eye, along with the vigor and sprightliness of the attack and the graceful coordination of all the movements into a single, seemingly effortless ballet, were required attributes of a dazzling courtier.

Female Curtsies

The woman's curtsy begins with one foot swept directly behind and to right angles to the other, with the swept-back heel landing directly behind and at right angles to the forward instep (the dancer's "open third" position). Both knees are then bent simultaneously, and the upper body slightly inclined forward, with the hands brought demurely together below the belly button, palms and (modestly curled) fingers facing inward.

For a more ostentatious curtsy, as to royalty, the same basic foot movement is used, but it ends with the legs further apart and further crossed (the left foot to the right of the right one); then, the body's weight is placed solidly on the back foot, and the woman sinks to a near-seated position, with the forward thigh "sitting" on the back one. This can go as deeply as can be managed, depending on the dress, the status of the person being curtsied to, and (very important) the woman's athleticism. With this curtsy, the arms may be stretched outward and may in fact hold the skirt, raising it gracefully an inch or two as the body sinks. (Be sure, in practicing this curtsy, that you can also rise to your feet when it concludes!)

A woman's curtsy in this and most other periods is generally much less assertive than the male bow (the word *curtsy* is simply a variant of *courtesy*), and the legs, completely hidden by the skirt, cannot even be seen. A demure expression, with eyes down and head inclined gracefully to the side, completes the submissive salutation. Needless to say, if you are playing an assertive woman (such as Kate in *The Taming of the Shrew,* prior to the final scene), you will probably want to parody or ridicule this curtsy, not merely employ it directly, and even in the last scene, where you "place your hand beneath your husband's foot," most actors and directors today will find movements to make a reverse commentary on this relic of medieval female submission. In a celebrated American Conservatory Theatre production in the 1960s, Kate curtsied and placed her hand beneath Petruchio's foot—and then, rising briskly without releasing his foot, upended him into a hilarious backward flip. Actors and directors ever since have sought to find new variations on this feminist-savvy theme.

◆ EXERCISE 2-4

Making Elizabethan Greetings

Learn bows (for men) or curtsies (for women); practice them with one or more partners. Then rehearse and play one or more of the following short greetings with a partner, varying the depth of your bow or curtsy with the perceived rank of your partner and the particular impression you want to convey to him or her. Men will want to get a floppy hat, and perhaps a "sword" to slip into a belt loop for this exercise; women might like to wear a long rehearsal skirt.

1.   HASTINGS: Good time of day unto my gracious lord!

     RICHARD: As much unto my good Lord Chamberlain!

Richard III Act 1, Scene 1

(Richard, the duke of Gloucester, angling to become king, has helped rescue Lord Chamberlain Hastings from prison—though he will later, as Richard III, have him executed.)

2.   DON JOHN: My lord and brother, God save you!

     DON PEDRO: Good den,° brother.   °*afternoon*

Much Ado About Nothing Act 3, Scene 2

(Though half-brothers, they are barely speaking to each other, as Don John, a bastard, is consumed with envy of his brother's higher rank and fortune.)

3.   TIMON: I am joyful of your sights. Most welcome, sir! [. . .]

     ALCIBIADES: Sir, you have saved my longing, and I feed
          Most hungerly on your sight.

     TIMON: Right welcome, sir!

Timon of Athens Act 1, Scene 1

(Timon, a rich man, welcomes General Alcibiades and his entourage to a party at his home; Alcibiades responds with an even more flowery greeting. "Saved my longing" means "Your appearance has saved me the anguish of missing your company." The overly effusive greetings between these two men become pivotal to the play's major action when, in a later act, both become embittered outcasts from their country.)

4.   FIRST LORD: The good time of day to you, sir.

     SECOND LORD: I also wish it to you.

Timon of Athens Act 3, Scene 6

(Two nobles meet in the Athenian equivalent of a Senate.)

5.   DUKE: Good morning to you, fair and gracious daughter.

     ISABELLA: The better, given me by so holy a man.

Measure for Measure Act 4, Scene 3

(Vincentio, the duke of Vienna, posing as a Franciscan friar, meets Isabella, a nun-in-training. The two characters, while restrained by their religious garb, are also quite possibly in love, thus making every action inwardly complex.)

6.   OTHELLO: O my fair warrior!

DESDEMONA: My dear Othello!

Othello Act 2, Scene 1

(A great general greets his new bride shortly after she debarks from a sea voyage on which they have had to travel separately.)

7.   GREMIO: Good morrow, neighbor Baptista.

BAPTISTA: Good morrow, neighbor Gremio.

The Taming of the Shrew Act 2, Scene 1

(Two older gentlemen meet in Padua; they are wary of each other because Gremio wants to marry Baptista's daughter—and Baptista has imposed stringent conditions.)

8.   KING OF NAVARRE: Fair Princess, welcome to the court of Navarre.

PRINCESS OF FRANCE: "Fair" I give you back again, and "welcome" I have not yet.

Love's Labor's Lost Act 2, Scene 2

(The characters, both royal, are in love but playfully quarreling. The princess may well not respond to the king's bow, since she doesn't accept his greeting. Or she may curtsy mockingly, with obvious exaggeration, to emphasize her repudiation of his welcome.)

9.   KING LEAR: Good morrow to you both.

CORNWALL: Hail to your Grace!

King Lear Act 2, Scene 4

(The king, having abdicated, is greeting his daughter Regan and her husband Cornwall, to whom he has given half his kingdom; he has, however, been profoundly disappointed with their loyalty since that event. They, correspondingly, feel it is he who has not lived up to his promise. Regan may also appear in this greeting, saying Cornwall's line simultaneously with him.)

10.   HERO: Good morrow, coz.

BEATRICE: Good morrow, sweet Hero.

Much Ado About Nothing Act 3, Scene 4

(Two female cousins, and best of friends, meet; *coz* is an affectionate nickname for *cousin* and can even be used between nonrelatives. No curtsy would be employed at this point, since the women are simply best friends, and nonroyal, so an appropriate Elizabethan embrace must be invented.)

11.   SIR TOBY: 'Save you, gentleman.

   VIOLA: And you, sir.

Twelfth Night Act 3, Scene 1

(Sir Toby, dissolute uncle of the rich homeowner Olivia, welcomes Viola, who is in man's disguise, to Olivia's home. In this greeting, Toby has to mask his inebriation, while Viola has to mask her femininity.)

12.   WILLIAM: Good ev'n, Audrey.

   AUDREY: God ye good ev'n, William.

As You Like It Act 5, Scene 1

(Young country people once in love. Now, however, with aristocrats visiting nearby, Audrey's eyes have opened to new possibilities, including the witty court jester, Touchstone, who is wooing her—and stands beside her during this exchange. William must recapture Audrey's love without embarrassing himself in front of the court-savvy Touchstone; Audrey must be polite to her ex-boyfriend without dismaying her new romantic interest.)

13.   THIRD CITIZEN: Neighbors, God speed!

   FIRST CITIZEN: Give you good morrow, sir.

Richard III Act 2, Scene 3

(Citizens meet hurriedly in the street just after hearing about the king's death and the accession of a new king. They need information fast and, as these are dangerous times, don't want to reveal their own political leanings.)

14.   PISTOL: God save you, Sir John!

   FALSTAFF: Welcome, ancient Pistol.

Henry IV, Part II Act 2, Scene 4

(In a tavern, these heavy drinkers and carousers meet again, each trying to impress their fellow barflies with their bravado and good fellowship.)

15.   NURSE: God ye good morrow, gentlemen.

   MERCUTIO: God ye good den, fair gentlewoman.

Romeo and Juliet Act 2, Scene 4

(Juliet's nurse, looking for Romeo, meets him on a street in Verona. But it is Romeo's friend Mercutio who replies, jesting—by calling her a gentlewoman, which she is not, being of humble birth—at the nurse's mistaking of afternoon for morning.)

16.   MISTRESS QUICKLY: Give your worship good morrow.

FALSTAFF: Good morrow, goodwife.

MISTRESS QUICKLY: Not so, an't° please your worship.   °*if it*

FALSTAFF: Good maid, then.

The Merry Wives of Windsor Act 2, Scene 2

(Mistress Quickly mockingly inflates Falstaff's title to "your worship." Falstaff mocks Quickly's marital/sexual status—she is an unmarried barkeep with a reputation for promiscuity. She agrees, making the point to all around them that Falstaff hasn't married her yet. Falstaff mocks her as a "good maid"—a virgin, which, since she is not one, becomes his rationalization for not marrying her.)

◆ EXERCISE 2-5

Ad-libbing Elizabethan Greetings

Make up some paper crowns, and bring in hats, rehearsal skirts, and walking sticks and staffs; distribute around the class so that each participant fashions a character of obvious status (such as royal, noble, peasant). Moving about the room, with classmates, engage in impromptu greetings with people of different ranks, using the appropriate physical greeting and any number of the lines below, all drawn from Shakespeare's plays. Your goal, in every case, is *at minimum* to convince the person you're addressing that you are comfortable in your own skin, conversant with the appropriate behaviors of your society, and *a person worth knowing better*. Do it! And keep doing it until you feel good doing it. Until you *enjoy* doing it!

All hail, my lords!

All health unto my gracious sovereign!

All health, my sovereign lord!

Brother, good day.

Brother, good night.

Fair sir!

Faith, sir, God save you!

Gentleman, God save thee!

God give you good morrow, master Parson.

God make your Majesty joyful, as you have been!

God save you gentlemen!

God save you, Madam!

God save you, sir!

'Save thee, Curan.

'Save your honor!

God speed fair Helena!

Good dawning to thee, friend.

Good day and happiness, dear Rosalind!

Good day at once!

Good day, my lord!

Good day, sir.

Good even, Varro.

Good morrow and God save your Majesty!

Good morrow to your worship.

Good morrow, fair ones!

Good morrow, fairest.

Good morrow, gallants.

Good morrow, gentle mistress.

Good morrow, good Sir Hugh.

Good morrow, ladies.

Good morrow, masters.

Good morrow, noble sir.

Good Signior Angelo.

Good sir!

Good time of day unto your royal Grace!

Hail to your lordship!

Hail, noble Prince!

Hail, Virgin!

Hail, you anointed deputies of heaven!

Happily met, my lady and my wife!

Happy return be to your royal grace!

How does my good Lord Hamlet?

How now, brother Edmond.

How now, spirit?

How now, fair maid?

How now, good fellow!

How now, how now?

How now, master Parson?

How now, my hardy, stout, resolvèd mates!

How now, my Lord of Worcester?

How now, my noble lord?

How now, Shylock?

How now, Signior Launce?

How now, sir?

Long live Lord Titus, my beloved brother.

Many good morrows to my noble lord!

Many good morrows to your Majesty!

My cousin Vernon, welcome, by my soul!

My excellent good friends! How dost thou?

My gracious lords.

My gracious prince, and honorable peers.

My gracious sovereign.

My honor'd lord!

My honorable lords, health to you all!

My ladies both, good day to you.

My lord!

My lovely Aaron.

My most dear lord!

My noble lords and cousins all, good morrow.

My very worthy cousin, fairly met!

O my good lords.

O thou good Kent.

O worthiest cousin!

Our old and faithful friend, we are glad to see you.

Sir Proteus! 'save you!

Sir Toby Belch! How now, Sir Toby Belch!

Welcome hither!

Welcome, dear Proteus!

Welcome, dear Rosencrantz and Guildenstern!

Welcome, gentlemen!

Welcome, good Messala.

Welcome, Harry!

Welcome, my good friends!

Welcome, pure wit.

Welcome, sweet Prince!

Well be with you, gentlemen!

Well met, honest gentlemen.

Well met, Mistress Page.

Why, how now, Dromio!

◆ EXERCISE 2-6

Ad-libbing Elizabethan Insults

Just so we don't get too exclusively touchy-feely in these greetings, let's re-peat Exercise 2-5, but instead of responding with a greeting, respond with your choice of Shakespearean insults. Really try to frighten your partner! Get him or her to fear crossing you again. Be really rude with any of the following:

A plague on thee!

A pox o' your throats!

Beetle-headed, flap-ear'd knave!

Blasts and fogs upon thee!

Comb your noddle with a three-legg'd stool.

Foul wrinkled witch!

Go thou and fill another room in hell.

Go, ye giddy goose!

Gross lout!

Hence, rotten thing!

Idol of idiot-worshippers.

Out, dog!

Pernicious blood-sucker!

Take thy face hence!

Thou art a boil, a plague-sore, an embossed carbuncle!

Thou art a wickedness!

Thou disease of a friend!

Thou full dish of fool!

Thou mongrel, beef-witted lord!

Thou rag of honor!

Vanish like hailstones; go!

Vengeance rot you all!

Were I like thee I'd throw away myself.

You mad-headed ape!

Your misery increase with your age!

◆ EXERCISE 2-7

Hamlet's Greeting to the Players

Learn and play Hamlet's very special greeting to the Players in Act 2 of *Hamlet*. Shakespeare never wrote another greeting like this one; Hamlet's words are profoundly simple, yet almost clumsy: He uses *well* and *welcome* no less than four times, and *friend/friends* twice, overdoing his greeting like Timon in Exercise 2-4, but with greater sincerity of friendship—as perhaps befits a prince who believes himself to be living in a prison, betrayed by those closest to him.

Greeting them with Hamlet's line, see if you can convince the Players of your profound joy at their arrival—and make them want to help you (even if it means defying the king).

HAMLET: You are welcome, masters, welcome all. I am glad to see thee well. Welcome, good friends. O, old friend!

Summary

Style—in life as well as in the theatre—describes real, not fake, behavior: that which is purposeful and not just showy. Both foreign languages and older versions of our own are—and must appear— as real to their speakers as ours is to us and our friends; likewise, foreign and ancient gestures, such as bows and curtsies, must seem to emanate from a desire to please, impress, and succeed—not merely to imitate. Even wholly imaginary or manufactured languages, such as pig Latin, must be played, in acting, as if your life depended on it—which, by the way, it *could*.

LESSON

3

Roses Are Red

Rhyme and Verse

We sometimes think of verse drama as something of a curiosity—a relatively minor form of theatre popular in "olden times." This perception is quite inaccurate: Verse has actually been the *major* form of dramatic language throughout history, including, in much of the world, the present day. All ancient drama, from the Egyptian to the Greek to the Roman, was in verse (often sung or chanted), often in rhyme as well, as was most medieval, Renaissance, and later European drama, including most of Shakespeare, Racine, Molière, Goethe, Calderón, and almost all their contemporaries, right up to the eighteenth century. Virtually every traditional Asian and African drama, from ancient to modern, is in verse and is quite often sung or chanted. And a significant proportion of modern European and American theatre contains verse or song or both, at least after Bertolt Brecht. Finally, musical theatre, often regarded as America's greatest contribution to drama, and increasingly popular worldwide today, is largely in (sung) verse.

Indeed, it is prose drama that is, historically at least, the curiosity, having appeared just occasionally from the Renaissance on, and dominating drama only during the past two centuries—and then only in the West.

But *playing* verse drama nonetheless seems foreign to American actors, generally raised on the notion (fostered by television and film as much as by the theatre) that acting should be "true to life." Since verse is artificially contrived, does it follow that verse acting must be artificial?

The answer is emphatically "No!"

Verse simply indicates a dramatic framework, like a proscenium (or an audience) surrounding a stage, or like the houselights going down at the start of the performance. It says "We're playing now," but it doesn't make the playing any less emotionally vivid or situationally intense. Indeed, emotions and situations can be made *more* dramatically powerful by the skillful use of verse, and rhyme as well, by both playwright and performer.

◆ EXERCISE 3-1

Roses Are Red

With a partner, quickly learn the following dialog:

A: Roses are red.

B: Violets are blue.

A: I'd like some bread.

B: I'd like some too!

Now imagine that you and your partner are playing two people sitting down at a coffee shop for lunch. Without discussing it beforehand, and without agreeing on any specific "situation" between the two of you, simply play the dialog as an ice-breaking conversation, looking each other in the eye most of the time and miming any props you may wish to introduce.

Now play it again, inventing a specific goal for your character: perhaps to set the stage to invite your partner to join your club, or to go to a party later that evening, or to leave the table so someone else can join you.

This "scene" is a bit of sheer nonsense, of course, but it introduces, at a very simple level, the near-magical charm of verse. For in playing the scene, which is virtually empty of practical content, a sort of relationship will probably emerge between you and your acting partner: possibly seductive, possibly argumentative or competitive, and almost surely probing playfully into your partner's mind and feelings. It is hard to play this scene without one or both partners cracking a smile at some point.

This is the power—and attraction—of verse. Verse is not spontaneous chatter; it is not ordinary daily discourse. Rather, it is a deliberately *contrived* language: thought-out, crafted, and controlled. To speak in verse is to announce that you have *designed the shape* of what you want to say and that you have chosen your words for their sounds as well as for their meanings. And for persons to *exchange* lines with each other in verse means that they seek to match each other in sharing sounds as well as ideas.

Two people exchanging lines with each other in the *same verse pattern* suggests they have, or want to have and, more important, want to *perform,* some sort of interpersonal relationship: either one-on-one (for example, a romantic relationship, a business relationship) or as part of a larger "world" that may include, in addition to style of language, mutual overarching interests and behavioral styles. So when two characters exchange lines in the "roses are red" pattern (or any other pattern), they are making an effort to "speak the same language," or to "be on the same page" with each other, regardless of the specific literal meaning of the lines.

The "roses are red" verse, of course, is extremely simple: four lines (a quatrain) in which each line has four syllables (as long as *violets* is pronounced "vi-lets" rather than "vi-o-lets"). And the stresses (the accents, or emphases) fall on the first and fourth syllables of each line:

RO-ses are RED.
VI(O)-lets are BLUE.
I'D like some BREAD.
I'D like some TOO!

The lines rhyme in an *ABAB* pattern: The last syllables of the first and third lines rhyme, as do those of the second and fourth.

The regular pattern of verse, with its alternation of stressed and unstressed syllables, creates a steady pulse that may be thought of as the heartbeat of speech. It provides a sense of drive and momentum, as well as composure and completion, to any spoken text. Stop this verse in the middle of a line—

RO-ses are RED.
VI(O)-lets are BLUE.
I'D like some BREAD.
I'D like . . .

—and the effect is unsettling—as though the speaker has had a heart attack. The absence of closure is so unnerving, in fact, that hearers will often shout out the missing words, even if they have to invent them, to fill the gap.

And rhyme creates, in the verse pattern, a ringing double-pulse, adding to the rhythm of stresses a rhythm of matching sounds. This emphasizes further the contrivance of verse: that the spoken words are deliberately rather than arbitrarily composed.

◆ EXERCISE 3-2

Roses Are Redder—Take One

Now play the "roses are red" scene a few more times, switching partners with others in your group and varying the situation. Look into your partner's eyes most of the time, but if you shift your focus, look at something else (that you imagine), not just "away." Some possible situations:

In a candle-lit restaurant: as a romantic overture

In a concentration camp: between starving inmates

At a gangster meeting: planning a heist

Contestants at a poetry-reading competition

Contestants at a bread-baking competition

At an English-as-a-second-language class competition

At a basketball game: as a romantic overture!

In a candle-lit restaurant: planning a heist!

Now repeat the exercise with a situation you and your partner create. Come up with simple goals—and subtle communications that might achieve them, which can be expressed by intonations, smiles, laughs, gestures, winks, muscle flexes, head tosses, touching your partner on the hand or shoulder, or anything that comes to mind—but that fall within the rules of decorum!

Remember to maintain eye contact with your partner most of the time—and to try to see what lies behind your partner's eyes. The forcefulness and magnetism of your acting will be a function not so much of how inventively you say your lines but how well you draw your partner out while saying them.

Eye Contact—And Looking Elsewhere

Eye contact—looking your partner directly in the eye—is a powerful acting tool because it makes clear, to your acting partner but also to an audience, that you are *really seeking your goal,* since you are studying your partner's responses to your speeches and actions for specific clues as to how you might proceed. If, for example, you are speaking with someone whom you plan to ask out on a date, you will generally be looking at his or her eyes to check the reaction to what you're saying, so as to determine the best time to pop the question or to adjust your tone and pace if you sense things aren't going quite as well as you'd hoped.

Maintaining eye contact is also a good way to let your partner know you're serious about something that involves him or her; you're genuinely inquiring, not just making a rote throwaway remark like "How ya doin'?"

But this doesn't mean you must *always* look your partner in the eye. It's an effective tactic to look elsewhere from time to time, toward, say, other people who, in the example suggested, you might turn your attention to if your partner doesn't want to go to the party. Showing that you have other fish to fry puts pressure on your partner and may help you achieve your goal. You can even look elsewhere for other people you don't know are there (and may not be) and achieve the same goal.

What you generally should *not* do, however, is simply look away. Looking merely away, at the floor for example, is not an active acting choice; it is usually just an unconscious avoidance of deep situational involvement. In-experienced actors glance at the floor mainly out of stage fright: fear of forgetting their lines, or embarrassment about looking foolish in some way. Whatever your acting goal is, it can rarely be achieved by staring at the floor or, for that matter, off into the flies. You can look at your partner, you can look at other people who might be useful to achieving your goal, you can look for other people who might be useful, you can look at or for God, you can look for a critical prop (such as a gun to shoot the intruder battering at your door) or at the set (such as the opulence of a room you have just entered, sizing up how likely its occupant will be to get you what you want), you can look out the window at people who might serve as role models ("Look at that man outside washing his car; Why can't my husband come here and see how a real man takes care of his family!"), but please don't look at the floor—unless the play is about a professional floor refinisher trying to impress a client!

◆ EXERCISE 3-3

Roses Are Redder—Take Two

Repeat the exercise, using any of these variant quatrains, again with a situation of your choosing and a specific environment (law office, bedroom, bar-room, city park) for that situation. Maintain constant eye contact with your partner and the useful persons or items in the environment of your situation.

A: Roses are red.

B: Violets are blue.

A: Honesty's dead!

B: What else is new?

A: Roses are red.

B: Violets are blue.

A: You look well fed!

B: What's that to you?

A: Roses are red.

B: Violets are blue.

A: What's that you said?

B: I'm teasing you.

A: Roses are red.

B: Violets are blue.

A: I'm off to bed.

B: Can I come too?

A: Roses are red.

B: Violets are blue.

A: Heard you were wed . . . ?

B: No, that's not true!

A: Roses are red.

B: Violets are blue.

A: What lies ahead?

B: I'll rhyme with you!

◆ EXERCISE 3-4

Roses Are Redder—Take Three

Starting with the opening gambit ("Roses are red / Violets are blue") and a situation and goal in your head, make up the final two lines, keeping them strictly within the pattern: four syllables, stressed on the first and fourth, with the "A" lines and "B" lines rhymed with their counterparts. Remember, again, to maintain eye contact, with your partner or useful persons and items in the environment, all the time, even when (*particularly* when) you are searching for your own line.

Take your time and don't feel rushed; this is not a cleverness contest.

And don't judge the appropriateness of the content of your line after you say it! Even if what you've come out with seems like total nonsense, the sound of your words conveys its own authority and will move you toward your goal. This is the power of style: Even sheer nonsense works if the style is confidently asserted.

Thinking Your Character's Thoughts

Choosing your own words makes this a more difficult assignment, but your skill at throwing yourself into this task, while still maintaining eye contact with your partner and environment, is a measure of your potential as an actor in a stylized play. The greatest difficulty of acting is to make those watching believe that you are not only saying your character's words but also *thinking them up* on the spot. The best acting always persuades us—the audience—that you the actor are the *creator* of your character's words, not just their interpreter (or, worse, their reciter).

For that matter, we like to believe that you are spontaneously creating your character's stage movements and have personally chosen your character's clothing. Of course we know that, normally at least, the words were written by a playwright, the moves arranged by a director, and the costume designed by a designer, but at the moment of performance we like to think that you, the character (which is also you, the actor, since you're the person we see in the role), are *initiating,* and not merely repeating, your part. This is why we are captivated—and not just entertained—by great acting.

And of course this illusion is generally more difficult to achieve when you are speaking in (and moving in, and dressing in) styles other than your own. But in the following exercise, you *are* coming up with your character's lines, so you can directly apply them to the goal (seductive? competitive? aggressive?) you seek to achieve with and through your acting partner. And your intonations, smiles, winks, and flexes will all be part of your integrated and goal-directed acting package in this mini–verse drama, *Roses Are Red*.

◆ EXERCISE 3-5

Roses Are Redder—Take Four

Bring a funny (or funky) costume, or simply a funny (or funky) hat, and an appropriate prop to class and repeat Exercise 3-4, folding them into the exercise—trying, all the while, to make the relationship interaction real within the context of the funny or funky accoutrements.

Playing the Play

You might think of the "Roses are red / Violets are blue" opening gambit, like "Knock, knock," as an invitation to *play*. Here it is useful to remember that the original English word for acting was *playing* and that we still call a single drama a *play* and a theatre a *playhouse*. The "roses are red" verse suggests a playful environment and a "play environment" as well; it is "dramatic." But that doesn't mean that it isn't real as well.

All dramas involve role-playing and, therefore, playing: "Roses are red" suggests an invitation to play much the same as a curtain rising announces a dramatic event. What "play" and "a play" have in common is that both are environments where we can be fully expressive and uninhibited—and not be held responsible for the consequences! Thus, the actor playing Romeo can try with all his might to "seduce" the actress playing Juliet—but since it is only "in play" he doesn't break her heart or his own when he goes home alone after the curtain falls. And the actor playing Othello can "strangle" Desdemona without going to jail for it. The play format makes the actions technically imaginary (there's going to be no actual heartbreak, no jail), but, conversely, it permits the *emotional and physiological actions* to be passionate and utterly uninhibited. In other words: Blood is not shed so that tears may be.

This is all said to make a single point: Stylized drama (including that written in verse) requires as much emotional realism in acting as modern "naturalistic" drama does. There is no question that Shakespeare's actors cried real tears in the performance of his plays, even though the plays were written largely in the "artificial" medium of verse. Shakespeare's actors were as believable as any in history, including today's. When Bottom the Weaver in *A Midsummer Night's Dream* is asked to portray the lover in a play within that play, he announces, "That will take some tears in the true performing of it"—as contrasted with a false performing of it. And while the "roses are red" exercise may not move you to a weepy state, some of the following exercises, from the world of actual plays, will quite likely do so.

But we shall start simply.

Summary

Verse—the contrived patterning of stressed and unstressed syllables in speech, often augmented by a regular rhyme scheme—creates a sort of steady heartbeat in speech, which conveys a regular momentum and sense of closure to the language and, when two or more characters exchange it, the sense that the characters live, or wish to live, in the same "world." Verse is also the mark of a deliberately "styled" language that implies playfulness, and playing, and has therefore been fundamental to theatre through the ages, permitting actors to act with total emotional authenticity while remaining within the framework of "playing" in "a play."

L E S S O N

4

Playing God

Now it's time to work on an actual play, one that happens to be among the very first plays in the English language. And let's look at a dramatic character who, while appearing in human form,* is as far from a normal human being such as ourselves as we can possibly imagine.

◆ EXERCISE 4-1

Playing God

Memorize and practice speaking the following lines. (Please note that while God is referred to as "he" in this play, both sexes may play this speech. No one—in acting class, anyway—should have a monopoly on "playing God." See further comment on this subject in the Preface.)

> Here 'neath me now a new isle I neven°   °*name*
> The island of Earth.[. . .]

This is the beginning of a speech by God in *The Creation of the Universe,* a play from the fifteenth century. It is written in Middle English (from which

---

* Medieval theology held that God literally created Adam in his own image; hence God was played, in medieval drama, as human in outward form.

it is here slightly adapted); the author is unknown. In this fragment, God creates the Earth, which he calls an island; he is speaking to a group of surrounding angels as he does so.

Standing on a low stool or bench, play God. Perform the line to your classmates, who now become your surrounding angels. As you say the words, imagine you are in the process of creating the Earth, giving it a name of your choosing.

At the same time, try to impress the angels with your divine power: your ability to create such a place and your authority to name it. This is not merely a matter of vanity; you are about to give them a code of ethics, and you want them—indeed, you *need* them—to heed your authority. So your goal in this line is not merely to convey the information of the lines, it's to make the angels *tremble*.

This is, obviously, a superhuman challenge. See the extent to which, in your own human imagination, you can rise to it.

As you play the line, notice how the playwright has, in the phrasing of the words, helped you achieve your goals.

First, well-chosen words reflect authority and dignity upon their user: words like *isle* and *neven* (rhymes with *heaven*), and the poetic contraction *'neath* (for *beneath*) all lend the line a melodious and awe-inspiring tone. (Note: the single apostrophe (') indicates a contraction, or a letter or letters missing, as in *e'er* for *ever* and *'tis* for *it is*.)

You will doubtless also notice the striking *alliteration* (repeated initial consonant sounds) in the line, which includes no less than four words beginning with the letter *n*. There is also marked *assonance* (the close juxtaposition of similar vowel sounds), as in the phrases "'neath me" and "isle I." These repeated sounds create a sense of harmony in the language, a pleasing and somewhat otherworldly pattern, appropriate for God (and, as we shall see, for God's creatures).

There is also a deliberate and definite rhythm to these words:

Dah dah dah DAH, d'dah dah dah DAH dah
D'DAH dah dah DAH!

This pattern of stressed and unstressed syllables, while not as regular as "Roses are red / Violets are blue," sets up a throbbing beat that continues through the entire line.

The normal order of subject, object, predicate, and adverb is reversed: instead of "I neven . . . a new isle . . . here," the author has written "Here . . . a new isle I neven." And a figure of speech is used: specifically, a *metaphor* (an implied comparison), whereby the Earth is described as an isle, or island.

This reversal of syntactical units and use of metaphor imply a formal and rehearsed declaration, rather than a spontaneous remark.

The various word choices, sound patterns, images, rhythms, and syntactical variations can radiate a very special sense of grace, authority, and intelligence for the character of God, whose words would thereby have seemed—certainly to a medieval audience—almost magically contrived and even divinely inspired. Indeed, the formality of the language is mainly what allows the audience to see the actor, who is in reality someone like themselves, as God, and even in some ways "godlike."

Thus the exalted style of the language creates a speech more persuasive than everyday phrasings could accomplish. Compare it, for example, with "I've made a planet down there, see? It's called . . . uhhh . . . Earth!" or "Hey! That new rock looks kinda like an island down there, duhdn' it? I'm namin' it Earth." Colloquial phrasing can convey the *content* of the original line but not the *character* (grace, authority, intelligence) of this speaker.

And what's wrong with that? Simply that the content isn't what makes the angels tremble—and thus doesn't truly deliver the totality of your line, which is an act that convinces the angels (and through them, the audience) that you are capable of creating and naming the human planet, and, therefore, you have godlike power. This, every bit as much as conveying content, is what acting requires. It's one thing to say you're creating the Earth; it's another to convince people you're actually doing it. The line stipulates a fact—that you have created the Earth—but it more profoundly creates an identity: you as God. Without the latter, we cannot be thrilled by the former. *We* want to tremble a bit too.

In other words God must not only make pronouncements, he must exude an aura of godliness—of divine power and moral authority. It is through the *style* of your assertions, not merely their content, that you will "play God" and thereby propel the angels to follow your divine leadership.

Thus the poetic images, alliterations, rolling assonance, formal (and surprising) syntactical structures, and rhythmic speech will indicate to the angels, and through them the audience, that your words were not arbitrarily summoned from the chaos of a human mind but were instead composed by the force of divinity itself. That the lines were in fact written by a human author, and are now spoken by a human (indeed, a student) actor, only indicates the tremendous challenge of making these characters come to life on stage.

So play this opening of God's speech again, and again, and yet again, seeking to do two things at the same time:

1. Convey the content (the meaning) of the line, which is the easy part.

2. Convey the "godliness" of your character—the grace and authority and divine leadership—that will make the angels want to do what you will soon be asking them to do.

How might you go about all this? How can you play God, for God's sake? Well, the good news is that everybody has a different notion of what "godliness" and "God's authority" might be, so you don't have to fit into any single ideal: God could be a saint, a brute, a spirit, a monster, an intellectual, a mystic, a fantastical poet: he (or she) has certainly been portrayed as all of these many times in the course of world literature. The deity you present will be like none other in the world, and the more freely you play the situation (impress the angels) instead of the stereotypes (your Sunday school teacher's view of God), the more unique and individual your God will be. But the words will send you in interesting directions. Let's study them a little more closely, to see what ideas they might generate.

Here . . .

You start the line with a declaration of absolute centrality, calling the attention of all the angels to yourself (the center of "Here") and the action you are about to do. This word, then, is a "grabber"—it implies "Don't look elsewhere, look here, look at me."

. . . 'neath me . . .

You must be "on high" if what you are about to describe is beneath you, so revel in your height. And by squeezing a syllable out of *beneath* to make the contraction *'neath,* you are (in addition to creating alliteration and regularizing the rhythm of the line) slighting the lower space, emphasizing that it isn't worth two whole syllables to explain its position.

. . . now . . .

Coupled with the initial "Here," you are defining not just spatial centrality but temporal immediacy, the "here and now" that lets the angels know that something is on the verge of happening—right at this instant, right in their midst.

. . . a new . . .

This suggests the possibility of a fresh start—that the hearers of your speech can have former sins forgiven. It also conveys excitement, for we are always astounded—and frightened—by the new. Here you must realize you are electrifying your angels, who presumably have been hanging around for most of eternity up to this point, with your novel creation.

. . . isle . . .

The word is deliberately poetic, suggesting a magical place, but it is also homonymic (sounds identical) with *I'll,* providing a subliminal suggestion of your (God's) activity in this renewal, and implying that you (God) will be the author of your hearers' renewal.

... I neven ...

Here you move to a formal, almost legalistic term, making it thereby clear that this is an important and perhaps permanent action you're engaged in; it's not a whim, not a brief experiment, but a cosmos-changing creation. (For a like reason, the traditional minister in the wedding ceremony says "I thee wed" rather than "I marry you.")

... The island ...

Your words now repeat, and expand upon, the designation of your creation as an isle. It's not just the doubling to two syllables; the new homonym expands to *I-land* and subliminally suggests your identification with, and thereby protection of, your new creation. The original English audience, of course, knowing that as an island itself, England was protected from invasion by sea, would be reassured by this image that the Earth would be protected by its creator, who considers the Earth an "I-land," that is, part of himself.

... of Earth.

Here you complete the naming action predicted by *neven,* thus fulfilling the action you have promised with the "here and now" opening. But note that the word is—to the angels—a surprise. And one question for you: *When* did you decide what it should be called? In acting, it is almost always more powerful and captivating if that decision is *fresh*: something you *do onstage,* in the moment, rather than a past decision you merely report on at the time we (the audience) see you.

Well, how then do you "play" these thirteen words, words so fraught with meaning that it takes several pages to gloss them?

No one can (or should) tell you exactly, since this is part of the actor's job, and each actor will (and should) do it a bit differently.

But you certainly want to:

- grab focus and attention with "Here"

- emphasize the immediacy of the situation with "now"

- encourage delight and excitement with "new isle"

- indicate the importance and gravity of your action with "neven"

- decide on a name for this new planet in real time, at the present moment, with your angels watching (and fearing, and admiring)

Try it!

Playing a Character

When you play a character, you are really playing *to* the other actors as though they were specific characters in relationship to yourself.

For example, in playing God, the starting point is to see the other characters as "not God." Specifically, in this case, you must see them as angels, as God's subordinates. By speaking to them as your subordinates, you will become their superior—and the only "person" superior to an angel is God. I call this playing a character *reciprocally*: finding your character not so much from how you appear but from how other characters appear to you when you are seeing through the eyes of your own character.

There is a very good reason for this approach: We do not, in life, see ourselves as characters—we see other people as characters. When you, a student, look at your professor, you are not thinking "I am a student"; but you are thinking "That is my professor." And so you act like a student. The veteran professor, meanwhile, is not up there thinking "I am a professor"; he or she is thinking "These are my students." And so he or she acts professorial.

Notice that I said "veteran professor." A beginning professor might very well be thinking "I am a professor," which will likely induce some rather unpleasant self-consciousness into the teaching process, either egotistical showing-off or awkward timidity—or both! But in the normal state of things, the way we see and categorize other people, and the ways we act toward them, determine *our* character—as seen by others.

We'll discuss this phenomenon further in the next lesson. But for the time being, look at your angels not as classmates but as characters craving your guidance and leadership. See them as loving you—and fearing you. See the adoration and awe in their eyes. And play to it.

Note that part of acting is seeing these emotions even if your fellow actors aren't showing them. Of course, it's wonderful if the other actors give you what you need in playing your part, but sometimes your seeing it, which is an act of your actor's imagination (which is what acting stems from), will induce it. See that idolatry and play to it! Love it, exploit it, work with it. Make them idolize you even more! Make them tremble! This isn't mere arrogance, you might want to realize; it dignifies them to be led by such a magnificent God as you are. It ennobles them, and they will love you the more for it.

It's only when you can do all this that the "God" in you will come alive. God must be supremely—nay, divinely—confident, and you must do all in your power to summon up that confidence in your divinity. There is simply no such thing as a diffident God.

As God, use your body as well as your voice. Imagine, for yourself, a posture, movements, and gestures. Do you stand tall? Do you stride? Do you swirl? Do you point? How? With a hand or with two hands or with a finger? Or with a down-turned thumb? Where do you look? And *how* do you look? With a glare? With a smile? Try several stagings of these thirteen words.

And your voice: Do you thunder? Do you bellow? Do you whisper? Do you resonate? Find the voice inside yourself that will inspire your angels with your godliness.

Costume yourself. Be creative. A giant robe and sandals? A sheet draped over you? A towering staff? A huge hat? Look at paintings and statues of deities from all ages and all religions (the play assumes a Judeo-Christian God, but you don't have to). Find garments and props that give you a grander-than-everyday scale. (But don't make the mistake of trying to please the class by undercutting or satirizing the authority you are trying to create. This is the easy way out. You are not trying to show how clever you are in this exercise; you are trying to appear godlike and all-powerful in the eyes of others. Mickey Mouse ears don't cut it here.)

If you feel unsuited to this task, don't worry: You *are* unsuited to it. Remember: You are *playing* God, but you *aren't* God. You're only *acting* (thank God!). Which is as far as you can go in this exercise.

But act up a storm: The role requires it. Actually, every role does. Professors not only profess, they also "play professors," as they must convince their students (and their deans) that they are *qualified* to teach, to be listened to, to be taken seriously. Merely holding a contract and title does not fully satisfy the job's basic demand: You will have to fill the role of professor with your own person. The same is true of any job, including that of a deity. And while I won't risk public sacrilege with a Judeo-Christian example here, I can say without qualification that in ancient Greek mythology, Zeus spent a great deal of time "playing the role" of King of the Gods, seeking to convince various demigods and attractive virgins that he was indeed all-powerful. Divinity, in theatre at least, is never self-evident.

Acting is doing your best to live up to a character, or style, that is not entirely your own; there will always be a tension between the character and yourself, between the style of the play and your own style of life. You are not God, and you aren't Oedipus or Amanda Wingfield, either. No one is. But you can try your hardest, using the tools the playwright (and, later, the director and costume designer) have given you. It is the *effort* to play God that is what, in the theatre, is godlike.

Summary

Playing God means not only delivering God's lines but persuading your on-stage hearers (the angels in this case) that you are godlike and carry the authority and dignity of God. If you don't, the lines will be out of context and meaningless. But, fortunately for you, everyone has a different notion of the authority and dignity of God, and your ideas are as valid as anyone else's. Moreover, you don't have to embody everybody's notion of God (which you won't in any case)—you only have to try (which is all you can do).

L E S S O N

5

Characterization

Reciprocal Characterization

The preceding lesson described a primary process of playing character, *reciprocal characterization,* whereby your character is determined chiefly by how you view other characters, and how you react in character to the way you view them. You are paranoid, for example, not because you're trying to be paranoid, but because you see other people as dangerous. Acting a character is not merely imitating the outward behavior of a certain kind of person but *thinking like* that person, and making the resulting actions that person would make. Your character behavior is then an *action,* not a demonstration of certain traits.

This, by the way, is how the notion of character or personality exists in real life. As human beings, we don't see ourselves as "characters," we see *other people* as characters. To ourselves, we are personality-neutral, behaving not according to the fixed character traits we notice in our friends but in response to ever-changing situations. This can be demonstrated scientifically.*

And therefore, paranoiacs do not think of themselves as paranoiacs but as normal people surrounded by assassins. Misers, to themselves, are would-be

---

* There's a classic experiment demonstrating this: When asked to rate themselves and others according to various personality scales, subjects invariably gave specific traits, such as stinginess, arrogance, happiness, to other people, while mostly rating themselves as "depends on situation," a category they rarely used to describe others. See my *Acting Power* (Mayfield, 1978), p. 18.

benefactors surrounded by swindlers. What distinguishes kings is not that they are tall, or rich, or old, or strong but that they see their countrymen as subjects. Character is thus all relative, which is why we understand that in the kingdom of the blind, the one-eyed man is king.

◆ EXERCISE 5-1

Reciprocal Characterization: Richard and Hastings

Let's go back to one of the Elizabethan greetings from Lesson 2. In this and subsequent cases in this chapter, in addition to bowing and curtsying, try to see the person you're greeting through the eyes of the person you're playing.

HASTINGS: Good time of day unto my gracious lord!

RICHARD: As much unto my good Lord Chamberlain!

Lord Hastings believes himself rescued from prison by Richard, whom he clearly sees as his savior. He's also obviously aware that Richard is aggressive, imaginative, and royal; clearly he hopes for further advancement from this distinguished patron.

Richard, by contrast, sees Hastings as a man of high status and title but, in reality, a weak, stupid sycophant, like the rest of the queen's courtiers.

With a partner, play the exchange, bowing deeply to each other as in Lesson 2. (Hastings, as a nonroyal bowing to royalty, should bow the more deeply of the two.) In the event a woman plays either role, she may be greeted as "gracious lady" or "Lady Chamberlain" if you wish, and she should then curtsy instead of bowing.

Allow the goals you play with each other, and the way you view each other, to affect your bows or curtsies. Also, recognize that the exchange takes place *in public*. So *perform* this exchange, and your bodily inclinations of (real or pretended) respect, to publicly announce your relationship with the other person in this greeting.

Intrinsic Characterization

Now let's take another step in characterization.

In addition to the characterizing that occurs by seeing other people differently from the way you see yourself, your own physical and psychological makeup obviously comes into play as well. We can call these the *intrinsic* aspects of character because they seem to exist whether other people are around or not. (Indeed, it is these intrinsic aspects of character that many beginning actors—and beginning directors—assume are all that characterization consists of!)

We can find intrinsic aspects of character from descriptions in the text, including stage directions by the author, verbal descriptions by other characters, the character's own self-reflections, or inferences we can draw from the lines or action of the play.

For example: When Hastings enters in an early scene of *Richard III,* another character remarks, "Here comes the sweating lord." This might suggest Hastings is corpulent, or at least out of shape.

And the action of the play indicates that Hastings several times fails to recognize the danger he is in, even when other characters warn him. "I know he loves me well," Hastings says of Richard when almost everyone else realizes that the duke is about to have him executed. This might suggest that Hastings is naive.

We know that Hastings boasts of having a celebrated mistress, which might suggest he is lascivious and foolhardy. He describes himself in the play as "triumphant," which might suggest that he is arrogant and self-important. He jests that other men are wimpy ("Where is your boar-spear, man? Fear you the boar?" he gibes), suggesting that he is pompous, hollowly heroic.

It is from the perspectives of Hastings's own intrinsic characteristics—physically unfit, naive, foolhardy, arrogant, and pompous—that he perceives Richard as his savior. The contrast between what we see in Hastings and what Hastings sees creates the dynamic tension—and human poignancy—of his character and role.

Richard, for his part, is repeatedly described as misshapen: History reports him "crook-backed" and "hard-favored of visage"; he admits in the play to being "deformed, unfinished," and the play's other characters describe him in even more grotesque terms: a "poisonous bunch-backed toad," a "bottled spider," an "abortive, rooting hog." Specifically, he is described as having a withered arm, an ugly face, a humped back, and one leg shorter than the other, and you may wish to incorporate all of these into your 'intrinsic" portrayal of the character. And then you would want to fold in his persistent drive to power and his psychopathic lust for evil ("I am determined to be a villain"), which will animate these physical deformities into a Richard that will intrigue, perplex, and thrill his allies and adversaries alike.

From this misshapen and intentionally villainous persona, Richard looks upon the fawning, pompous Hastings, and they exchange pleasantries. And we can sense what is going to happen.

◆ EXERCISE 5-2

Intrinsic Characterization: Richard and Hastings

Play the simple exchange, again, with a variety of partners, switching back and forth between the roles. Create the intrinsic characters by letting your imagination take off from any of the above points. Give each role a costume: a cape for Richard, perhaps, which could (for class purposes) be a blanket draped over your shoulders; a sword in your belt; a crutch under your arm (or arms: Anthony Sher made a famous choice of giving Richard two crutches with which he hopped about the stage); and perhaps shoes of unequal sizes. And for Hastings, a pillow under your shirt, perhaps; a blanket or a sheet draped over you; a floppy hat, say; and perhaps a staff of office. (If this two-line exchange intrigues you, you might want to work up the entire scene, still a short one: which is Act 1, Scene 1, 122–44; or even the more murderous "Off with his head!" final scene between the two: Act 3, Scene 4, 59–79.)

Intrinsic Characterizations: Extensions and Stereotypes

There are many ways in which actors can create an intrinsic characterization—developing character voices, character walks, character tics, for example—but these methods are also a minefield. Extending yourself into behaviors you cannot convincingly perform, particularly in a realistic play, can result in mere stereotypes and caricatures. That's one reason for looking at reciprocal characterization first.

But you certainly can explore intrinsic characterization, subtly in realistic plays and more aggressively in comic plays that include farcical or stock characters, such as those derived from Roman comedies (Italian *commedia*; certain works of Molière and Shakespeare) or modern farces, musical comedies, and TV sitcoms. Here are exercises and discussions to get you started.

Centering

The Russian teacher Michael Chekhov (nephew of the famed playwright and disciple of Stanislavsky) popularized the teaching of "finding your center" in the 1930s and '40s; it is one way of extending your body into at least the image of another. Using Chekhov's technique, an actor playing Hastings might choose to mentally center his body in his chest, puffing himself up with the pride of his position as Lord Chamberlain, while the actor playing Richard might choose to mentally find his body's center in the sour pit of his stomach, longing for power and recognition, or perhaps in his twisted arm, which has so forced a reorganization of his life's goals. In any case, the place where the actor chooses to center his or her movement will affect that movement—and the implicit character that is observed by both the other characters and the audience.

◆ EXERCISE 5-3

Centering

Stride about the room, concentrating on the fullness and grandness of your chest. Greet people you see with Hastings's line ("Good time of day . . .") and a more modest bow but always concentrating on *showing off your magnificent chest*.

Stride about the room, concentrating on the sour pain in the pit of your stomach. Greet people who greet you with Richard's line ("As much unto . . .") and a commensurately reduced or distorted bow.

Play these characters, and play other Elizabethan greetings from Lesson 2, while striding around the room and concentrating on various other parts of your body: your loins, your fingertips, your knees, your sinuses, your belly, your tongue, your chin.

See how this affects your speaking, your breathing, your walk, your posture, and your general attitude.

Our bodies are not all alike. Chances are, if you could magically inhabit someone else's body, you would start thinking, moving, and acting differently. Well, acting a role *is* inhabiting someone else's body, even if a fictitious one, and the opportunity to re-center your body, through your creative imagination, can extend you into a different aspect of yourself—which, in the theatre, we call "character."

Character Postures and Walks

People stand and move in different ways—for all sorts of reasons unassociated with a psychological center. Physical realities (height, weight, strength, health, injury) are invariably factors, as are certain psychological traits (confidence, recklessness, timidity, specific phobias). Occupational identities play a role in, say, the cowboy's lope, the gambler's stealth, the pimp's swagger, the nurse's stride. And cultural codes probably induce the surfer's shuffle, the party girl's sashay, the jock's guffaw, and the scholar's scowl—all of which, at least at the unconscious level, we use to signal likeminded souls.

◆ Exercise 5-4

Character Walks

Imagine that you are applying for a job as a professor at your own college or university and are walking across your campus to a job interview. Walk around the room as though it were the route to the interview, greeting people you know and silently acknowledging others that you assume know you, while at the same time imagining that you:

1. Are much taller than you are.

2. Are much shorter than you are.

3. Are much fatter than you are.

4. Are much leaner than you are.

5. Have one leg shorter than another.

6. Have a pain in one hip.

7. Are always sore from riding horseback all day.

8. Always carry large sums of cash on your person.

9. Are blind.

10. Are afraid of people.

11. Are extremely pigeon-toed.

12. Have just had a sex-change operation resulting in your becoming a man (even if, in real life, you are a man).

13. Have just had a sex-change operation resulting in your becoming a woman (even if, in real life, you are a woman).

14. Have an extreme need to find a bathroom.

15. Are extremely afraid of spiders, which are known to be present around you.

16. Have just had a nose job.

Try to project whatever image you think will help you get the job.

Character Voices

In Lesson 4 you were asked to find God's voice within yourself. Of course, no one knows what God's voice sounds like—nor do we know what Hamlet's voice, Jocasta's voice, or Stanley Kowalski's voice sounds like either: These are all fictional characters, even if based on real people, and your voice, if you're playing the part and speaking the lines, is going to be delivering the character's voice no matter what happens.

But *which* of your voices? You have many: one you use with your parents, another with small children, another with your closest friends, perhaps another with the officer who stops and questions you. And then there are the voices you can create and employ for special occasions: football games, rave concerts, church services, parties, council meetings, special prayers to God or some other deity. And surely you have rehearsed, in your mind at least, a few voices you have never yet had to use: addressing a political rally on behalf of your cause, telling someone you love him or her, demanding the overthrow of an intolerant regime, energizing your teammates before the final quarter, giving your Academy Award acceptance speech.

So by finding, and sometimes then extending, your varied voices, you will find your version of God's voice, and the devil's voice (see Lesson 7), and maybe Hamlet's or Jocasta's voice as well.

How do you extend your voice? This is a danger area: Even minor extensions of your voice lead quickly to caricature and are best limited to plays involving farcical, abstract and nonhuman (such as God, witches, dolls), or highly stereotyped characters. Moreover, developing an artificial "stage voice" can come back to haunt you by suddenly showing up in realistic roles (or at auditions for realistic roles!) when you don't intend it to. Extending your voice can also damage your vocal instrument, if overdone. You may, however, conduct some *judicious* experiments, perhaps with coaching from an instructor, by varying the normal placement of your vowels (far back in the throat, or right up behind the teeth) or the formation of your consonants (give yourself a lisp or overaspirated plosives), or altering your resonation (by pinching up your face, increase your nasality). All of these changes can create hilarious character voices suitable for certain kinds of plays. But, finally, note that your voice develops its own character over many decades, and as a young actor you are probably quite far from the mature voice you will have years from now. Don't try to duplicate the voice of an actor twice your years; this will happen on its own, in good time.

◆ EXERCISE 5-5

Finding Your Voices

These exercises do not require you to extend your voice artificially but to find the voice within you specific to the situation, and expand it in its own direction.

1. Face a (real or imaginary) ocean and speak to it in Byron's famous apostrophe:

    Roll on, thou deep and dark blue ocean—roll!

    Repeat three to five times, until you feel you are commanding the waves.

2. Face a (real or imaginary) thunderstorm and challenge it in Lear's cry:

    Blow, winds, and crack your cheeks! Rage! Blow!

    Repeat, challenging the very heavens to topple you—if they dare.

3. Look out into an imaginary night and, hoping that your loved one might be there, speak to him in Juliet's words,

    Romeo, doff thy name,
    And for that name, which is no part of thee,
    Take all myself.

    Repeat, inducing Romeo, should he magically be there, to fall as deeply in love with you as you are with him.

4. Dance around a cauldron and make it bubble with the witch's words from *Macbeth*:

    Double, double toil and trouble;
    Fire burn, and cauldron bubble.

    Repeat three times (as the witches do!), letting your voice and movements be the fire that makes the cauldron heat and boil over.

5. Drop to the floor and summon black vengeance from hell in Othello's oath:

Arise, black vengeance, from thy hollow hell!
Yield up, O love, thy crown and hearted throne
To tyrannous hate!

Repeat, seeking to catch the devil's ear with your voice, your roaring vowels, the resonance of your own name, hidden in a near anagram in this speech: Othello as o - the - hell - o)

6. Kneel before your aging, dying, deeply confused father and seek his blessing using Cordelia's words from *King Lear:*

O look upon me, sir,
And hold your hands in benediction o'er me.

Repeat, seeking to penetrate the old man's confusion and guilt for earlier quarrels and fury.

7. Protect yourself from the blows of your master, who is displeased with you, in Dromio's words from *The Comedy of Errors:*

What mean you, sir? For God's sake, hold your hands!
Nay, an° you will not, sir, I'll take my heels!   °*if*

Repeat, pleading—with voice and gestures—to induce your master to love you again and stop beating you. Find your voice of absolute supplication.

Character Descriptions

Since the late nineteenth century, dramatists have often included in the texts of their plays descriptions of the characters, giving them specific appearances, voices, and behaviors in stage directions, usually at the point of the character's first entrance. The following exercises contain several such stage directions, plus a line or two of dialog from characters in well-known American plays. (Some of the stage directions and lines are slightly edited for this exercise, as indicated with bracketed ellipses.) Each selection is from the character's first scene. These are difficult: You are not normally going to be able to give a full-on version of the character in the classroom, as you will lack the costume, scenery, dialect, and age makeup support that you could count on in a professional situation. But as a learning exercise, try to slide into one of these characters and give your best impression—voice, body, movement, attitude—of your chosen role. Or go outside this text and find dramatic characters of your own.

◆ EXERCISE 5-6

Playing Out Character Descriptions

Find clothing from your own wardrobe, or borrow some from friends or perhaps a costume storage shop you may have access to (realizing that few college costume departments lend out costumes for classroom purposes!), or rummage through thrift shops that might have what you need, and costume yourself as best you can for the following parts. Then find the most appropriate voice within yourself, and, consulting a full-length mirror where possible, create the silhouette and movement pattern matching the following characters in their opening lines and movements. Then perform them.

1. Eddie, in Sam Shepard's *Fool for Love*, is talking to May (his girlfriend and half sister) whom he has previously abandoned.

[Stark, low-rent motel room on the edge of the Mojave Desert. (. . .) EDDIE wears muddy, broken-down cowboy boots with silver gaffer's tape wrapped around them at the toe and instep, well-worn, faded, dirty jeans that smell like horse sweat. Brown western shirt with snaps. A pair of spurs dangles from his belt. When he walks, he limps slightly and gives the impression he's rarely off a horse. There's a peculiar broken-down quality about his body in general, as though he's aged long before his time. He's in his late thirties. (. . .) He wears a bucking glove on his right hand and works resin into the glove from a small white bag. (. . .) He pulls his hand out and removes gloves.]

EDDIE: *[seated, tossing glove on the table]:*   May, look. May? I'm not goin' anywhere. See? I'm right here.

2. Margaret (Maggie), in Tennessee Williams's *Cat on a Hot Tin Roof*, is talking to her husband, Brick, who is offstage showering.

[A bed-sitting-room of a plantation home in the Mississippi Delta (c. 1955). (. . .) A pretty young woman, with anxious lines in her face, enters. (. . .) Margaret's voice is both rapid and drawling. In her long speeches she has the vocal tricks of a priest delivering a liturgical chant, the lines are almost sung, always continuing a little beyond her breath so she has to gasp for another. Sometimes she intersperses the lines with a little wordless singing, such as "Da-da-daaaa!" (. . .)]

MARGARET: *[shouting above the roar of water]:*   One of those no-neck monsters hit me with a hot buttered biscuit so I have t'change. [. . .] it's too bad [. . .] you can't wring their necks if they've got no necks to wring! Isn't that right, honey? [. . .] Yep, they're no-neck monsters, all no-neck people are monsters. [. . .] Hear them? Hear them screaming? I don't know where their voice-boxes are located since they don't have necks.

3. Brick is responding to Margaret in #2.

[He stands there in the bathroom doorway drying his hair with a towel and hanging onto the towel rack because one ankle is broken, plastered and bound. He is still slim and firm as a boy. His liquor hasn't started tearing him down outside. He has the additional charm of that cool air of detachment that people have who have given up the struggle. But now and then, when disturbed, something flashes behind it, like lightning in a fair sky, which shows that at some deeper level he is far from peaceful. Perhaps in a stronger light he would show some signs of deliquescence, but the fading, still warm, light from the gallery treats him gently. (. . .) A tone of politely feigned interest, masking indifference, or worse, is characteristic of his speech with Margaret.]

BRICK: Wha'd you say, Maggie? Water was on s'loud I couldn't hearya. . . . Why d'ya call Gooper's kiddies no-neck monsters?

4. Herald Loomis, in August Wilson's *Joe Turner's Come and Gone*

[August 1911. A boardinghouse in Pittsburgh. (. . .)From the deep and near South the sons and daughters of newly freed African slaves wander into the city. Isolated, cut off from memory, having forgotten the names of the gods and only guessing at their faces, they arrive dazed and stunned, their heart kicking in their chest with a song worth singing. (. . .)Enter Herald Loomis and his eleven-year-old daughter, Zonia. Herald Loomis is thirty-two years old. He is at times possessed. A man driven not by the hellhounds that seemingly bay at his heels, but by his search for a world that speaks to something about himself. He is unable to harmonize the forces that swirl around him, and seeks to recreate the world into one that contains his image. He wears a hat and a long wool coat.]

LOOMIS: Me and my daughter looking for a place to stay, mister. You got a sign say you got rooms. *[pause]*   Mister, if you ain't got no rooms we can go somewhere else.

5. Mattie Campbell, in August Wilson's *Joe Turner's Come and Gone*

[Enter Mattie Campbell. She is a young woman of twenty-six whose attractiveness is hidden under the weight and concerns of a dissatisfied life. She is a woman in an honest search for love and companionship. She has suffered many defeats in her search, and though not always uncompromising, still believes in the possibility of love.]

MATTIE: I'm looking for a man named Bynum. Lady told me to come back
    later. [. . .] Are you the man they call Bynum? The man folks say can fix
    things? [. . .] Can you fix it so my man come back to me?

6. Lawrence Garfinkle, in Jerry Sterner's *Other People's Money*

*[Andrew Jorgenson's office. The present (1987). Lights up on Garfinkle. He
is an immense man of forty, though he looks older. He is always elegantly
dressed, surprisingly graceful for his bulk. He is, in some way, larger than
life. His deep, rich voice fills the stage. He speaks in a New York rhythm.
He looks about.]*

GARFINKLE: Haven't seen a place this shitty since I left the Bronx.

7. Laura Wingfield, in Tennessee Williams's *The Glass Menagerie*

*[The Wingfield apartment. Laura is seated at the table. Laura's situation is
even graver (than her mother's). A childhood illness has left her crippled,
one leg slightly shorter than the other, and held in a brace. This defect need
not be more than suggested on the stage. Stemming from this, Laura's sepa-
ration increases till she is like a piece of her own glass collection, too exquisitely fragile to move from the shelf.]*

LAURA: *[rising]*   I'll bring in the blanc mange.*

8. Maxine, in Tennessee Williams's *Night of the Iguana*

*[The play takes place in the summer of 1940 in a rather rustic and very
Bohemian hotel (. . . in) Puerto Barrio in Mexico. (. . .) Mrs. Maxine Faulk,
the proprietor of the hotel, comes around the turn of the verandah. She is a
stout, swarthy woman in her middle forties—affable and rapaciously lusty.
She is wearing a pair of Levi's and a blouse that is half unbuttoned. (. . .)
Mrs. Faulk looks down the hill and is pleased by the sight of someone coming up from the tourist bus below.]*

MAXINE: *[calling out]*   Shannon!   *[A man's voice from below answers:
    "Hi!"]*   Hah!   *[Maxine always laughs with a single harsh, loud bark,
    opening her mouth like a seal expecting a fish to be thrown to it.]*   My
    spies told me that you were back under the border!

9. Mary Tyrone, in Eugene O'Neill's *Long Day's Journey into Night*

*[Living room of James Tyrone's summer home on a morning in August,
1912. (. . .) Mary is fifty-four, about medium height. She still has a young,
graceful figure, a trifle plump, but showing little evidence of middle-aged
waist and hips, although she is not tightly corseted. Her face is distinctly
Irish in type. (. . .) She uses no rouge or any sort of make-up. (. . .) What*

---

*   A custard dessert, pronounced "blaw mawnj."

strikes one immediately is her extreme nervousness. Her hands are never still. They were once beautiful hands, with long, tapering fingers, but rheumatism has knotted the joints and warped the fingers, so that now they have an ugly crippled look. One (. . .) is conscious she is sensitive about their appearance and humiliated by her inability to control the nervousness which draws attention to them. She is dressed simply but with a sure sense of what becomes her. Her hair is arranged with fastidious care. Her voice is soft and attractive. When she is merry, there is a touch of Irish lilt in it. (. . .)

MARY: *[Turns smilingly to (her sons), in a merry tone that is a bit forced.]* I've been teasing your father about his snoring. [. . .] *[She stops abruptly, catching Jamie's eyes regarding her with an uneasy, probing look. Her smile vanishes and her manner becomes self-conscious.]* Why are you staring, Jamie? *[Her hands flutter up to her hair.]* Is my hair coming down? It's hard for me to do it up properly now. My eyes are getting so bad and I never can find my glasses.

10. Jamie is responding to Mary, his mother, in #9.

[Jamie (. . .) is thirty-three. He has his father's broad-shouldered, deep-chested physique, is an inch taller and weighs less, but appears shorter and stouter because he lacks (his father's) bearing and graceful carriage. (. . .) The signs of premature disintegration are on him. (. . .) His hair is thinning and already there is indication of a bald spot. (. . .) His nose is (. . .) pronouncedly aquiline. Combined with his habitual expression of cynicism it gives his countenance a Mephistophelian cast. But on the rare occasions when he smiles without sneering, his personality possesses the remnant of a humorous, romantic, irresponsible Irish charm—that of the beguiling ne'er-do-well, with a strain of the sentimentally poetic, attractive to women and popular with men.(. . .)]

JAMIE: *[Looks away guiltily]* Your hair's all right, Mama. I was only thinking how well you look.

11. Miss Roj (a man) in George C. Wolfe's *The Colored Museum*

[Electronic music. A neon sign which spells out THE BOTTOMLESS PIT. (. . .) There is a blast of smoke and, from the haze, Miss Roj appears. He is dressed in striped patio pants, white go-go boots, a halter, and cat-shaped sunglasses. What would seem ridiculous on anyone else, Miss Roj wears as if it were high fashion. He carries himself with total elegance and absolute arrogance.]

MISS ROJ: God created black people and black people created style. The name's Miss Roj . . . that's R.O.J. thank you and you can find me every Wednesday, Friday and Saturday nights at "The Bottomless Pit," the watering hole for the wild and weary which asks the question, "Is there life after Jherri-curl?"

12. Blanche du Bois, in Tennessee Williams's *A Streetcar Named Desire*

[(New Orleans, c. 1947.) Blanche comes around the corner, carrying a valise. She looks at a slip of paper, then at the building, then at the slip and again at the building. Her expression is one of shocked disbelief. Her appearance is incongruous to this setting. She is daintily dressed in a white suit with a fluffy bodice, necklace and earrings of pearl, white gloves and hat, looking as if she were arriving at a summer tea or cocktail party in the garden district. She is about (thirty). Her delicate beauty must avoid a strong light. There is something about her uncertain manner, as well as her white clothes, that suggests a moth.]

BLANCHE: *[with faintly hysterical humor]*   They told me to take a streetcar named Desire, and then transfer to one called Cemeteries and ride six blocks and get off at—Elysian Fields!

13. Stanley Kowalski, in Tennessee Williams's *A Streetcar Named Desire*

[Stanley throws the screen door of the kitchen open and comes in. He is of medium height, about five feet eight or nine, and strongly, compactly built. Animal joy in his being is implicit in all his movements and attitudes. Since earliest manhood the center of his life has been pleasure with women, the giving and taking of it, not with weak indulgence, dependently, but with the power and pride of a richly feathered male bird among hens. Branching out from this complete and satisfying center are all the auxiliary channels of his life, such as his heartiness with men, his appreciation of rough humor, his love of good drink and food and games, his car, his radio, everything that is his, that bears his emblem of the gaudy seed-bearer.]

STANLEY: H'lo. Where's the little woman?

Animal Imagery

In the last two stage directions in the previous exercise, Blanche du Bois is said to suggest a moth, and Stanley a richly feathered male bird. The character of Mitch in the same play is described as a dancing bear, and another character is described as "rooting" through a dropped purse, as a hog might do. Actors can make use of animal imagery as well, by discovering or creating animalistic metaphors (or residual traits!) in their characters, which will help make those characters both highly specific (as to a given species) and archetypal. Robert de Niro, for example, imagined Travis Bickle in the film *Taxi Driver* as a crab, "moving awkwardly, sideways and back."* Using animal images also helps *animate* character, and by so doing we recognize the common origin of those words: What is finally "animal" and "animated" in your character is precisely what you, the actor, provide—and what the text on the page cannot.

◆ Exercise 5-7

Animate (Animalize) Your Character

Replay the Hastings–Richard greeting from Exercise 5-1 with Hastings as a peacock and Richard a spider. You needn't give a literal impression of the animal—just your impression of the animal's essence, hybridized onto your own.

Try it with different animals. A lion and a serpent. An ostrich and a hyena. A walrus and a fox. A giraffe and a warthog.

Take any of the speeches from Exercise 5-6 and animate it with an animal of your choice. And don't rely on your memory of animals: Do what many actors do, go to the zoo!

Intrinsic and Reciprocal Characterization

Intrinsic and reciprocal characterization work as a team, as two sides of the same coin. But they are seen from two different perspectives: Intrinsic character is that which we gather from reading the play; reciprocal is that which we gather from playing the part. Critics, who read the plays but don't usually act them, mainly write about intrinsic characteristics. And since the actor reads the play before playing it, intrinsic characterization generally comes to the actor's mind before the other type; you read the play and arrive at some conclusions about what sort of person you are about to portray. Many beginning actors, as mentioned earlier, simply stop there and go no further.

But reciprocal characterization—the way your character perceives other characters—is what drives the role *during the performance itself*; it is what evokes the telling characteristics from you. It is not the reader's view, nor the

---

* Doug Tomlinson, *Actors on Acting for the Screen* (Garland, 1994), p. 143.

critic's; it is the actor's view in the real time of the play. So if these two aspects of characterization are to function as a team, teamwork is required. You will create the intrinsic character through studying the way the part is described and appears on the page. And you will create the reciprocal characterization through your imagination: by getting *inside* that character to see other people not as you do in your own life, but as you do with your character's eyes. Put these aspects of character together and you will have the kernel of characterization. A few more exercises will get you started.

◆ EXERCISE 5-8

Character Greetings

Let's replay some of the greetings in Exercise 2-4 aided by our discussions of characterization. Comments below each dialog will guide you to possible text considerations (refer to Exercise 2-4 for basic descriptions of the situations), and you can flesh these out, now, with extensions: You might try bodily recenterings, animal imagery, or other intrinsic characterizing techniques.

Caveat: These are not to be thought of as scenes, just simple exchanges. Likewise, comments on the characters are only "get-you-started" suggestions; they don't involve character development, nor do they assert "official" or "definitive" statements about these characters—each of which may be played in hundreds of different ways.

Don John/Don Pedro

DON JOHN: My lord and brother, God save you!

DON PEDRO: Good den, brother.

Don Pedro is a prince of Arragon, recently returned from a victorious military battle. He sees his half-brother as an embarrassment to his family name. Don John is a bastard, resentful of the legitimate and more noble Pedro, and, like Richard, admits to villainy ("I am a plain-dealing villain," he tells a friend). Don John sees his brother as an obstacle to his advancement, though at this point he is trying to lure him into a trap. Both actors can imagine themselves wearing formal garb, either as military officers (with Don Pedro the more distinguished) or as party guests.

If you want to extend this exchange to a fuller scene, it's *Much Ado About Nothing* Act 3, Scene 2, lines 80–91 (at which point another character joins the dialog).

Duke/Isabella

DUKE: Good morning to you, fair and gracious daughter.

ISABELLA: The better, given me by so holy a man.

The text indicates that the duke, disguised as a friar, is attracted to Isabella (to whom he will propose marriage) and preoccupied with profound moral and religious questions. Isabella, a young woman, having begun training as a nun, now finds herself in a deeply compromised moral position with her brother and the duke's deputy. The duke sees her as a beautiful and endangered young woman; she sees him as a potential savior for her desperate situation. Both actors can imagine themselves in religious vestments.

The scene, which is intense, continues at *Measure for Measure* Act 4, Scene 3, lines 112–148.

Othello/Desdemona

OTHELLO: O my fair warrior!

DESDEMONA: My dear Othello!

Othello is an African general flush with great victories and a new bride. From the text we gather that he sees Desdemona as a beautiful and sainted woman ("my soul's joy" he calls her moments after this), brave enough to follow him, against her father's direst warnings, into an interracial marriage. Desdemona, a virtuous but in some ways naive Venetian socialite, clearly adores her magnificent husband. They both see the crowd of soldiers surrounding them as loyal supporters of what they foresee as a long and illustrious life together. The actors should imagine Othello garbed as an officer—the text describes him as holding a sword—and Desdemona as a discreet bride forced to travel separately from her husband aboard a ship, from which she has only recently debarked. Their greeting would presumably be some form of embrace.

The scene continues at *Othello* Act 2, Scene 1, lines 181–198.

Mistress Quickly/Falstaff

MISTRESS QUICKLY: Give your worship good morrow.

FALSTAFF: Good morrow, goodwife.

MISTRESS QUICKLY: Not so, an't please your worship.

FALSTAFF: Good maid, then.

Mistress Quickly (Libby George) and Sir John Falstaff (Dennis Robertson) greeting each other in the 2000 Utah Shakespearean Festival production of *The Merry Wives of Windsor*. (© 2000 Utah Shakespeare Festival; photo by Karl Hugh)

Sir John Falstaff, who appears in three of Shakespeare's plays, is famously outsized. He is middle-aged or older, fat, and long fallen (or risen?) into drinking and womanizing. The text shows him to be garrulous, amoral, whimsical, a leader among his drinking buddies, and brilliant at avoiding commitment. Mistress Quickly, his steady woman friend and eventually his wife, is his true counterpart, somewhere between a barkeep and a brothel madam. Each sees the other as a formidable challenge, and the gender difference, with all it implies socially and politically, ignites fireworks.

If you'd like to continue the scene, which is a long one, it's *The Merry Wives of Windsor* Act 2, Scene 2, lines 33–136. But I recommend holding off until you've progressed through Lesson 12 of this book.

William/Audrey

WILLIAM: Good ev'n, Audrey.

AUDREY: God ye good ev'n, William.

A shepherd and shepherdess in *As You Like It*, neither educated, both presumably fit and hardy from working in the fields. He sees her as a beautiful

Mercutio (Jeffrey Binder) and the Nurse (Anne F. Butler) parry words in the 1997 production of *Romeo and Juliet* at the Colorado Shakespeare Festival. (Courtesy Colorado Shakespeare Festival; photo © P. Switzer)

princess; she sees him as a rustic ignoramus; both of them see the court jester, Touchstone, who is watching this encounter, as a distinguished and admirably learned celebrity.

Nurse/Mercutio

NURSE: God ye good morrow, gentlemen.

MERCUTIO: God ye good den, fair gentlewoman.

The nurse was Juliet's wet nurse, having lost her own daughter in or shortly after childbirth; we know from the text that she is gabby, affectionate, and loves to laugh and joke. We infer that she is heavyset because, like the "sweating" Hastings, she is out of breath when she returns to the Capulet home after this scene. Mercutio is an unattached young nobleman, quick to jest and pun with his friends and to fight with his enemies. Clearly she sees him as one of a group of thoughtless young aristocrats—the sort she deals with only when necessary, as is the case today—and he sees her as a bulky servant-class woman useful only as a target for his playfulness and showing off.

From left to right: Sir Toby Belch (Ray Porter), Feste (G. Valmont Thomas), and Sir Andrew Aguecheek (Dan Donohue) in the Oregon Shakespeare Festival's 2000 production of Shakespeare's *Twelfth Night*. (Courtesy Oregon Shakespeare Festival; photo by Andrée Lanthier)

You might like to continue the exchange for three more lines, until Romeo interrupts it:

NURSE: God ye good morrow, gentlemen.

MERCUTIO: God ye good den, fair gentlewoman.

NURSE: Is it good den?

MERCUTIO: 'Tis no less, I tell ye, for the bawdy hand of the dial is now upon the prick of noon.

NURSE: Out upon you, what a man art you?

Sir Toby Belch/Viola

SIR TOBY: 'Save you, gentleman.

VIOLA: And you, sir.

Sir Toby is not unlike Falstaff; enamored of his "cakes and ale" (and therefore presumably fat and somewhat addled), he spends much of his time drinking with his men friends, cavorting with the housemaid (whom he eventually marries), and playing practical jokes on his adversary in his niece Olivia's household, where he lives as a family retainer. Viola is a young woman who, stranded in a foreign country, has taken on the disguise and name (Cesario) of a man. Toby regards "him" as a lower-class servant; Viola perceives Toby as a man just unorthodox enough, as a man's man, to see through her disguise.

You could continue this scene, if you wish, with lines that follow almost immediately at *Twelfth Night* Act 3, Scene 1, lines 74–83.

Summary

Character is composed of two fundamental aspects: the *intrinsic* aspects that we infer from the dialog and the stage directions, and the *reciprocal* aspects that the actor plays while performing the character and seeing other people in the play as characters. By blending these two interrelated aspects, you can actively play, not merely demonstrate, a character's personality, and you can look through the eyes of the character.

More God

Here's more of the speech you worked on in Lesson 4.

Here 'neath me now a new isle I neven,
The island of Earth. And see: Now it starts—
Earth, wholly, and Hell; this highest be Heaven,
And those wielding wealth° shall dwell in these parts.　°*enjoying well-being*
This grant I ye, ministers mine°　　　°*my angels*
To-whiles° ye are stable in thought.　　°*as long as*
But to them that are nought°:　　　°*not (stable)*
Be put to my prison—and pine°!　　　°*suffer*

This is not an easy text; it includes now-unfamiliar words (*neven, to-whiles*), familiar but archaic words (*ye*), and tricky phrasing ("those wielding wealth"). But you should know that some of the language and phrasing was unfamiliar and archaic even in the fifteenth century; the point of playing in style is to open up lives and worlds other than our own, and the medieval authors and actors who wrestled with this material (as you do) were seeking to depict a world they thought to be four thousand years before their own time. Thus they used words that were archaic even to them, and phrasings that imposed a certain distance between the dialog and daily speech. So don't be discouraged: Difficult tasks generate hard work, but often spectacular results.

In the continuation of the speech, you (as God) now create Hell and Heaven; then you tell the angels (here called your "ministers") that they may live happily ("wielding wealth") in Heaven, so long as they remain level-headed ("stable in thought"). But, you then warn them, they will be sent to

Hell, to endure endless suffering (to "pine"), if they wander from the straight and narrow path you have ordained.

Now we see a larger aspect of the design of God's speech. There is a continuation of the alliteration in line 1; now we have several series of words in a single line that begin with the same (or close to the same) consonant: "wholly/Hell/highest/heaven" (line 3), "wielding/wealth/(d)well" (line 4), and "put/prison/pine" (line 8). But we can also see that the speech is composed in a verse form, with repeated patterns of vocal stress (for example, "but to them that are nought"—dah dah DAH dah dah DAH), and of rhyme (ABAB—"neven, starts, Heaven, parts"—as well as ABBA—"mine, thought, nought, pine"). The dramatist's complex verse patterning creates a firm sense of carefully *composed* language, appearing not as spontaneous chatter but as measured, virtually *musical* thought.

And the rhyme makes the language particularly *entertaining*—as we saw in the "roses are red" exercise—which is why rhyme continues to play such an important role in popular music, light verse, and advertising jingles. A well-fashioned rhyme pattern also conveys an appealing sense of harmony, wholeness, finality, and, in the medieval mind, something approaching magic or divinity. It is a fundamental strategy for convincing its audience that these words are, if not divinely created, then at least divinely inspired.

◆ EXERCISE 6-1

A Stanza, by God

Study and memorize the longer speech. Now—play the speech to the angels.

This time, you have multiple goals to achieve during the course of the speech. During the first lines, as before, you want to impress the angels that you are qualified to give them rules of moral instruction—and that these rules are more important, and more central to their future existence, than, say, advice in a newspaper column. These words, you want them to understand, are backed by *divinity;* by the universe itself, not just by an ordinary person or committee.

Then you make your charge to the angels: If they remain levelheaded, they can live as your personal assistants in Heaven, enjoying the full wealth of your divine spirit. Should they reject that stability, however, you will make them suffer in Hell!

Using the language of the author, and your own tactics and skills in speaking it, *encourage* the angels to accept your authority and to keep to the path you have shown them. And, conversely, *discourage* them from veering off the path and landing in Hell.

THE CHARACTER OF GOD

This is an acting, not a religious, exercise, nor is it meant to be a sacrilegious one. The "God" referred to is not necessarily your God, nor your teacher's God, nor the author's God, nor, for that matter, any living person's God. Rather, he—or she—is a dramatic character conceived by an anonymous medieval writer, quite possibly a Christian monk, six hundred years ago, in this particular play. Your task—which would be fundamentally no different if you were playing Zeus in a Greek tragedy—is to understand *what* this specific character of God is trying to achieve with the other persons in the scene (here, for the time being, imaginary), and just *how* you are going to try to achieve this. You will also, inevitably, seek to understand how your character thinks and feels while doing this. But you are not "the" God, you are only playing (that is, acting) *a* God. So don't confuse your character's behavior with your own religious beliefs, or even your disbeliefs.

No, do more than that. Scare the Hell out of them!
Go ahead: Play it now.

Have you made some headway? Good. Let's make even more.

Why did the dramatist choose the particular words in this speech? Or, to put it another way, why didn't the dramatist use simpler language? Why didn't he (if it was a he) simply "say what he meant"?

Words are not merely the sum of their semantic content (their "meaning"). They also transmit sound, imagery, feeling, and, through these, the intelligence and seriousness of the speaker. Well-turned phrases become calls to action that can live on long after they have first been uttered. If Lincoln had begun his Gettysburg address in the simplest possible way, "Eighty-seven years ago, the constitutional drafters declared that a portion of North America would become an independent country," no one would have remembered his speech by the following morning. But "Fourscore and seven years ago, our fathers brought forth, on this continent, a new nation" will live in the hearts of Americans for centuries to come.

Look at how the medieval dramatist chose words that gave richer meaning, and denser texture, to the speech you have learned.

"Earth, wholly, and Hell" introduces a fascinating intervening adverb: *wholly* is homonymic with *holy* and also *hole-y*, which suggests on the front end that the Earth is not only whole (complete and contained, as an island) but holy (tied to Heaven); while, on the back end, Hell is a "hole" (or even a "Hell-hole").

"[T]hose wielding wealth shall dwell in these parts" is a complex phrase, which basically suggests that persons selected for Heaven will enjoy happiness and well-being (the original meaning of *wealth*, as in *commonwealth*). But it also, perhaps subliminally, suggests that such persons will also have riches and prosperity—the more modern meaning of *wealth*, even in the fifteenth century. The phrase is deliberately ambivalent as to which comes first: whether those wielding earthly wealth will eventually go to Heaven, or those who go to Heaven will consequently wield wealth; but both meanings are clearly put forward as God's gift to humankind.

"This grant I ye" is a formal, almost legal phrasing. Compare the word order and word choice with the more common "I give you this," or, more simply, "Here, take this!" This is *ritualizing* language, which sanctifies what it pronounces; it is similar to the traditional line in wedding ceremonies, "With this ring I thee wed," conveying content (information) in a format used to solemnize (and therefore make unbreakable) sacred covenants.

In "ministers mine," you reverse the normal order of noun and modifier, placing yourself in the line-ending, climactic position, which emphasizes your authority over your angels (as does the scansion: "MIN-is-ters MINE"); while at the same time your alliteration on those two words emphasizes your shared friendship with those well beneath you in the celestial hierarchy. And by thus taking the angels into your bosom, as your personal ministers (suggesting that they might minister to you), you are providing them with something very special: your love and trust.

The stipulation "stable in thought" reminds the angels that they are already right-thinking, and you are only insisting that they remain so; however, you don't exactly define what right-thinking is. The deeper meaning is, perhaps, "Don't question, don't change, don't let this new planet give you any new ideas." It is not entirely irrelevant that a "stable" is also a place where animals are kept: Both meanings derive from the Old French *estable*, meaning "standing firm," and you are suggesting that the angels, like domesticated animals, are not to think for themselves. (One of them, Lucifer, will of course disobey this command—and suffer grave consequences!)

With "But" at the start of line 7, you make an emotional turn, shifting from blessing to threatening the angels, and heightening the importance of your message. Having secured their attention by your beneficence, you now seek to ensure their obedience.

The phrase "them that are nought" is a euphemism: You don't define the sins they might commit (so as not to give them ideas), you merely promise punishment to those who take a negative attitude toward your instructions.

"My prison" refers to Hell, of course, which you mentioned in the first quatrain. *Prison* also carries the meaning of capture (from the Latin *prehen-*

sion, "apprehension, seizure"); you are suggesting you will personally grab them—in a grip so fierce they will never escape.

To the medieval mind, the word *pine,* which originally meant "to suffer," had immediate resonance with the wooden cross (from a Jerusalem pine tree) on which Jesus was crucified. So the suggestion is not merely "longing," as we use it today, but truly excruciating pain.

See how many of these notions you can play effectively to your listeners, who are the angels, played by your classmates. Try to inspire them with trust—while at the same time putting "the fear of God" into them.

Go back to what you did (or the discussion) in Lesson 4: Find your "voice of God." Create "God's costume."

And stage yourself as God.

♦ *Point to* the places you are naming and/or creating: Point out the island of Earth, and then Hell, and then "this highest," which is Heaven, as you name them. Let the angels know precisely what you are talking about— "'neath me" is a pretty big place; you can be more specific as to what you're identifying with an appropriate gesture. And the word *this* is what grammarians call a demonstrative pronoun (along with *that, these,* and *those*); such pronouns virtually *require* some sort of visual indication, or your listener will say "*Which* highest?"

♦ *Look* in the direction of "those wielding wealth." Again, *those* being a demonstrative pronoun, be sure to demonstrate to the angels those among them whom you expect to be their role models.

♦ *Gesture* on the phrase "This grant I ye," supporting the future granting of "this" (another demonstrative pronoun, referring to Heaven but also to God's—your—love) by a symbolic handing-over. What sort of gesture? It could be specific, to "this highest . . . Heaven," but you've already made that part clear; perhaps you might try here an open-handed gesture of emphatic affection, referring simply to "everything you see here." Ritualized gestures solemnize important transitions: a tap of the queen's sword to award knighthood, the tender placing of a wedding ring on a bride's finger, the handing over of the America's Cup to the world's yachting champion.

♦ *Move to* your angels, perhaps circling or touching them or both, on "ministers mine" to show them the warmth of your love.

♦ *Glare at* any angel of whom you may be suspicious (and know that Lucifer is among this crowd).

♦ *Emphasize,* with a swift and sudden gesture or posture of absolute conviction, that you are disciplined enough to mete out any punishment necessary, on "pine."

▼ INDICATING ▼

This is a good time to clear up a misunderstanding about the word *indicating*. I, and virtually all other acting teachers (including Stanislavsky in his later years), urge actors not to indicate a character's emotion, but rather to play the action of the scene (try to win the character's goal) with energy, focus, and intensity, in which case you will experience the emotion of your character. The audience will sense your (character's) emotion much better, and more authentically, if they don't see you trying to "indicate" or "push" that emotion out in a technical fashion.

But that doesn't mean you should avoid physically gesturing to objects, or people, by way of explaining—or indicating—exactly what you mean. You cannot, for example, say "Sit in this chair" without somehow pointing out the specific chair you mean: The word *this* doesn't carry the burden of explaining "which," and an indicative gesture of some sort is absolutely necessary to successfully complete the speech act. Not only is there nothing wrong with this form of indicating, it is essential. It is also helpful in supporting the actor's sense that artificial props represent the real thing; when you say "this highest be Heaven," merely pointing, at the same time, to a wooden scaffold, or whatever the scene designer has fashioned, will make the fake Heaven much more real to you as well.

So don't indicate emotion, but *do* feel free to indicate the facts—the people, places, things—that support your point, clarify your argument, and help you win your character's goals with the other characters on stage.

Let whatever costume you have chosen for this role (see Lesson 4) flow with these moves and gestures; indeed, choose your costume so that its movements extend your own.

Is all this hokey? Yes it is, if you don't do it with conviction, or if you do it simply because you are told to do it. No it isn't, if you are an actor and convince us that you *want* to do it—and, in fact, *need* to do it. This is what acting is: It's getting inside a presumably fictional being—a character—and playing his or her part. Obviously, lighting, scenery, sound enhancement, special effects, and a real costume and wig will help a lot, but no amount of technical support will make you God, and no fabric or fog machine will be necessary for the other actors or audience to accept you as God if you want them to.

Playing "God" is an inexhaustible exercise; you can play it many times and make it better each time. Rising to the challenge of this role helps you deliver qualities we rarely explore outside of the stage: grandiosity, unlimited authority, charisma. Merely exploring them—if you can do so without inhibition—can extend your personality as well as your acting ability, as long as you don't let it get out of hand when you leave the theatre!

Summary

Playing a character requires, after a searching analysis, an attempt to master not merely the *meaning* of your words and actions but also the *nature* of the language the playwright has given you, its sounds and shapes and natural progressions. And mastery includes both vocal and physical expressiveness, which you can draw from yourself by seeking to meet the challenges of the role. The role of God, in particular, poses more challenges than most of us rise to in a lifetime—offstage, anyway.

Playing the Devil

Had enough of playing the good guy? Try playing Lucifer (later known as Satan) in the play we've just been working on, *The Creation of the World*. In addition to being evil, Lucifer is probably also the first *comic* character in English drama.

Only a few pages ago, you were basking in the brilliant light of Heaven, where you were a beloved angel in God's company. But since you overreached—demanding to be seen as God's equal—you and your followers have been suddenly cast down into the lower world: into Hell. This is your first speech to the other devils:

Out! Out! Harrowed!° Helpless! Such heat is there here!	°*torn apart*
This is a dungeon of dole° in which I can't delight.	°*unhappiness*
What has my kind become, so comely° and clear?	°*handsome*
Now I am loathsome, alas, who was light.	
My brightness is black and blue now,	
My bale° is e'er° beating and burning.	°*sorrow* °*forever*
I hie° me a-howling and churning.	°*run around*
Out! Ay, welaway!° I wallow in woe now!	°*alas*

For what purpose do you say all this? And to whom are you speaking?

These, by the way, are *the two most important questions* you can ask about *any* acting speech. The playwright may have written the speech primarily to give the audience information, but it's *your* job to create the reasons why *you*, the character, are speaking it in the here and now. Or, in this instance, why you are saying anything at all under these hellish conditions.

The answers are more complex than you might at first think. From the playwright's point of view, of course, you are simply explaining what, in a theatre without contemporary scenic and lighting technology, would be otherwise hard for an audience to discern: that you have just fallen from Heaven into Hell. But you cannot act from the playwright's point of view—only from the character's. Therefore, you must turn the playwright's task (advancing dramatic exposition) into a character's passion, and therefore the actor's task: to fulfill a goal. And what goal might that be in this case?

Let's say, for a start, that your goal is to protest your fate so vigorously, and with such articulate and imaginative description, that you gain the loyalty of the other devils. Think of the situation not as something already wholly determined but as a chaos of new possibilities: The angels falling with you could kill you in revenge for having brought them to this fate, or they could find another leader, or, if you play your cards right, they could come to admire and even worship you once again. As an actor, you know how this is supposed to come out, at least if you've read your Milton, but as Lucifer, your character, you don't. Which would you prefer: being hated or being worshipped? The choice is obvious—so go for it.

Seeking the loyalty of the other devils is obviously a sensible goal, but it is also the sort of positive, active, and, most important, *interactive* goal that makes for vigorous and vibrant acting. Given the choice of goals to play— and every actor has this decision to make—it is virtually always preferable to find those that are positive and interactive: where you can make strong actions to improve your lot, no matter how dismal.

So don't just complain about your fate; rather, seize control of your Hell! Infect your fellow fallen angels with your charisma, your authority, your brilliant invective, your absolute power!

◆ EXERCISE 7-1

Playing the Devil

Students can take turns presenting the Lucifer speech while the others play the other fallen angels.

Give yourself a satanic body for the role of Lucifer, a body broken by the long fall, twisted by evil, and tormented by the fires of Hell. (This character reappears in Renaissance dramatic history as a so-called Vice role, which includes characters such as Mery-reporte in John Heywood's *Play of the Weather,* Avarice in Nicholas Udall's *Respublica,* Covetous in the anonymous *Enough Is as Good as a Feast,* and as Richard III, whom you worked on in Lesson 5).

Find your satanic voice, one that can command respect and fear from devils and is authoritative enough to defy God. It's not your everyday voice,

Devils force a sinner into Hell in a production of the medieval drama *Doomsday* by the Focused Program in Medieval Drama at the University of California, Irvine. (Photo © Phil Channing)

but then you don't have to frighten devils or defy God every day, so find, in yourself, something special.

Costume yourself for the fall and the fire. Imagine that your angel clothes have been burned off; you are now in your satanic undergarments.

And look about you: Who are you looking at? These other devils: What sort of devils are they? Imagine them as cowards, imbeciles, sycophants; allies but decidedly underlings. They adore you; use them mercilessly. Exploit them. And God is a pompous old fart, full of long-winded homilies; he's powerful but dismally stupid. (Note: Scurrilous language is necessary here; you must animate a satanic irreverence in yourself to play this role!)

Play the speech to the devils, and to God.

What did you find out?

Was it funny on occasion? Good: This should not be surprising; remember we noted that Lucifer was, in these early English dramatic incarnations, largely a comic character. This is because, in medieval drama, villains were portrayed as foolish, as ludicrously overreaching dolts. That's not to say medieval audiences took evil lightly; they, instead, felt confident of the supremacy of what they believed to be God's values and believed that no truly intelligent person would challenge them. They also knew, in watching *The Creation of the Universe,* that they were merely at a play, one performed by people they knew well from their own home town.

Should you "play" the comedy then? No. You need play only the overreaching. And it might be even better to say you need play only the reaching, since the "over" is fully latent within the speech.

Look at the language closely for clues:

Out! Out! . . .

You are both yelling to the devils to flee the punishment they have fallen into and yelling in protest to God for kicking you and your fellows "out" of heaven. You are also trying to establish yourself as the leader of the fallen angels. Your first words have a very simple semantic content; they are as much sound as meaning: an ear-splitting howl (with the same vowel sound as *howl*) that shocks, protests, and commands at the same time.

Indeed, having these three different goals for your howl will make it more visceral, more emotionally profound, as it has an ambiguous meaning. Cry it from the bottom of your tortured soul, in grief and fury. Words with little semantic content are an actor's dream, for the *sound* of the word, as amplified and colored by the actor's emotional response to an immediate situation, produces virtually all its "meaning."* So howl your heart out, and you will, by that means, also justify your claiming to be "a-howling" by the end of the speech.

And, as you howl, hurl yourself around Hell. Don't just talk about trying to get out of there, or away from the other devils, try to *do* it. *Run!*

. . . Harrowed! Helpless! Such heat is there here!

The alliteration (*harrowed, helpless, heat, here*) and assonance (*harrowed, there, heat, here*) common in medieval verse is repeated throughout this speech, which in Lucifer's case (in contrast to God's in Lesson 6) is comical, as if Lucifer is trying to copy God's language but gets silly in the process.

The emphatic word of the line is, of course, *heat,* as that's what we first think of when we think of the physical condition of Hell. Let the word present you (as Lucifer) the opportunity to show your fellow devils, perhaps by a giant tremble, a giant shrugging-off with arms flailing, how you can

---

* In Shakespeare's *Othello,* for example, Othello's cry of "O! O! O!" as he realizes the extent of his error in killing his wife—a line possibly added to the text by the role's first actor, Richard Burbage—has little semantic content but can potentially deliver a searing emotional impact.

finally beat the heat, and overcome the feeling of helplessness with which you began the line.

What's your goal here? To show, perhaps, that you are bold enough to call hellfire by name (or at least by a euphemism), brave enough to challenge it, and wise enough to show your former followers that you are yet unbowed. Now move to your devils.

This is a dungeon of dole in which I can't delight.

This is more alliteration (*dungeon, dole, delight*), and more comedy in the ludicrously understated "in which I can't delight." *This,* another demonstrative pronoun, should be supported with some sort of gesture (perhaps pointing wildly with all ten extended fingers?) that shows just what dungeon you are referring to.

What has my kind become, so comely and clear?

This rhetorical question (one which you don't expect to be answered) allows you to throw your focus directly on your fellow devils and show them that you share their lot. In early English, *kind* shares the modern meaning "sort" as well as the adjective "nice, gentle," but also an older meaning of "kin, kinship, family." Thus all three meanings are involved here: Persons of "kindred" are of the same certain "sort" and, because of that, "nice"—at least to each other.* So having yelled at them, perhaps now you can reach out to them—or one or two of them—and touch their (now tormented and misshapen) faces on *comely* and *clear.* Appeal to your fellow devils' sense of loyalty to your kinship and kindness, as well as your own former beauty and brilliance (clarity).

Your ability to rhyme (*here/clear*) also shows that you haven't lost your great agility with words, despite the pain you're experiencing, and thus poetic eloquence is part of the package of your appeal. If you can state their anxieties better than they can themselves, if you can even entertain them with your and their distress, they will almost certainly continue to accept you as their leader.

Now, having gained the initial respect of the devils, it's time to turn your focus back to God in Heaven above. While still speaking to your fellow devils, be sure that God overhears your anger and defiance. Challenge your fate vigorously. Make God sweat! Impress your fellow devils with your sacrilegious audacity! No one hearing you now should doubt who your future target will be.

---

* Thus when Hamlet calls Claudius a "kindless villain" in Shakespeare's play, he is calling him "unkind" in the modern sense and also "without kindred," Claudius having murdered his own brother.

A medieval devil   A devil messenger prods the monster's mouth that opens to become the gateway to Hell, with Satan perched above the head, in a drawing of a 1539 production of *The Vineyard of the Lord* in Zurich, Switzerland. Devils had fantasy animal characteristics, here tusks, snout, and horns, and so would probably move in ways that showed an exaggerated, fantastical, animalistic ferocity. Satan's giant ears and claws made him a fearsome but also somewhat comic figure to the medieval audience.

Now I am loathsome, alas, who was light.

Starting with *Now* (a word you will repeat twice again in the next four lines), differentiate yourself from your past identity and move forward to what you will do in the present time. Bring the action to the here and now.

Know that "who was light" refers to your own name: Lucifer, from the Latin *lux,* "light," means "one who brings light."* Let that word *light* ring

---

* In England, a fireplace match was until recently called a "lucifer."

in your fellow devils' ears and remind them of what you did for them: You lighted their way.

My brightness is black and blue now,
My bale is e'er beating and burning.

For the first time, your alliteration carries over two lines (*brightness, black, blue, bale, beating, burning*), characteristic of your overreaching. Hammer your devil pals with these six words and their opening plosive consonants: You are, of course, describing them as well, and what they have now become. Make them as enraged at God as you are.

I hie me a-howling and churning.

Do this: Hie (run about) howling, trying to get the other devils to follow you! If they follow you, you will have reemerged as their leader; you will be the Head Devil in a battle for control of the Earth.

Out! Ay, welaway! I wallow in woe now!

This time your "Out!" can be addressed directly to God above, with a devil-ish gesture of defiance. Your "Ay, welaway" might be a reaction (fear? increased defiance?) to the retaliation you may sense coming down on you from on high. And "I wallow in woe now" may be played not merely as a lament but as an even more urgent invitation for your fellow devils to follow you—and wallow around in Hell with you.

Thus what looked at first like an undifferentiated lament actually has four distinct, and sequential, units, or "beats" as actors often call them:* first your protest and attempt to escape further torment, then a sympathetic reaching out to your fellow devils for support, then a bold defiance of God in an effort to start a revolution, and finally a reaction to God's presumed retaliation, coupled with a deepening of your invitation to avenge your fate.

In all these suggested objectives, you are encouraged to find active goals that will animate your performance and make you connect physically and emotionally as well as vocally with not only your fellow actors in Hell (the devils, as played by your nonspeaking classmates) but also God, who might be imagined or who might be played by an actor in Heaven. (In the original medieval play, the character of God is indeed positioned above during this speech.)

---

* *Beat* is often thought to be Stanislavsky's term for an acting unit. The word, however, seems to derive from a mishearing of the simpler word *bit*, meaning the same thing, as pronounced by Richard Boleslavski (in his Polish accent) when teaching Stanislavsky's system in New York during the early 1920s.

◆ EXERCISE 7-2

Playing the Devil—Take Two

Play the speech again with, as special "punishments" of Hell, one of the following:

1. You find your right wrist tied to your right ankle.

2. You are wearing fifty-pound boots.

3. You can feel dozens of ants crawling underneath your clothes.

4. You are being attacked by drops of acid rain.

5. You can hear the angels above laughing at you.

Your instructor and fellow students can suggest many more punishments which will intensify Lucifer's anguish—and your consequent defiance—all the further.

Summary

Your task as an actor is to *act out a situation,* not to narrate a text. And to do this, you must interact with other actors, even with non-present actors (such as God, in this case), as if you didn't know the final outcome of the dramatic story. Find and use the rhymes and rhythms of the language to help you achieve your situational goals; create a devilish costume from simple wardrobe items; and find within yourself a satanic voice, posture, and gestural repertoire. And play the Hell out of it!

L E S S O N

8

The Battle of the Sexes: Noah and His Wife

It's time to play some human beings. Since this is a book on style and character, they aren't exactly going to be the human beings next door—but they are certainly going to have things in common with all humanity.

Let's look at one of the first true masterpieces of English drama: the Noah play in the Wakefield cycle of the fourteenth century, an expansion of the famous Bible story written by an author who, while anonymous, is known to us as the "Wakefield Master," a title honoring the Yorkshire city where he (presumably) lived and the particular excellence of his craftsmanship.

As you will quickly see, the scene selected—an argument between Noah and his wife—owes far less to Genesis than to the eternally humorous "battle of the sexes" we see in comedies from all ages. Furious marital disputes and lovers' quarrels, comic while bordering dangerously on the abusive, are familiar in both the Old and New Comedies of ancient Greece, and subsequently in Roman, medieval, Renaissance, and modern drama. They were standard in *commedia dell'arte* and early English Punch and Judy puppet shows; they surface in Shakespeare's *Taming of the Shrew* and *Much Ado About Nothing*, Molière's *Bourgeois Gentleman* and *The School for Wives*, Congreve's *The Way of the World* and Wycherley's *The Country Wife*; and in more modern times in classic television sitcoms (*The Honeymooners, I Love Lucy, Roseanne*) and Broadway comedies (Neil Simon's *Barefoot in the Park*) and musicals (Frank Loesser's *Guys and Dolls*).

The medieval era, an age when the status of women was rapidly rising (owing to increased literacy and urbanization), was particularly attuned to the plight of women seeking their independent voices, opposed by men trying to retain their historic prerogatives.

Otto Coehelo and Mehr Mansouri play Noah and his wife in a production by the Focused Program in Medieval Drama at the University of California, Irvine. (Photo © Phil Channing)

Thus, in this scene where Noah is struggling to get his wife to board the ark as the rain begins, Noah's wife is cockily asserting her freedom and independence. I have added stage directions so that you can readily follow the action.*

NOAH: Now are we there as we should be.
Do get in our gear, our cattle and fee°,   °possessions
Into this vessel here, my children free.

[Noah's children—his three sons and their wives—enter the ark. Noah's wife remains outside.]

NOAH'S WIFE [looking at the ark]:
I was ne'er barred up before—as ever might I thee—
In such a hostelry as this!
In faith, I cannot find
Which is the front, which the behind.
But shall we here be impined°,   °imprisoned
Noah, as thou have bliss°?   °if you want to be happy

---

* Adapted from the original and edited by Robert Cohen and Edgar Schell.

NOAH: Dame, if we have skill, here must we abide grace.
   Therefore, wife, with good will come into this place.

NOAH'S WIFE *[standing her ground, outside the ark]*:
   Sir, for Jack nor for Jill will I turn my face
   Till I have on this hill spun a space
   On my rock°.   °*tool for spinning thread*
   Well were he that might get me!
   Now will I down set me;
   And reck° I no man stop me   °*reckon*
   For dread of a knock°!   °*a hit on the head*

[She sits down on a hill and spins.]

NOAH *[within the ark, hearing thunder and seeing rain]*:
   Behold to the heavens! The cataracts all,
   They are open full even, great and small,
   And the planets all seven have left their stall.
   These thunders and lightnings down here fall
   Full stout
   On both halls and bowers,
   Castles and towers.
   Full sharp are these showers
   That rain hereabout.

   Therefore, wife, have done; come into ship fast.

NOAH'S WIFE *[still sitting on her hill and spinning]*:
   Yea, Noah—Go clout thy shoon°!   °*go fix your shoes*
   The better will they last.
   . . .

NOAH: Now is this twice: Come in, dame, on my friendship!

NOAH'S WIFE: Whether I lose or I win, in faith, thy fellowship
   Set I not at a pin°. This spindle will I slip°   °*I consider worthless*
                                                    °*spinning tool I will toss aside*
   Upon this hill,
   Ere I stir one foot.

NOAH: Peter°! I trow we dote°.   °*St. Peter (an oath)* °*I believe we will go mad*
   Without any more note°,   °*if we keep quarreling*
   Come in if ye will.

NOAH'S WIFE *[seeing the water rising near her]*:
   Yipes! Water nighs so near that I sit not dry!

Into ship with my gear, therefore will I hie
For dread that I drown here!

[She struggles onto the ark but stays right by the door.]

NOAH: Dame, surely
It be'est brought full dear° ye abode so long by   °*It's too bad*
Out of ship.

NOAH'S WIFE: I will not for thy bidding
Go from door to the midding°.   °*center of the boat*

NOAH: In faith, and for your long tarrying,
Ye shall have a lick of the whip.

NOAH'S WIFE: Spare me not, I pray thee, but e'en as thou think;
These great words shall not flay me.

NOAH: Abide, dame, and drink°:   °*listen to my response*
For beaten shalt thou be with this staff till thou stink.

[He strikes her with his "staff," a harmless baton.]

Are my strokes good? Say me.

NOAH'S WIFE: What say ye, Fred Fink°?   °*a made-up name*

NOAH *[striking her]*:
Speak! Cry me mercy, I say.

NOAH'S WIFE: Thereto say I, *nay!*

NOAH: If thou don't, by this day,
Thy head shall I break!

NOAH'S WIFE: Lord, I were at ease, and heartily I'd heal,
Might I once have a mess of honest widow's meal,
For thy soul, no less, a mass penny should I deal

[pointing to, and addressing, the women in the audience]

And so would all of these, here in the commonweal°,   °*village*
These wives that are here,
For the lives they have led,
Wish their husbands dead.
For, as ever I ate bread,
So wish I our sire were.

NOAH *[addressing the men in the audience]*:
Ye men that have wives, while they are young,
If ye love your lives, chastise their tongue.
Me thinks my heart rives°, both liver and lung,   °*breaks*

Medieval wear   A man and woman in the late thirteenth century. These are probably the sort of clothes Noah and his wife—as well as members of the audience—
would be wearing in the plays of that period: for the men, a knee-length tunic with
overlong sleeves gathered at the wrists, and hose and boots beneath; for the women,
a floor-length, long-sleeved, loose-fitting woolen gown or robe. Both men and
women wore hoods or caps. The voluminous costumes do not restrict bold movements, but may limit the effectiveness of subtle or delicate gestures.

To see such strives°, wed-men among   °*arguments*
But I,
As have I bliss,
Shall chastise this.

[He strikes at her; she dodges.]

NOAH'S WIFE: Yet may ye miss,
    Simple Si°!   °*a made-up name, possibly a reference*
                    to the Simple Simon of the nursery rhyme

NOAH: I shall make thee still as stone, beginner of blunder°!   °*first sinner*
    I shall beat thy back and bone, and break all in sunder.

NOAH'S WIFE *[as they resume fighting]*:
    Out, alas, I am gone! Out upon thee, man's wonder!

[She rolls on top of him in victory.]

NOAH: See how she can groan, and I lie under!
    But wife,
    Let us halt this ado,
    For my back is near in two.

NOAH'S WIFE: And I'm so black and blue
    That I may lose my life.

Clearly the scene, though biblically inspired and from a play with deeply reverential passages, is a farce. Its wife-beating theme would be appalling—except that it's the husband who begs for mercy and we know nobody has really been hurt. The language is far more fluid and informal than in *The Creation of the Universe,* with comic names and homely invectives ("Go clout thy shoon!"), verse lines from as few as two to as many as thirteen syllables, a wide range of rhyme schemes (including the rare AAAA), and alliteration which is present only in spurts, invariably indicating failed pomposity.

◆ SCENE 8-1

Noah and His Wife

Play the scene with the following suggestions:

- ◆ Use a stool or a chair for the hill on which Noah's wife sits, and simply mime the ark and the entrance to the ark.

- ◆ Use a mat or carpeted floor for the fight between Noah and his wife, and use a harmless baton (such as a toy plastic baseball bat) for the staff with which Noah hits his wife. Use another plastic baton for the wife's spindle, as she will use this for her weapon. Use imaginary string and an imaginary rock for the spinning of the wool.

- ◆ Stage the fight in a very simple way, emphasizing the reactions to the blows rather than the force of the blows themselves and working out how Noah's wife ends up sitting on top of him.

- ◆ Stage the scene with the audience around it, in a circle or semicircle, and the men and women in the audience grouped separately. Each gender can cheer on their own representative.

- ◆ Imagine your three sons and three daughters-in-law have gone into the ark and are watching you both.

- ◆ Here's the kicker: Play the scene with the goal of convincing your three sons and three daughters-in-law that your gender is the smarter one!

If you can do this, you will enjoy the liberating experience of medieval comedy, which is essentially a mass public spectacle, not a drama for an elite-only audience.

Notice that everything in the text of the scene is a tool to demonstrate how smart you are. The rhymes, which in Lesson 6 could be construed as demonstrating the character's divinity, now demonstrate your cleverness at matching words. See how the wife trumps Noah with this rhyme:

NOAH: Speak! Cry me mercy, I say.

NOAH'S WIFE: Thereto say I, *Nay!*

Her "I, Nay!" both repeats his "I" and counteracts his "say," giving her a double victory: absorbing his word and turning it around on him. Noah's earlier rhyme

Abide, dame, and drink
For beaten shall thou be with this staff till thou stink

pairs a five-syllable line with a twelve-syllable one (a technique revived by American poet Ogden Nash five centuries later). It is a delightfully comic insult.

The wife's made-up names for her husband, Fred Fink and Simple Si, show her mastery of the art of the insult, deploying both alliteration and rhyme.

Noah's alliteration ("I shall beat thy back and bone") is calculated to show his unyielding stamina in assault; his employment of gratuitous facts ("the planets all seven") seeks to establish that he is graced with vast knowledge, while the wife's metaphoric epithets ("Go clout thy shoon!") show her a woman of inventive linguistic imagination. These are combatants who love the battle and are evidently well practiced at it. Playing these roles challenges you, the actors, to let loose a barrage of medieval verbal flourishes—all in the service of humiliating your spouse and convincing those around you (children and theatre audience) that yours is the superior sex.

And your blows—let them appear to be ferocious! (This is the reason to use a harmless, featherweight plastic baton.) Flex your muscles: Show that you are not to be made a fool of!

In all this, speaking and moving, *be a role model for your same-sex children*! Noah, show your boys how to handle their wives! Wife, show your daughters-in-law how to stand up to their husbands! And both of you: Never think that you are trying to win this fight just for yourself. Rather, understand that you are trying to win to better influence your same-sex children! You are trying to show them how to have a happier life.

Notice that I suggest, regarding your blows, "Let them *appear to be* ferocious," not simply "Let them be ferocious." It is the appearance of ferocity that will impress your children. Real ferocity could, by harming your wife or husband, backfire into creating sympathy for the other gender.

Now let's go one step further: Play the scene with the goal of convincing the surrounding *audience* that your gender is the smarter one. Be a role model for all the men, or all the women, in the audience. In fact, try to convince *both* sexes that your ways are the best. Noah's wife: Try to make all the men stop abusing their women. Noah: Try to make all the women stop defying their men.

Play shamelessly to the audience in order to get them on your side. And I mean *shamelessly* quite literally: Play to the audience without shame—because *they are where your goal must be won.* You are not playing to entertain the audience (in the ordinary sense) but to win them over to the belief that your sex, of the two, is the brighter, the more imaginative, the more ferocious, and the one more qualified to exert leadership.

In doing this, paradoxically, you will entertain the audience. But remember, the word *entertain* doesn't just mean "to amuse." Fundamentally, it means to "capture their attention," deriving from the French word *entretenir,* or "to hold together" (from *entre,* "between," and *tenir,* "to hold"). So capture the attention of the audience by involving them in your debate about which sex is more qualified to lead.

The relationship of the play to the audience, though, is an issue complicated enough to have a lesson of its own; indeed, it is the thorniest issue in the study of acting. Even Stanislavsky was puzzled by it, considering pleasing the audience as the "super-super-objective" of the actor but also considering that he "could not yet define it." We'll take our crack at it in the next lesson.

Performance

In his most famous paradox, Konstantin Stanislavsky, the great Russian actor and acting teacher, said that acting was "doing something private in public." Since everyone already knew that acting is public, taking place in front of assembled audiences, Stanislavsky's work became celebrated for his emphasis on the private half of this paradox. Indeed, in America, the private aspect of acting—which he also called "public solitude"—was mainly what Stanislavsky was known for during the great era (1935–1975) of naturalistic (or "method") acting that, through his books and followers, changed the style of American acting for both stage and film.

Lee Strasberg, Stanislavsky's most noted American disciple and the long-time head of the Actors Studio, developed his best-known exercise out of this paradox. Called "the private moment," Strasberg's exercise asked students to do something on stage that they would never do if they were being observed in real life, without regard to whether it was "theatrical." An entire generation of actors was surprised to discover that these private moments often proved publicly captivating.

Strasberg's private moment is a wonderful opportunity for actors to understand—in their hearts as well as their heads—that great acting, while it may be supported by exquisitely perfected theatrical technique, ultimately emerges from a performer's emotional core. What transports an audience and centers the theatrical experience, Strasberg demonstrated, is the *authenticity* of actors within their roles and the full engagement of actors in the dynamics of their actions.

Virtually all actors—and acting teachers—agree with this basic principle. Great acting, as it is widely understood, does not merely entertain the audience with virtuosity; it also expresses a personal and truthful humanity. The ability to touch private feelings (and fears, and fantasies) is, more often than not, what makes a stage interaction—whether an argument, a romance, or a shared experience—memorably intense. Such acting also conveys the inherent uniqueness of each actor, making the role personal as well as dramatic. Acting that reaches down into your private self is fundamental to that level of performance and was, therefore, all but worshipped by Stanislavsky, Strasberg, and the (primarily American) actors who have since fallen under its influence.

But neither Stanislavsky nor Strasberg invented this notion. Drama has *always* had a private character. According to ancient records, the fourth-century Greek actor Polus placed an urn containing the ashes of his own dead son in front of him when he knelt to sing the lamentation of Electra; this encouraged him to tap in to his most private, personal grief, lending authenticity to his performance of the depths of despair. Quintilian, a first-century Roman orator, imagined "visions" of his wife and children dying to achieve the same effect. In even the most formal theatre genres, personal authenticity has always been prized: The celebrated eighteenth-century actor of the elaborately stylized Japanese *kabuki*, Sakata Tojuro, said the best way to act "is to forget the audience and to concentrate upon playing the play as if it was really happening," which is to say with a private rather than public focus.

But of course acting is also a *public* interaction, not only because it is performed before a theatre audience but because people in real life give public performances much of the time. As the sociologist Ervin Goffman has persuasively demonstrated (in *The Presentation of Self in Everyday Life*, 1959), they perform for their friends, their employers, their families, and their known or imagined "public." Some perform for their God.

And if the characters we play on stage are to be truly authentic, *they* must perform publicly as well. Let's explain this in practice rather than continuing this rather abstract philosophical discussion!

In Lessons 4 and 6, God, in *The Creation of the Universe*, is speaking publicly to a group of angels. Immediately afterward, he turns and addresses one of them individually:

> Of all the mights I have made, most next after me
> I make thee as master and mirror of my might.
> I build thee here boonly° in bliss for to be   °*happily*
> I name thee for Lucifer, bearer of light.

Here, God is addressing the angel Lucifer directly, but he is also "naming" Lucifer to the other angels, who are overhearing these remarks. Thus God's speech may be described as both a *private interaction* with Lucifer and, simultaneously, a *performed public pronouncement* to the angels. God is, therefore, speaking both privately and publicly at the same time.

We can then say that God has two levels of audience for these remarks: Lucifer is his primary audience; the collective angels are his secondary audience.

And while these audiences exist simultaneously, God is speaking to them on different levels. He is speaking directly to his primary audience (Lucifer) but indirectly (by their overhearing him) to his secondary one (the angels). The *performative* aspects of his behavior (such as the versification and rhyme pattern of his thoughts) come into play with this indirect inclusion of the secondary audience.

We can also identify God's third, or tertiary, level of audience: those other angels who, though not in sight, may be presumed elsewhere in Heaven— and therefore still within range of an all-powerful (and thus universally heard) God.

◆ EXERCISE 9-1

A Performative God

Play this speech, referring back to the commentary in Lessons 4 and 6 for suggestions on "playing God," but now in the context of three different levels of audience. Speak directly to Lucifer, looking him straight in the eye, but be certain the angels around you are also paying attention—and make certain they revere the ceremony you are performing for their edification.

And let your words cascade throughout all Heaven as well. Make certain that all the angels in the cosmos hear and respect you. Command attention with your posture, gestures, tone of voice, and phrasing. Find the voice, and the resonance, and the cadences that can spread your godliness throughout the divine universe.

Performative Aspects of Dramatic Scenes

◆ EXERCISE 9-2

Performing Your Greetings and Insults

Return to Exercises 2-4, 2-5, and 2-6: the Elizabethan greetings and insults. Replay these exercises with a partner but in an actual crowded courtyard or city plaza. Play them with your partner, as before, but at the same time *perform* them to the crowd. Show everybody just how warm, and welcoming, and eloquent, and noble you can be in greeting your partner, and how terrifying you can be in insulting him or her. Make a public statement about *yourself* with your greeting or insult. Make passersby admire you, or fear you, as the case may be. Make your greeting or insult a public performance!

When we experience these exercises, we soon realize that personal communication almost always includes a performative element. To hail someone graciously is not merely to interact graciously with that person but to demonstrate to anyone who might be within earshot that you are a gracious person. And to insult someone is not merely to inflict a measure of pain upon him but to let the world know you are not a person with whom to be trifled. We are always, in our interactions with a particular individual, projecting an image of ourselves to everyone who may happen to be watching or listening. Indeed, we may often be seeking—consciously or unconsciously—to induce these bystanders to pay attention to us. This is at the heart of performance in life—and in the theatre.

In the scene from the Noah play in Lesson 8, Noah and his wife are, at the primary level, interacting with each other (trying to change each other's behavior of the moment), while at the secondary level they're performing for their children (trying to teach them how to treat the opposite sex). And at the tertiary level Noah is hoping that God will hear that his effort to get the ark under way is proceeding apace, as God had instructed.

And Noah and his wife are also performing for a *fourth* level of audience, the imagined community of their fellow citizens—some doubters, some admirers—who have gathered around them. But of course this community is represented, in the theatre, by the live theatre audience! And here is the major linking between the private and public levels of acting—interacting with your partner and giving a performance to an audience—that Stanislavsky was thinking about.

The Audience in the Theatre

Theatre was a more openly public event in ages past, and the audience was more openly evident in the theatrical event. Ancient Greek theatre, which was performed to audiences numbering in the several thousands (17,000 at Athens and Epidaurus), featured a chorus, representing citizens or demigods, who would both witness and comment on the actions of the principal characters. The physical design of the Greek theatre placed the chorus between the principal characters and the audience, so that characters speaking to the chorus were also speaking directly to the audience immediately behind them. In medieval theatre, audiences gathered freely around the action on at least three sides of the stage—sometimes all four—and actors would and could talk directly to them (as Noah and his wife do), sometimes walking among them while speaking. Most of this mingling was carried over into Renaissance theatres as well: In Italian plazas and gardens where *commedia* was performed, in Spanish *corrales,* and in English innyards and aptly named public theatres during the time of Shakespeare, where the spectators not only surrounded the stage but sometimes sat right on it, the audience was part of the picture.

And all of these theatres operated outdoors in full daylight, where audiences and actors could see each other equally. Even after theatre moved indoors somewhere around the seventeenth century, the audience area was never darkened during the performance but remained fully lit so that the actors and audience were all bathed in the same light. It has been barely a hundred years that the theatre audience has sat, like voyeurs, in a dark space watching spotlighted actors.

Correspondingly, pre-nineteenth-century drama largely features public rather than private discourse, as well as moments of direct public performance, in which actors face and speak directly to the audience. Prologues, epilogues, monologues, soliloquies, songs, dances, and covert asides to the audience are features of virtually all drama from the ancient Greeks to the Romantics of the nineteenth century, and when these methods reappear in contemporary drama, they may seem avant-garde but are actually as old as Aeschylus and Aristophanes.

Thus, acting, prior to Stanislavsky's time, was more openly public than it had become in his time. Which is one of the reasons Stanislavsky, whose actors were initially trained in the nineteenth century, was considered revolutionary for asking them to become "private" in the twentieth.

But privatization was not merely a theatrical revolution, it was a social one. Life itself was more publicly lived in earlier times. It is easy for us to forget that the privacy we treasure today is a recent luxury. The notion of a free-standing family home that could be maintained without live-in servants or workers, much less a soundproofed, insulated apartment free from the commotion of its surrounding neighborhood, was a rarity in centuries past. In a pre-industrial world without the central heating, air conditioning, indoor plumbing, refrigeration, telephones, and electronic entertainment that make staying at home attractive, waking life was almost entirely lived in public: among servants and workers at home (where the home often doubled as a place of business) and in the streets, plazas, churches, theatres, schools, assemblies, baths, washhouses, and open-air markets outside the home. City dwellers lived mainly in vast warrens of tiny, interconnecting rooms; country people boarded their parents, children, animals, and workhands in their farmhouses; and even the nobility maintained estates that were shared with dozens, even hundreds, of servants, retainers, extended family members, and often domestic animals. And with little public transportation to speak of until the 1800s, most people before that time simply lived where they worked, in the public environment of their social communities.

Thus, in the era before Stanislavsky, the idea of doing something "in private" was a rarefied one; few people ever experienced such a treat. Real solitude barely existed: Taking a bath, and even using the toilet, were often public activities. It is difficult, therefore, to conceive of an Elizabethan actor even imagining how to create a "private moment." Or a playwright writing one. When Hamlet, famously, says "Now I am alone," it is a rare moment of theatre, and he is soon burst in upon by friends who don't even bother to knock.

The retreat to a private mode of communication, however, was relatively shortlived, at least in the theatre. Today, actors are expected to explore the public as well as the private interactions of their characters. The regular revivals of pre-naturalistic plays, both on stage and in films; the growing popularity of post-naturalistic, directly performative theatrical techniques, exemplified by the plays of Bertolt Brecht (as well as by musical theatre, dance theatre, and many other widely popular dramas and dramatic forms); the sociological studies of Goffman and newer postmodern theorists; and the development of globalized entertainment and communications through film, television, and the Internet have led to a fresh study of the nature of the role that *audience* plays in the behavior of dramatic characters and in the acting of the actors that play them.

Let's experiment further with this notion, using excerpts from three great dramatists (with whom you will work further in later lessons): Sophocles, Shakespeare, and Chekhov.

◆ SCENE 9-1

The Performative Context: Oedipus and Creon

Here is a portion of a scene from Sophocles' *Oedipus Tyrannus* (also known as *Oedipus Rex* and *Oedipus the King*), first performed around 430 B.C., where Oedipus, the mythical tenth-century-B.C. ruler of Thebes, is arguing with his brother-in-law, Creon, to the point that Oedipus seeks Creon's death. Memorize and, with a partner, perform this exchange, which takes place in or in front of the palace. Oedipus has accused Creon of trying to undermine his authority, while Creon has defended himself.*

---

* The *Oedipus* scenes here and in Lesson 10 are from the translation by Luci Berkowitz and Theodore F. Brunner, published in the Norton Critical Edition, 1970. They are slightly edited and abridged, and I have added stage directions.

CREON: Do you intend to banish me?

OEDIPUS: No. No, not banish you. I want to see you *dead*—to make you an example for all aspiring to my throne.

CREON: Then you won't do as I suggest? You won't believe me?

OEDIPUS: You have not shown that you deserve belief.

CREON: No, because I see that you are mad.

OEDIPUS: In my own eyes, I am sane.

CREON: You should be sane in mine as well.

OEDIPUS: No. You are a traitor!

CREON: And what if you are wrong?

OEDIPUS: Still—*I* will rule.

CREON: Not when you rule treacherously.

OEDIPUS: O Thebes! My city! Listen to him!

CREON: My city too!

It is easy to see that this scene, like all Greek drama, occurs in a public context: When Oedipus cries "My city! Listen to him!", he is appealing to the chorus—a representing group of Theban citizens—to take his side. And Creon's response, though directed to Oedipus, is likewise an appeal to those same citizens, reminding them that he, too, is a member of Theban society. Indeed, as the play makes clear, Creon has lived in Thebes all his life, while Oedipus only arrived there after he had grown to maturity.

This exchange, though framed as an argument between two characters, is in fact a public debate between two political rivals, with each trying to gain the chorus's sympathy and respect for his own position. When Creon calls Oedipus mad, he is trying to get the chorus to accept this definition of Oedipus's behavior in order to weaken Oedipus's authority. When Oedipus says "*I* will rule," he is trying to demonstrate such fierce authority that Creon will have to back down.

Moreover, Oedipus is also trying to forestall any further uprisings. When he says he wants to make Creon "an example for all aspiring to my throne," the "all" is specifically directed to anyone in the chorus who might be thinking of supporting Creon or his allegations.

So, the characters are arguing with each other (interacting at the primary level) but also performing for the chorus of citizens of tenth-century-B.C. Thebes (the secondary level), seeking to win approval of their positions and righteous authority. And, as this scene plays in the Theatre of Dionysus in Athens, they are also performing for a theatre audience (the tertiary level) of fifth-century-B.C. Athenians. One can easily draw the analogy of a televised debate between presidential candidates, who are simultaneously arguing with each other's positions, performing for the applause of the studio audience, and, at the tertiary level, seeking the votes of the television audience.

Play the scene in front of a "chorus" of your classmates. Try at one and the same time to *humiliate* your rival and *impress* the citizenry. Try to persuade the chorus to believe that you are the most authoritative and righteous leader in all Greece. Try to win their vote, as though you were competing in a forthcoming election. Try to win their applause—or even shouts of approval! And chorus: Feel free to murmur sounds of encouragement to these competitors. Inspire them to work for your vote—and your applause.

◆ EXERCISE 9-3

The Performative Context: Shakespeare

Memorize one of the following speeches from Shakespeare's *Hamlet*. Each of the two characters, Queen Gertrude and King Claudius, is trying to persuade Prince Hamlet (who is Gertrude's son and Claudius's nephew and stepson) not to go back to school. Each speech takes place at the Danish court, not long after King Hamlet, Prince Hamlet's father, has died suddenly.

QUEEN: Good Hamlet, cast thy nighted° color off,   °*gloomy*
    And let thine eye look like a friend on Denmark.
    Do not for ever with thy vailed° lids   °*half-closed*
    Seek for thy noble father in the dust.
    Thou know'st 'tis common; all that lives must die,
    Passing through nature to eternity.

              . . .

CLAUDIUS: For your intent
    In going back to school in Wittenberg,
    It is most retrograde to our desire:
    And we beseech you, bend you to remain
    Here, in the cheer and comfort of our eye,
    Our chiefest courtier, cousin, and our son.

Now play the speech you have chosen to someone playing Prince Hamlet, surrounded by a host of other nobles and attendants. Your goals are twofold: On the primary level, you must appeal to your son/nephew to stay by your side; on the secondary level, you, as a ruler, must show your court that you have the authority to command your own family (if you don't, how can you command a kingdom?).

Note that the situation for both of you, Gertrude and Claudius, is very perilous. King Hamlet has just died, under somewhat mysterious circumstances, and, as his widow and brother have married with "unseemly haste" immediately thereafter, a foreign prince now holds "a weak supposal" of your "worth" and thinks your kingdom may be "disjoint[ed]." He is openly planning a military attack. It is essential, then, since your reign is beginning with an international crisis, that you assure the court of your capacity for strong leadership and of the security of your royal marriage. Neither of you can afford to publicly look like a pushover to your son/nephew's wishes.

Combining the appeal to your son/nephew with the show of political and marital strength, however, is a tricky task. The appeal is based on loving concern, expressed in your words "good Hamlet," "friend," "we beseech you," "cheer and comfort," "cousin," "son." But beneath these kindnesses you must convey to the court the capacity for effective rule; your tone and body language under the phrases "it is most retrograde to our desire" and "all that lives must die" must suggest the iron fist beneath the velvet glove. Indeed, Claudius's "our son" contains strong elements of both affection and authority, since by publicly assuming the parental role, he emasculates Hamlet's own adulthood, and by using the royal "we" to indicate himself, Claudius also reinforces his bond with Gertrude—while at the same time replacing Hamlet's real father with his own personage.

Try your speech several times, seeking to influence both audiences simultaneously: encouraging Hamlet (your primary audience) to stay in your home, while simultaneously assuring the court (your secondary audience) to accept your authority on all upcoming political and military matters.

And there is a tertiary audience as well. Although Hamlet doesn't yet know it, Claudius murdered Hamlet's father; moreover, he secretly feels guilty about it (as we later discover). And Gertrude, though perhaps unaware of her first husband's murder by her second, is almost certainly guilty of the earlier adultery of which she is later accused. Both of these characters are, though not openly, seeking to make their peace with God and perhaps hoping that they can do so by the "love" they show their son/nephew.

Playing at these three levels at the same time is not easy—but it's essential if you are to capture what's really happening in these moments of the play. All these communications would be going on simultaneously if the situation were experienced by real people, and so they must be seen as going on among characters who are played by real people. This is how acting reaches into the complexity of human personalities. The ability to speak effectively and at different levels to multiple audiences is a skill that all trained actors have— and all successful public figures (such as Gertrude and Claudius) have as well.

And finally: Playing to the onstage onlookers is the link with which the actor—without arbitrarily pushing "projection"—connects with the theatre audience as well. In speaking to the nobles in the room, and to those listening in from (hypothetical) adjacent rooms as well, and to God even beyond that, the actors playing Claudius and Gertrude will authentically and convincingly reach the farther audience: the one watching the play in the theatre. They will be not merely private in public but public in public.

♦ SCENE 9-2

The Performative Context: Chekhov

With a partner, memorize the following brief scene from Chekhov's *Three Sisters,* between Kuligin, a schoolteacher, and his younger wife, Masha. The scene takes place in the midst of a crowded birthday party for one of Masha's sisters.*

KULIGIN *[to everyone, with his arm around Masha]:*   Today I feel cheerful and in the best of spirits.   *[turning to Masha]*   Masha, at four o'clock this afternoon we have to be at the headmaster's. An excursion has been arranged for the teachers and their families.

MASHA: I am not going.

KULIGIN: Dear Masha, why not?

MASHA: We'll talk about it afterwards.   *[pause]*   Very well, I will go, only let me alone, please.   *[walks away]*

KULIGIN: And then we shall spend the evening at the headmaster's. In spite of the delicate state of his health, that man tries before all things to be sociable. He is an excellent, noble personality. A splendid man. Yesterday, after the meeting, he said to me, "I am tired, Fyodor Ilyitch, I am tired."   *[looks at the clock, then at his watch. Turns to one of Masha's sisters]*   Your clock is seven minutes fast. "Yes," he said, "I am tired."

Here the dissonance between the performative and private voices is particularly glaring, creating discomfort for both characters and for the family members and friends at the party as well. It is a classic awkwardness: a spousal quarrel in public.

Play this scene with the rest of your class playing the surrounding party guests. Try to win over your spouse (your primary audience), while at the

---

* This and Scene 15-2 are from Constance Garnett's translation, first published in 1916.

same time projecting a good image to the guests (your secondary audience). If you are Kuligin, that image is probably that of the well-spoken, locally respected schoolteacher. If you are Masha, that image might well be that of the artistic, passionate, restless wife—for indeed, Masha has already begun to fall in love with one of the other guests, with whom she will have an affair before long.

Play the scene again, reaching to be heard, and understood, by your public audience in every corner of the room—and any people that might be outside the room as well. Play to everyone in the house—and therefore to everyone in the theatre house as well. Imagine that there are servants eavesdropping everywhere! You desperately want to win the respect and admiration of *all* of them—even as you truthfully address your remarks to each other.

The Scenes

THE SECOND HALF OF THIS BOOK PRESENTS A VARIETY OF SCENES from seven major periods—Greek, *commedia*, Elizabethan, neoclassic, Restoration, Belle Epoque (1890–1914), and contemporary—each of which has made a profound contribution to Western theatrical history.

These periods are presented in chronological order, and with attention to the cultural and theatrical patterns that are reflected in the writing of the scenes, with the idea that it is essential for the actor to understand what sort of world the dramatist was imagining when writing the play. That world includes discrete aspects such as clothing, manners, social etiquette, prevailing religions and philosophies, and attitudes toward sexuality, money, politics, morality, social class, and lifestyle issues: urban versus rural, for example.

But you should have absolutely no thought of concretizing any specific or universally accepted "period style" for any period play. The reasons for this are multiple and various:

◆ Culture and style evolve rapidly within every historical period. Significant changes in English clothing, for example, can be identified almost annually back to the reign of Edward III (1327–77). Thus there can hardly be a set notion of what constituted a "medieval sleeve," or an "Elizabethan bonnet," for there would have been dozens of sleeves and bonnets during those periods.

♦ Stylistic differences among individual authors writing at the same time are vast in virtually every historical period. No Athenian theatregoer would ever mistake a play of Sophocles for one of Euripides, though both were Greek tragedians of the same era. The same is true of later contemporaries, such as Shakespeare and Ben Jonson, George Bernard Shaw and Oscar Wilde, Margaret Edson and David Mamet.

♦ We know far less about actual production methods prior to 1650 than is generally admitted. History provides only tantalizing hints as to the staging, costuming, and acting of plays in Greek, medieval, Renaissance, and Elizabethan times; stage directions are rare, theatregoing descriptions rarer, and contemporary visual reproductions virtually nonexistent (or of doubtful reliability). Contemporary reconstructions (including my own) of early drama are educated guesses, and while they provide a general over-view, they cannot be construed as authoritative with regard to details.

♦ Styles from the past are taken both from daily life and from the theatre, but these are not the same; the clothing of a period is not identical with its costuming, nor does daily speech correspond with the stage speech of the era. So in trying to conjure the world of a dramatist's imagination, we must look at both the daily world in which the dramatist ate and slept and the theatrical one in which he or she worked.

◆ Authors in the past often set their plays in periods different from those in which they were written. Most Greek tragedies written in the fifth century B.C. concerned characters and events from a much earlier mythic history, perhaps five to seven hundred years in the Attic past. Medieval mystery plays were set in biblical times, and Shakespeare's plays were set in ancient Rome, early Britain, and Renaissance Italy, among other ages and locales. So today's producers must consider at least two "period styles" for any such dramatic work: the one of authorship and the one of the author's intended setting.

◆ Dramatists are not historians and have never sought to present to their audiences historic documents or dioramas. Rather, they interpret the period they have chosen and often deliberately incorporate elements from other periods (including their own), or no period at all, in order to provide a critique of the historical characters or actions they portray.

◆ Finally, contemporary directors rarely stage plays from past eras with external fidelity to their perceived period style; indeed, in the current theatre, classic plays are more often than not staged in periods radically different from the ones in which they were written or set. Or such plays are set in no historical period at all, or periods that change during the course of the play.

The outward manifestations of historical styles, therefore, are subject to radical reexamination and revision in contemporary performance. Nonetheless, these historical styles remain embedded in dramatic texts of every period and resonate through the play's action and language. Historical foundations will continue to serve as a key to understanding—and exploiting—how the play can be effectively performed on today's stage, no matter how or where it is "set" by the contemporary director or designers.

The scenes in Part II are presented with suggestions as to how a contemporary actor might capture the essence—*from the inside* more than from mere mimicry of superficial details—of their stylistic and character elements. Suggestions, therefore, come from possibilities of movement, voice and speech production, costume, staging, and—particularly in those plays that have come down to us in their original English rather than translation—text analysis.

Greek Tragedy

The Greeks did not actually invent drama. Indeed, Egyptians were staging plays on the banks of the Nile a full twenty-five centuries before the Greeks donned their masks in Athens, which means that Egyptian drama was as ancient to the Greeks as Greek drama is to us.

Still, Greek drama is the earliest from which we actually have scripts. And those surviving plays include several dozen that are produced today in virtually every language of the theatrical world. Many of them also serve as the jumping-off point for later dramas, from Roman (Seneca's *Oedipus*) and neoclassic (Jean Racine's *Phèdre*) to modern (Eugene O'Neill's *Mourning Becomes Electra,* Jean-Paul Sartre's *The Flies,* Jean Anouilh's *Antigone*) and contemporary (Neil LaBute's *Medea Redux,* John Barton's *Tantalus*).

In addition, we have a body of criticism (chiefly from Aristotle), various theatrical anecdotes (from Athenaeus, Plato, and others), hundreds of sculptures and vase paintings, and the actual ruins of dozens of Greek theatres. The classical Greek theatre, therefore, is a vast, rich treasure from which we steadily draw scripts, source material, and inspiration.*

Delving into Greek drama, however, means that we must move into a world radically different from our own—different in its culture, its performance spaces, and its drama.

---

* Actually, when we say "Greek" in most of these contexts, we really should be saying "Athenian" because virtually all the playwrights, philosophers, artists, and architects we are referring to, wherever they may have hailed from, plied their trade in the independent city-state of Athens.

Modern face-fitted masks are used to stunning effect in Peter Hall's production of *Tantalus,* a compilation by John Barton of several Greek plays and legends. Annalee Jeffries (left) is Clytemnestra and Greg Hicks is Agamemnon. (Courtesy Denver Theatre Center; photo © P. Switzer)

As to culture, the ancient Greeks worshipped gods of fiery passions and uncertain morality, whom they balanced with a philosophy that valued self-knowledge ("Know thyself!") and the golden mean ("Nothing to excess!"). Economically, Athenian citizens operated a slave society at home and wide-spread trade abroad; politically, they alternated among democracy (which they invented), oligarchy, and empire; militarily, they were aggressive and often exploitative; scientifically, they made giant leaps in mathematics, medicine, history, and astronomy; artistically, they revered music, dancing, the human body, vivid illustration, and grandiose architecture.

As best we can determine, by the middle of the fifth century B.C. Greek plays were performed in and around a circular *orchestra,* which contained a chanting and dancing chorus (ranging from twelve to fifty members), a raised stage for the principal actors, and a building (*skēnē*) behind the stage, whose doors provided entrances and exits for the principals. The actors, all male, wore long gowns (*himatia*), elevated shoes (*kothornoi*), tall head/hairpieces (*onkoi*), and full-face masks. It is believed that no more than three actors played all the parts, by changing masks offstage. The audience, seated in

Greek ladies   Three ladies of classic Greece, as drawn by Thomas Hope from a Greek vase and originally published in 1812. The Greek *himation,* a long tunic worn by both men and women, went all the way to the ground; often, for women, an overgarment was also wrapped around the upper body, held in place by two clasps. This drapery, which was also the style of classical Greek stage costumes, required skilled moment-to-moment management by the (male) actor, who had to continually adjust the hang and sway of the garments.

a circular stone *theatron,* was by today's standards gigantic: upwards of 17,000 persons.

The tragic dramas were written in unrhymed verse, sung or chanted rather than spoken, and each play was formally divided into a series of episodes between principal characters that alternated with choral odes addressed to the audience. There was also a prologue, generally spoken by an actor playing a god or demigod, and an epilogue, chanted by the chorus. Such tragedies were normally presented in groups of three on related themes (a *trilogy*) in a single day; the trilogy was normally followed by a briefer "satyr play," which mocked the concerns of what preceded it.

None of this adds up to a single "Greek style" or even "Greek tragic style," for reasons described in the introduction to Part II. But every one of these factors—culture, theatre, and drama—influences the nature of acting in these masterpieces.

A Greek philosopher   Greek men who prided themselves on their austerity would merely drape their naked bodies in a simple cloak, gathered over the left shoulder, concealing the left arm and hand. This garment, the predecessor of the Roman toga, severely restricted athleticism. Roman actors were consequently instructed to gesture primarily, or even exclusively, with right hand only, and, moreover, to keep all gesturing below eye level.

◆ Scene 10-1

Politician vs. Prophet: Oedipus and Teiresias

This scene from *Oedipus Tyrannus* follows the excerpt in Lesson 9. Thebes has been visited by a plague, and Creon has been sent to the oracle at Delphi to find a cure. He returns and announces that the plague has been sent by the gods because the murderer of Laius, the last Theban king, has not yet been found and punished. Creon suggests that Oedipus send for the blind prophet, Teiresias, for advice, but the seer, we soon find, knows a terrible secret: that Oedipus, believing he was the child of distant parents, was actually the long-abandoned son of Laius! Moreover, Oedipus had murdered Laius—whom he of course did not recognize—in a long-forgotten quarrel and had subsequently come to Thebes and taken his father's throne. Worst, he had then married Laius's widow, Jocasta—Oedipus's own mother! Naturally, Teiresias does not want to speak about these things.

Classical gesture   These animated characters appear in two ancient productions of Terence's *Phormio* (above) and *Eunuchus* (below), Roman comedies modeled after Greek New Comedy. The voluminous costumes do not suppress vigorous hand and finger gestures, even with the left hand occasionally buried in the drapery of male attire. From drawings in the Vatican museum.

With a partner, memorize, stage, and perform this scene, considering the spectators to be the chorus of Theban citizens. You can use a chair for Oedipus's throne if you wish, and Teiresias may enter with a walking staff and be led on and off stage by a servant. (The actor playing Teiresias may also wish to be blindfolded, in which case safety precautions should be observed in the staging.)

[Oedipus sits or stands before a chorus of Theban citizens. The blind Teiresias, whom he has summoned, arrives, led by a servant.]

OEDIPUS: Teiresias, all things are known to you—the secrets of heaven and earth, the sacred and profane. Though you are blind, you surely see the plague that rakes our city. My Lord Teiresias, we turn to you as our only hope. We must find Laius' murderers and drive them out. Then, only then, will we find release from our suffering. I ask you not to spare your gifts of prophecy. Look to the voices of prophetic birds or the answers written in the flames. Spare nothing. Save all of us—yourself, your city, your king, and all that is touched by this deathly pollution.

TEIRESIAS: O God! How horrible wisdom is! How horrible when it does not help the wise.   *[turns to leave]*   I should not have come.   *[He starts away.]*

OEDIPUS: Why?   *[restraining him]*   What's wrong?

TEIRESIAS: Let me go! It will be better if you bear your own distress and I bear mine.

OEDIPUS: This city gave you life and yet you refuse her an answer? You speak as if you were her enemy!

TEIRESIAS: No! No! It is because I see the danger in your words. And mine would add still more.

OEDIPUS: For God's sake, if you know, don't turn away from us! We are pleading, we are begging you!

TEIRESIAS: Because you are blind! No! I shall not reveal my secrets. And I shall not reveal yours!

OEDIPUS: What? You know, and yet you refuse to speak? Would you betray us and watch our city fall helplessly to her death?

TEIRESIAS: I will not cause you further grief. I will not grieve myself. Stop asking me: I will tell you nothing!

OEDIPUS: You monster! You could stir the stones of earth to a burning rage! You will not tell? What will it take?

TEIRESIAS: Know thyself, Oedipus! You denounce me, but you do not yet know yourself!

OEDIPUS: Ah, yes! You disgrace your city, and then you expect us to control our rage!

TEIRESIAS: It does not matter if I speak; the future has already been determined.

OEDIPUS: And if it has, then it is for you to tell me, *prophet!*

TEIRESIAS: I shall say no more. Rage if you wish.

Ken Ruta as the masked Teiresias in *Oedipus Rex*, led on stage by a young boy. (Courtesy American Conservatory Theatre)

OEDIPUS: I *am* enraged. And now I will tell you what *I* think. I think this was *your* doing. *You* plotted the crime, *you* saw it carried out, it was *your* doing. All but the actual killing. And had you not been blind, you would have done *that,* too!

TEIRESIAS: Do you believe what you have said? Then accept your own decree. From this day on, deny yourself the right to speak to anyone. For you, Oedipus, are the desecrator, the polluter of this land!

OEDIPUS: Traitor! Do you think that you can get away with this?

TEIRESIAS: The truth is my protection.

OEDIPUS: Who taught you this? It did not come from prophecy.

TEIRESIAS: *You* taught me. *You* drove me, *you* forced me to say it against my will.

OEDIPUS: Say it again. I want to make sure I understand you.

TEIRESIAS: Understand me? Or are you trying to provoke me?

OEDIPUS: No, I want to be sure, I want to know. Say it again!

TEIRESIAS: I say that you, Oedipus Tyrannus, are the murderer you seek.

OEDIPUS: So! A second time! Now twice you will regret what you have said!

TEIRESIAS: Shall I tell you more? Shall I fan your flames of anger?

OEDIPUS: Yes. Tell me more. Tell me whatever suits you. It will be in vain.

TEIRESIAS: I say you live in shame with the woman you love, blind to your own calamity.

OEDIPUS: Do you think you can speak like this forever?

TEIRESIAS: I do, if there is any strength in truth.

OEDIPUS: There is—for everyone but you. You—you cripple! Your ears are deaf, your eyes are blind, your mind—your *mind* is crippled!

TEIRESIAS: You fool! You slander me when one day you will hear the same . . .

OEDIPUS *[interrupting]*:   You live in night, Teiresias, in night that never turns to day. And so, you cannot hurt me—or any man who sees the light.

TEIRESIAS: No, it is not I who will cause your fall. No, Oedipus, you are destroying yourself.

OEDIPUS: How much of this am I to bear? Leave! Now! Leave my house!

TEIRESIAS: I would not be here had you not sent for me.

OEDIPUS: I would never have sent for you had I known the madness I would hear.

TEIRESIAS: To you, I am mad; but not to your parents . . .

OEDIPUS: Wait! My parents? Who are my parents?

TEIRESIAS: This day shall bring you birth *and* death.

OEDIPUS: Why must you persist with riddles?

TEIRESIAS: Are you not the best of men when it comes to riddles?*

OEDIPUS: You mock the very skill that proves me great.

TEIRESIAS: A great misfortune—which will destroy you.

OEDIPUS: I don't care. If I have saved this land, I do not care.

TEIRESIAS: Then I shall go.

OEDIPUS: Go. You won't be missed.

TEIRESIAS: I am not afraid of you. You cannot hurt me. And I tell you this: The man you seek—the man whose death or banishment you ordered, the man who murdered Laius—that man is here, living in our midst. Soon it will be known to all of you—he is a native Theban. And he will find no joy in that discovery. His eyes see now, but soon they will be blind: rich now, but soon a beggar. Holding a scepter now, but soon a cane, he will grope for the earth beneath him—in a foreign land. Both brother and father to the children that he loves. Both son and husband to the woman who bore him. Both heir and spoiler of his father's bed and the one who took his life. Go, think on this. And if you find the words I speak are lies, *then* say that I am blind.   *[Teiresias leaves, and Oedipus goes into the palace.]*

Here, as in the *Oedipus* scene in Lesson 9, the two actors are playing for the opinion of the chorus. Each is promoting his own virtue while also trying to discredit the other, as we can see every time they use the words "this city" or "our city" or "this land" in front of the very same people who constitute "this city" and who live in "this land." For example:

OEDIPUS: *This city* gave you life and yet you refuse her an answer? [. . .] Would you betray us and watch *our city* fall helplessly to her death? [. . .] You disgrace *your city* [. . .] If I have saved *this land,* I do not care.

. . .

TEIRESIAS: [Y]ou, Oedipus, are the desecrator, the polluter of *this land!*

But their appeals, and their performative behaviors, are quite different. Oedipus's argument with Creon in Lesson 9 is essentially political; it is a power struggle between two would-be rulers. (The Greek word *creon,* in fact, means "ruler," and Creon will succeed Oedipus as king by the end of

---

* The citizens of Thebes had chosen Oedipus as their king because he had solved the riddle of the Sphinx, thus saving the city from destruction.

the play.) And so here, as in the excerpt in Lesson 9, you will want to perform the public role of a great *professional* leader, politician, dictator, impressing your hearers (the chorus) with your authority, wisdom, logic, control of the agenda, political courage, determination, and capacity to employ military force that will get them—and through them Teiresias—on your side. Imagine yourself in a presidential debate, as you did in the Creon–Oedipus scene, and while responding to the charges of your opponent (Teiresias in this case), you are exerting every effort to win the public's support for your candidacy.

But Teiresias is not a politician, and his appeal to the chorus is quite different; to win their respect, he must inspire them not with his political might but with his divine wisdom and gift of prophecy.

But how do you, a mere earth-bound actor, do *that*? It's hard enough to perform the role of national dictator, but it's twice as hard to convincingly perform that of a future-knowing prophet with direct access to divine wisdom.

Or is it? Here's where imagination joins with your acting instrument: You must find *the voice within you* that convinces others your words come directly from the gods. You must find and develop, as you did in Lessons 4 and 6, a voice that suggests to all observers that you are divinely inspired and that you bring truthful and irrevocable messages from a supernatural world. (And you will need this voice in many other parts: Shaw's St. Joan, Bolt's Sir Thomas More, Pirandello's Stepfather, Kushner's Angel, or any of Shakespeare's witches, ghosts, and soothsayers, for example.)

Do you have such a voice? Of course you do—but it's not the one you use every day. In fact, it's not the one evangelical preachers or tribal shamans use every day. Rather, it's the professional *job* of prophets, as well as preachers and shamans, to find, refine, and then employ the voice in their work that will successfully relay the (assumed or real) supernatural forces they believe are latent in their words.

And you must find and develop not merely the voice but the physical behavior—the bearing, movement, and gestures—that will also reflect your oneness with the divine world.

Know that Teiresias—though this is not manifest in this play—is a transsexual: born as a man but now sporting a woman's breasts. This can stimulate your most surreal imagination to create the supernatural world from which seers must emanate.

Without the otherworldly voice and behavior, Teiresias would be seen not as a prophet but simply as an educated guesser, and thus he would be no match for Oedipus, the king. You can confront Oedipus successfully only if your *spiritual* power matches (or even tops) his *political* might.

Think of Teiresias, then, as a *professional* prophet. Prophecy is your job, and you must perform your job convincingly. It is not enough merely to know the future; you must convince the chorus that you're the kind of person who, unlike them, *could* know the future. Otherwise, they will laugh you off.

Imagine that you've been training yourself in prophetic speeches for many years and before many audiences. That you have studied your prophetic speaking skill does not mean that your prophecies are insincere; theological and rabbinical seminaries give courses in preaching theory and practice and rehearse their beginning preachers to help them perfect their deliveries. The magnificently stirring cadences of Martin Luther King, Jr., were learned and practiced at his father's knee for years before he mesmerized the millions at the Lincoln Memorial.

So, as Teiresias, convince the chorus that your words are stronger than those of Oedipus because they come from another world: a world of gods and prophecy, a world where the future is as clear as the past, and where the truth is absolute and irrevocable. And since this feat can't be achieved with words alone, create and develop the reverential tones, cadences, movements, gestures, and godlike bearing that will simply shock and awe the chorus, silencing the powerful (but woefully human) leader who opposes you. A supernatural text requires supernatural delivery: Find your deepest resonance, your most forthright builds and crescendos. In movement, extend your arms, whirl about, wave your walking staff, and enter a conjurer's state of rapture, of magical fascination. Call upon the gods, the clouds, the sky; summon the thunder! And know that you can do it because you speak and move with the inspiration of Apollo, Zeus, Athena, and Dionysus!

Is this silly? Well, of course it would be—if we were in a rational, skeptical, empirical world, such as a science classroom or a coffee shop. But it's not at all silly in an ancient Greek hillside theatre, where *Oedipus* was first performed, and it's not silly in a modern theatre when we have been effectively transported to that earlier and more mystical world. Your commitment to the power of Teiresias's actions will transport us to a world where prophets spoke confidently of the future and with the force of what they fully believed (and/or persuaded others to believe) to have been divine inspiration.

So you must assume the mantle of prophecy to play this role and not worry about how outlandish it might seem on the campus quad. And assume the mantle literally: Fashion yourself one with an ordinary blanket and safety pin and use this "cape of divination" to accentuate your rapturous, Dionysian movements as you deliver Teiresias's words.

Remember: A professional prophet could never take his audience for granted even in ancient times—there were skeptics aplenty in Athens; indeed, Sophocles' colleague Euripides was one. So you have to believe in the strength of your prophecy (or as Jean Giraudoux said, you have to "believe that you believe" in it) for the duration of the scene. That belief, if you fully engage it, will transport us, the audience beyond the chorus, to a world where prophets could stun to silence any merely mortal king.

Create the battle between Oedipus's political muscle and Teiresias's spiritual authority. Each of you must try your hardest to get the chorus on your character's side. Then switch parts and try it again.

◆ SCENE 10-2

The Personal Context: Oedipus and Jocasta

Shortly after Teiresias leaves, Creon returns and Oedipus rages at him as well, rashly condemning him for siding with Teiresias. Then Jocasta enters to calm Oedipus down.

Gown yourselves for this scene, either in some approximation of the Greek *himation* or simply in a robe. Walk barefoot on the imagined sand of the *orchestra* (as early Greek actors would have done), or give yourself platform shoes—or a platform—to stand above your classmates performing as the chorus.

Work out movement around a throne, or two thrones, or an imaginary idol or ceremonial firepit. Thrash yourself with wheat stalks if the spirit moves you, or create your own Attic ritual through a combination of research and imagination.

Do you have a friend who plays the flute? Let him or her accompany you on an approximation of the Greek aulos, a two-pronged recorder. Don't be too concerned about the tune—no one has any idea what the music in Greek classical drama sounded like, though we know it existed. Or find another musical instrument that will help you reach the multileveled audience, from spouse to public to divine, that attends your words.

Create a style from the text, and from your imagination, and from your interpretation of the suggestions given.

Play the scene.

JOCASTA: In the name of Heaven, my Lord, tell me the reason for your bitterness.

OEDIPUS: I will—because you mean more to me than anyone. The reason is Creon and his plot against my throne.

JOCASTA: But can you *prove* a plot?

OEDIPUS: He says that I—Oedipus—bear the guilt of Laius' death.

JOCASTA: How does he justify this charge?

OEDIPUS: He does not stain his own lips by saying it. No. He uses that false prophet to speak for him.

JOCASTA: Then, you can exonerate yourself because no mortal has the power of divination. And I can prove it. An oracle came to Laius once from Apollo's priests—that he would die at the hands of his own child, his child and mine. Yet the story which *we* heard was that robbers murdered Laius in a place where three roads meet. As for our child—when he was three days old, Laius drove pins into his ankles and handed him

The Stratford Festival in Canada pioneered in mounting a repertory of classic plays in North America, exemplified by this masked production of *King Oedipus* directed by Sir Tyrone Guthrie, the festival's founder, in 1955. Shown are the crowned Oedipus and his wife Jocasta. (Courtesy Stratford Festival Archives)

to someone to cast upon a deserted mountain path. And so, Apollo's prophecy was unfulfilled—our child did not kill his father. And Laius' fears were unfulfilled—he did not die by the hand of his child. Yet these had been the prophecies. You need not give them any credence.

OEDIPUS: Jocasta—my heart is troubled at your words. Suddenly, my thoughts are wandering, disturbed . . .

JOCASTA: What is it? What makes you so frightened?

OEDIPUS: Your statement—that Laius was murdered in a place where three roads meet. Isn't that what you said?

JOCASTA: Yes, that was the story . . .

OEDIPUS: Where is this place where three roads meet?

JOCASTA: In the land called Phocis where the roads from Delphi and from Daulia converge.

OEDIPUS: How long a time has passed since then?

JOCASTA: We heard it shortly before you came.

OEDIPUS: O God, what have you planned for me?

JOCASTA: What is it, Oedipus? What frightens you?

OEDIPUS: Do not ask me! Just tell me—what was Laius like? How old was he?

JOCASTA: He was tall and his hair was lightly cast with silver tones, the contour of his body much like yours.

OEDIPUS: O God! Am I cursed and cannot see it?

JOCASTA: What is it, Oedipus? You frighten me.

OEDIPUS: It cannot be—that the prophet sees! Tell me one more thing.

JOCASTA: You frighten me, my Lord, but I will try to tell you what I know.

OEDIPUS: Who traveled with the king? Was he alone? Was there a guide? An escort? A few? Many?

JOCASTA: There were five—one of them a herald—and a carriage in which Laius rode.

OEDIPUS: O God! O God! I see it all now! Jocasta, who told you this?

JOCASTA: A servant—the only one who returned alive.

OEDIPUS: Is he here now? In our house?

JOCASTA: No. When he came back and saw you ruling where once his master was, he pleaded with me—begged me—to send him to the fields to tend the flocks, to be a shepherd far from the city.

OEDIPUS: Could we arrange to have this shepherd here—now?

JOCASTA: Yes, but what do you want with him?

OEDIPUS: I am afraid, Jocasta. I have said too much and now I have to see him.

JOCASTA: Then he shall be brought. But I, too, must know the cause of your distress. I have the right to know.

OEDIPUS: Yes, you have the right. And I must tell you—now. You, more than anyone. Jocasta—I was in that place where the three roads meet. There was a herald leading a carriage drawn by horses, and a man riding in the carriage, just as you described. The man in front, and the old one in the carriage, ordered me out of the path. I refused. The driver pushed. In anger, I struck him. The old man reached for his lash, and struck me on the head. But he paid—oh, yes, he paid. He lost his balance and fell from the carriage and, as he lay there on his back, I killed him. I killed them all. But if this stranger had any tie with Laius—O God!—who could be more hated in the eyes of Heaven and Earth? *I* am the one who must be driven out! *I* am the one for whom my curse was meant! What cruel god has sent me this torture? My only hope is waiting for this shepherd.

JOCASTA: Why? What do you hope to find with him?

OEDIPUS: This—if his story agrees with what you say, then I am safe.

JOCASTA: What did I say that makes you sure of this?

OEDIPUS: You said he told of *robbers*—that *robbers* killed the king. If he still says robbers, then I am not the guilty one. But if he names a *single* traveler, there will be no doubt—the guilt is mine.

JOCASTA: You can be sure that this is what he said—the whole city heard him, not I alone. But even if he alters what he said before, he cannot prove that Laius met his death as it was prophesied. For Apollo said that he would die at the hands of a child—of mine. And, as it happens, the child is dead. So prophecy is worthless. I wouldn't dignify it with a moment's thought.

OEDIPUS: You are right. But still—send someone for the shepherd. Now.

JOCASTA: I shall do what you ask. But now, let us go inside.

Although it takes place in front of the chorus (who speak immediately before and after it, and to whom Jocasta refers when she says "the whole city heard him"), this is an intensely private scene between a wife and husband—who also happen to be mother and son. And the gradual truth of their original relationship dawns on each of them, though at different moments, as the scene progresses; indeed, what makes the scene psychologically fascinating (and dramatically suspenseful) is how each character deals with the emerging truth. Oedipus, for example, is alarmed to hear about Laius's being killed at the same intersection where he once killed a man, but he ignores, perhaps because his mind has already started to "wander," as he says, the subsequent description of Laius's driving pins into his child's ankles—which should ring a bell, since Oedipus has been troubled by mal-formed ankles all his life (his name, in fact, means "swollen ankle"). And Jocasta is alarmed by seeing his alarm—so much so that she is already pre-paring her backup story in case the shepherd changes his report about the number of killers. These are *subtextual* developments—no one speaks of them in the text of the play—but they are as important as they would be if they were spoken of directly.

Indeed, there are deeply emotional issues throughout this dialog. Oedipus says at the outset that Jocasta "means more to him than anyone"; theirs is clearly a tender relationship, not merely a formal or royal one. And while Jocasta never mentions how she felt when her child was mutilated and taken away from her, to be left for dead by Laius, she clearly was devastated—which profoundly colors the way she recounts this horrific episode to Oedi-pus now, leading to her savagely repressed conclusion, "And, as it happens, the child is dead." Emotional words like *fear, afraid, troubled, distress,* and *frighten* occur regularly in this scene, revealing the anxious feelings of both characters and their dependence on each other for reassurance.

And, finally, that such reassurance hangs on a fragile shred of evidence—whether a servant, twenty years ago, had said *robber* or *robbers*—leaves both characters beginning to fear the worst, both for themselves and for each other.

The emotion in this scene extends toward the divine presence as well. On several occasions Oedipus calls out to God ("O God!").* Unlike the throw-away expression of today ("Oh God, I can't find my car keys"), this *apos-trophe* (a brief statement to a physically nonpresent person or object) is a direct invocation to the gods on Mount Olympus to intervene in—or to stay out of—human affairs.

This scene, therefore, has a very powerful private subtext between the two characters (who are each other's primary audience). And just who are these characters? On the purely human level, they are simply a married couple, parents of at least four grown or nearly grown children, and individuals troubled by mysteries in their separate pasts. Oedipus, obviously a rash man at times (he once murdered apparent strangers essentially out of road rage), is nonetheless relentless in seeking the truth about himself, even if this will lead to his destruction. Jocasta, grieved about the apparent death of her three-day-old son (of which she has presumably never spoken until this scene), is torn between loyalty to aiding her husband's search and anguish about the tragic end that search might ultimately provoke. It's the sort of problem that, with different specific details, faces millions of couples in every

---

* In the Greek, he calls out to "Zeu," which means both Zeus, the king of the gods, and the generic notion of God.

era. When Jocasta begins the phrase "As for our child," she is every mother dragging to the surface her memory of a parent's most horrific dread. Does she unconsciously wrap her forearms around her abdomen when she says these words? Any woman, even a Greek queen, might well do so.

But they are also tyrannic royalty, used to summoning servants, leading rather than following events, and getting what they want. And they are used to having their discords, marital and political, observed by their servants and subjects. Thus their private lives, while crucially motivating their decisions, play out in the presence of the chorus, "citizens of Thebes" (the secondary audience) who will eventually influence as well as witness the tragic outcome, and in the presence of the gods (the tertiary audience) who control human destiny and have the power to determine the course of events.

And so when Oedipus says "[S]end someone for the shepherd," who is he talking to? Most literally, to Jocasta, who by her answer will send a servant to fetch the man. But Oedipus is also performing to the chorus, letting his citizens know that he is fulfilling his professional office by seeking to find the killer of Laius, no matter what the consequences may be to himself. And he is performing to the gods, saying, in effect, "I do not shrink from my fate; I am willing to face whatever destiny you have in store for me." This is what makes Oedipus more than a faithful husband to his wife, and more than an honorable king to the chorus; it makes him a tragic hero in the eyes of the gods and and the theatre audience.

More Greek Scenes

Is this all there is to Greek tragedy? Hardly. We have looked only at one play and little in the way of Greek costumes, props, or staging effects. But the public and political arena represented by the chorus, and the cosmos of ancient gods that you will have to find in your imagination are the key ingredients of this seminal dramatic form. Master these and you will be prepared for the theatrical worlds that ancient Greek drama can propel onto the contemporary stage.

Other Greek scenes you might explore are:

Ismene–Antigone in *Antigone* by Sophocles

Hecuba–Menelaus in *The Trojan Women* by Euripides

Creon–Haemon in *Antigone*

Prometheus–Hermes in *Prometheus Bound* by Aeschylus

Commedia

Greek and Roman drama all but disappeared with the fall of the Roman empire in 476 A.D. and the consequent rise of the Catholic church as the preeminent intellectual and cultural force throughout Europe. But classical theatre was reborn about a thousand years later, during what we now call the Renaissance, during which time the long-forgotten classic plays of the Greeks and Romans were rediscovered and, thanks to the invention of movable type in the mid-1400s, published for general readers, first in their original tongues, then in translation, and finally in modernized adaptations. By the early 1500s, emerging troupes of professional actors were performing both these and new plays in the public squares and royal courts of Europe, starting in the home base of the old Roman Empire (and the medieval Holy Roman Empire), Italy.

Commedia Styles and Scripts

One of the most exciting of the new emergent styles was the Italian *commedia,* comic drama based on the plays of Roman-era dramatists, chiefly Plautus. We now recognize two forms of *commedia: commedia erudita,* which was an adaptation of a Roman comedy (written by a dramatist "erudite" enough to read Latin), and the subsequent *commedia dell'arte,* which, starting from the same stories, embroidered them with improvised dialog and recurring characters, most of them masked, who have since become famous: Arlecchino (Harlequin), the scamp; Pantalone, the rich old codger; Dottore

Scapino.   *Cap: Zerbino*

A *commedia* greeting   The scamplike Scapino and the pompous Capitano Zerbino meeting on the street in a 1618 *commedia* illustration by Jacques Callot. Notice the out-turned legs, the expressive finger gestures, the swords, and the angled postures.

(Doctor), the pretentious intellectual; Capitano, the bragging soldier; Zanni, the clown; and Colombina (Columbine), the lovely damsel.

Since it was largely improvised, no complete *commedia dell'arte* scripts survive, although we have many fragments, illustrations, derivations, and descriptions. But we do have several plays of the earlier *commedia erudita* type, from which *commedia dell'arte* was directly derived.

Commedia Performances

Commedia performances of both sorts almost always took place outdoors, with both men and women actors, on a simple trestle stage with the audience gathered around on at least three sides. Like the Roman comic playwrights before them, *commedia* dramatists limited themselves to simplistic and universal comic themes (superheated lust, marital discord, social climbing), stock characters (the wily servant, the audacious maid, the bombastic soldier, the sweet young girl, the foolishly amorous old geezer), and conventional plot devices (mistaken identity, hiding and spying, the reunion of long-lost

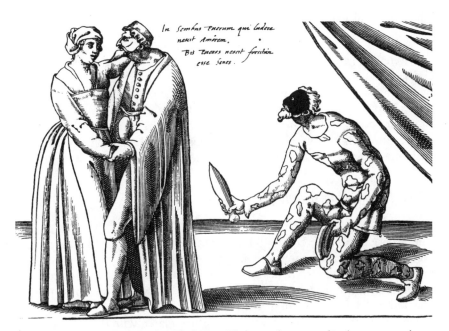

Francischina, Pantalone, and Arlecchino   Three stock *commedia* characters—the servant woman, the self-important older man, and the rascally servant—appear in a 1577 illustration by Sieur (Sir) Fossard. Pantalone, the model for Nicomaco in Machiavelli's *Clizia*, often pursues younger women; Arlecchino usually intervenes—both on the woman's and his own account. The full gown and beard of Pantalone indicate his elevated social rank, though not any intelligence; the tight-fitted patchwork costume of Arlecchino, plus his black mask and sneaky crouch, are traditional to his portrayal, and reflect his crafty mind and slippery nature.

relatives). Since characters and plot were predictable, the plays succeeded mainly through the skill of the actors: their comic imagination, verbal and physical dexterity, charm, and timing.

Indeed, the necessity for acting genius is built into *commedia dell'arte,* which brags of a glorious performance mastery in its very name. The *arte* must be lived up to at every moment—even at the expense of other theatrical values (plot credibility, human sensitivity, thematic profundity, poetic beauty) that earlier and later ages would consider more important.

Though there is no chorus in either form of *commedia,* the characters often address the audience directly, giving the audience the role of chorus and asking them for their judgment of key issues. The setting is almost always presumed to be a public one, generally a street or plaza, facilitating this form of direct audience address. Characters in *commedia* often break into song, or comic bits of business (called *lazzi*), or independent speeches that bear little relationship to the plot.

Commedia and Renaissance Ideals

The Renaissance was a rebirth not merely of secular literature but of many classical ideals, of which the most important was doubtless the one uttered by Protagoras, a pre-Socratic philosopher: "Man is the measure of all things." After a thousand years of medieval Christianity, the secular humanist culture brought the return of paintings, sculptures, and plays drawn from contemporary life—and not just biblical history—along with a fascination with human scheming, intrigue, and debate.

Acting Commedia: Machiavelli's Clizia

The two speeches in Exercise 11-1 are from Niccolò Machiavelli's *commedia erudita* called *Clizia*, written about 1524.

This play has characteristically ancient roots. It began as a Greek comedy by Diphilus, from the fourth century B.C., now lost, which was subsequently adapted into Latin by Plautus, the Roman comic dramatist, a century later. Machiavelli's version comes seventeen centuries later, with the author translating Plautus's version into contemporary Italian, setting the play in Florence, and making many plot and character changes.

The author is the same Niccolò Machiavelli who wrote *The Prince*, which is considered the world's greatest textbook on political power. But Machiavelli is also regarded as one of Italy's greatest playwrights—perhaps, in fact, the greatest until Luigi Pirandello. In both his political and dramatic writings, Machiavelli had the Renaissance gift of looking clearly and closely at human interactions, unfiltered by mythic fantasy, religious moralizing, or gothic obscurities and sentimentalism.

◆ EXERCISE 11-1

Commedia: Direct Address

The two speeches that follow, which are from different parts of *Clizia,* are monologues addressed directly to the theatre audience. Cleandro, a young man, is telling us how much he loves a pretty girl named Clizia, who has been a lodger in his home since childhood. And Sofronia, Cleandro's mother, is complaining that her husband, Nicomaco, loves Clizia as well, and he is indeed going crazy over her. The setting is a city street. The translation is my own.

Memorize, prepare, and present either one.

CLEANDRO: Who was it said that lovers are like soldiers? He sure was speaking the truth! The general wants his men young and sturdy; so do women. Old soldiers are a dirty joke; so are old lovers. Soldiers get chewed out by their sergeants; lovers by their ladies. Soldiers sleep out in the rain on the battlefields; so do would-be Romeos, who get sopping wet under the balconies of their Juliets. Soldiers pursue their enemies with total ferocity, just as lovers attack their rivals. Secrecy, faith, and courage are the emblems of both the soldier and the lover: neither blackest night, nor iciest cold, nor driving-est wind, nor rain, sleet nor hail shall halt either one on their road to conquest! So that, at the end of his lonely struggle, the soldier dies dismembered in a ditch: and the lover dies strung out in despair! And so it is with me: Clizia lives in my house. I see her, I eat with her. The closer she gets, the more I want her; the more I want her, the less I have her; the less I have her, the more I am overwhelmed by the agony of passion! But where is my servant Eustachio? Oh, wait, there he is! Eustachio! Eustachio!

. . .

SOFRONIA: *[speaking about Nicomaco, her husband]*   It's amazing, the change in this man! Why, right up through last year, he was serious, consistent, respectful, honorable! He woke up early, got dressed, went to church, and went about his work! In the morning he'd make his rounds: to the market, city hall; maybe a business call or two; then to a quiet lunch with a few friends, perhaps a visit with his son, to give the boy a few words of advice—worthwhile lessons from history, you know, sage observations on current affairs—and then he'd come home for his afternoon chores, evening prayers, and a quick visit to his study to plan the next day's events. Then, at nine o'clock, we'd have a big family dinner in front of the fireplace. He was a model husband, father, and citizen; an exemplar of family values. But now look at him! All of a sudden, he's lost in fantasy: All he thinks about is this girl, Clizia! He ignores his business, neglects his properties, and forgets his friends! Instead, all he does is yell and scream! About what, nobody knows; most of the time he doesn't even know himself! A thousand times a day he comes home and then goes right out again, for no reason at all! He's never here at mealtime: If you talk to him he doesn't respond—or if he does, he doesn't make any sense! The servants laugh at him, his son's completely written him off, and everyone in the house now feels they can do whatever they want! Well, I'm going to church and pray things get better. Hey: There's Eustachio!

First question: Was your monologue funny?
Second question: Should it have been?

It's obvious that anything labeled *commedia* would be expected to be funny. And it certainly is. But what does this have to do with playing the goal of the character? How is playing *commedia,* or playing comedy, consistent with basic acting technique, which teaches you above all else to try to achieve your character's goals?

The best answer is this: Since these speeches take place in a public setting—a street with presumed passersby—both Cleandro and Sofronia want the passersby, who (conveniently) also include the theatre audience, to support their arguments. That way, the passersby, or audience, can help them achieve their individual goals. It's always easier to win an argument with someone if the people who happen to be around you are on your side. It's even easier if they are openly rooting for you: cheering your remarks and laughing at your jokes. The other person is virtually bound to give in.

So you can simply make the presumed passersby, and the theatre audience, into characters in your play—that is, into sixteenth-century Florentines—and then do whatever you can to get them to see things your way. Persuade them to support you in winning Clizia's love (if you are playing Cleandro) or shaming Nicomaco into giving up his absurd quest (if you are playing Sofronia). Inspire them to laugh at your jokes and cheer your insights. You know your goal; let the audience help you win it. If an analogy would help, imagine you are arguing with someone who has cut in line ahead of you to buy one of the last available tickets to a rock concert. Let all the other people in line hear—and believe—your explanation of who's first in line! Get them to send the interloper to the back!

Still, why must you be "entertaining"? Why can't you simply state your case and expect us to agree? Because your case—as an objective legal argument—isn't by itself all that interesting! Why should we, the audience, care whether you get Clizia or someone else does? Or whether your husband behaves properly or improperly? Indeed, young men fall in love all the time, husbands stray all the time, and there's no particular reason why we should care about your problems rather than our own. So you have to make us care, and the only way you can do that is by grabbing our attention—by *entertaining* us!

Remember: The word *entertain* does not simply mean "to amuse." It also means "to hold in the mind." We use the word in this sense when we say "I will entertain your suggestion." *Entertainment,* then, basically means capturing the minds of the audience. And the easiest way of doing that, in an ordinary quarrel at least, is to amuse them—to make them laugh and enjoy themselves.

So Cleandro and Sofronia must entertain the public in order to win their goals; consequently, you the actor (through the character) must, in struggling to achieve your character's goal, entertain the theatre audience. You must make your character, and your character's plight, worth our time. Remember, the audience is not paid to watch a play—quite the reverse: They pay to

Acrobatics and pratfalls   Physical comedy is a prominent feature of all *commedia,* and the handstand by Arlecchino mocks the tumbled comic servant Cornetto in this drawing of the period.

watch it. So they have to *want* to watch it. And you have to make them want to watch it—or you will be all alone in hoping that Clizia returns your affection or that Nicomaco is shamed into changing his errant ways.

So go ahead. *Entertain* us with the arguments of Cleandro or Sofronia—and go ahead, be funny! Make us forget our own problems, so that we will pay attention to those of your character.

How? Look for clues in the dialog. Italian comedy is filled with puns and other wordplays, quotations and misquotations of famous lines, mini-poems of alliterations, assonance, and rhymes, and an entire repertoire of nonverbal utterances: stutters, blusters, bawdy innuendo, linguistic indecencies, mispronunciations (particularly of foreign languages), pseudomelodramatic posturing, gasps, wheezes, and inventive throat-gaggings (hence the word *gag* for "joke").

And try the bits of comic business suggested in the stage directions, provided by me, in the versions of the two speeches that follow, perhaps augmenting them with a study of the illustrations in this chapter—which, though idealized by their draftsmen, date from the sixteenth and seventeenth centuries. Or invent better ones! *Commedia* is famed for its physical sight gags, known in Italian as *lazzi* (singular: *lazzo*), a near-infinite assemblage of pratfalls, double takes, exaggerated trembles (like knocking knees and chattering teeth), rowdy (yet harmless) battles, sexual gropings and gestures, and elaborate comic miming (for example, Arlecchino swats and stuns an imaginary fly on his forehead, then carefully plucks off its wings and eats it—with great fanfare). The *commedia dell'arte* "slapstick"—a trick baton made of two wooden slats, hinged together to make a sharp sound when struck on an object, such as Zanni's bottom—has indeed become the word we use to describe all such physical stage buffooneries. Many of these comic *lazzi* have found their way directly into contemporary stage comedies and farces; many more are seen nightly on television sitcoms. Granted, the humor of such *lazzi* can be viewed as merely *stupido*, which is in a sense inevitable, as they are hundreds of years old and originally designed for an illiterate audience; on the other hand, the greatest comic actors reinvent classic *lazzi* all the time, making them original and particular to themselves.

So act out these speeches and get the audience to laugh with you—and at your adversaries!

CLEANDRO: *[looking the audience right in the eyes, looking for someone to accuse]*   Who was it said that lovers are like soldiers?   *[finding the person, and smiling at her or him]*   He sure was speaking the truth!   *[puffing himself up as a pompous Italian general, perhaps Mussolini]* The general wants his men young and sturdy;   *[suddenly going goo-goo-eyed; his version of an infatuated young girl]*   so do women.   *[tottering about with an imaginary rifle on his shoulder]*   Old soldiers are a dirty joke;   *[tottering about making limp sexual overtures]*   so are old lovers.   *[cowering in mock fear]*   Soldiers get chewed out by their sergeants;   *[cowering further in mock terror, hands across his nether regions]* lovers by their ladies.   *[falling to the floor with his imaginary rifle, as a soldier in a rainstorm]*   Soldiers sleep out in the rain on the battlefields;   *[rolling over in the rain trying to serenade a girl on a balcony, the "rifle" now becoming a "guitar," batting off the raindrops falling in his eyes]* so do would-be Romeos, who get sopping wet under the balconies of their Juliets.   *[responding to a sudden downpour, then rising ferociously]* Soldiers pursue their enemies with total ferocity,   *[roars to his left]* just as lovers attack their rivals.   *[roars even more fiercely to his right, and then to his rear, and then to the audience. Catches himself up short, as if stopping himself before getting too carried away. Then, miming the nouns as he says them]*   Secrecy, faith, and courage are the emblems of both the soldier and the lover: neither   *[miming nouns as before]* blackest night, nor iciest cold, nor driving-est wind, nor rain, sleet nor hail shall halt either one   *[exaggerated heroic bravado]*   on their road to conquest!   *[directly to the audience, as if summing up philosophically]*   So that, at the end of his lonely struggle, the soldier   *["dying" vaingloriously, hand on head wound]*   dies dismembered in a ditch: *[rolling over, hand on heart wound]*   and the lover dies strung out in despair!   *[up and charming]*   And so it is with me: Clizia lives *[points to his house]*   in my house.   *[starts to house, quickly returns]*

I see her, I eat with her.   *[starts further to house, quickly returns]*   The closer she gets, the more I want her;   *[starts even further to house, quickly returns]*   the more I want her, the less I have her;   *[starts even further to house, quickly returns]*   the less I have her, the more I am overwhelmed by the agony of passion!   *[glances in opposite direction, returns]*   But where is my servant Eustachio?   *[glances in opposite direction, returns, glances back—a double take]*   Oh, wait, there he is!   *[hollering in his direction]*   Eustachio! Eustachio!

SOFRONIA: *[advancing directly toward the audience, while pointing back to her left to where her husband has just run away from her]*   It's amazing, the change in this man!   *[turning back toward her husband, and, leaping in the air, pretending to spit at him with a loud "Ptooooie!" Then turning back to the audience, indicating him with her thumb as in an umpire's gesture for "Out!"]*   Why, right up through last year, he was   *[showing her thumb as in "one"]*   serious,   *[showing her index finger as in "two"]*   consistent,   *[showing her middle finger as in "three"]*   respectful,   *[starting to show her fourth finger, but instead re-raising her middle—indecent—one again]*   honorable! He woke up early, got dressed, went to church, and went about his work! In the morning   *[suddenly speaking rapidly, while miming all this in exaggerated imitation of an old man]*   he'd make his rounds: to the market, city hall; maybe a business call or two; then to a quiet lunch with a few friends, perhaps a visit with his son, to give the boy a few words of advice—   *[employing a pretentiously sanctimonious voice]*   worthwhile lessons from history, you know, sage observations on current affairs—   *[back to exaggerated miming and fast speaking]*   and then he'd come home for his afternoon chores, evening prayers, and a quick visit to his study to plan the next day's events.   *[miming exhaustion, sitting on a bench and spreading out]*   Then, at nine o'clock, we'd have a big family dinner in front of the fireplace.   *[exaggerated eating noises and miming]*   He was a model husband, father, and citizen; an exemplar of family values.   *[rising in presumed anger, and pointing over the audience's heads at her "husband," who is presumed walking about town]*   But now look at him! All of a sudden, he's lost in fantasy: All he thinks about is this girl,   *[sashaying around like a dim-witted, sex-crazed girl, and stuttering her name]*   Clizia!   *[building this sentence in intensity with each verb]*   He *ignores* his business, NEGLECTS his properties, and *FORGETS HIS FRIENDS!*   *[now yelling and screaming]*   Instead, all he does is yell and scream!   *[suddenly realizing she should modify her own behavior; quieting down]*   About what, nobody knows; most of the time he doesn't even know himself!   *[miming this, tiptoeing home and turning around]*   A thousand times a day he comes home and then goes right out again, for no reason at all! He's never here at mealtime: If you talk to him he doesn't respond—or if he does, he doesn't make any sense!

[leaping into the air spitting, "Ptooooie!" "Ptooooie!"]   The servants laugh at him   *[laughing uproariously, then suddenly stopping],*   his son's completely written him off   *[miming huge Xs on a page],*   and everyone in the house now feels they can do whatever they want!   *[one more "Ptooooie!"; gathering her things and heading off to the left]*   Well, I'm going to church and pray things get better.   *[looking back at the audience, seeing her servant to her right and swinging back to him]*   Hey: There's Eustachio!

In all this behavior, understand that you are putting on a performance for your fellow citizens, inciting them to side with you. Win them over with your humor, your self-assurance, your witty descriptions, your physical and vocal elaborations of your case. If you can do this, you are beginning to appreciate the style of old Italian comedy: You are a "commedia-n."

Commedia Lazzi

In his wonderful book *Lazzi: The Comic Routines of the Commedia Dell'Arte* (Performing Arts Journal Publications, 1983), Mel Gordon describes two hundred *lazzi* known to have been used in *commedia* performances between 1550 and 1750. These are usually performed by the Zanni characters (clowns—this is where we get our word *zany*), most usually pot-bellied Pulcinella, or Arlecchino, the cunning and acrobatic rascal eternally familiar in his black mask and multicolored, diamond-patterned costume.
Some of the simpler ones:

- *Lazzo of the Hands Behind the Back*   Arlecchino, attempting to hide behind Scaramuccia, places his arms around him, making all the hand gestures for him. In this way, Arlecchino torments Scaramuccia by slapping his face, pinching his nose, and so forth.

- *Lazzo of Eating the Cherries*   While Scapino is speaking, Arlecchino shows his indifference by taking imaginary cherries out of his hat, eating them, and throwing the pits at Scapino.

- *Lazzo of Imitating a Dog*   To frighten Scaramuccia, Arlecchino snarls and snaps at him like a dog.

Some of the more complex:

- *Lazzo of the Rope-Macaroni*   Attempting to smuggle a rope into a jail to help a friend escape, Pulcinella tries to convince the jailer that the rope is only a long strand of macaroni.

- *Lazzo of the Hatching Egg*   Arlecchino, hatched from an egg, learns to coordinate each part of his independently jointed body.

Cap. Babeo.   *Cucuba.*

Ribaldry   *Commedia* was a ribald and often riotous comic form, as exemplified by this Callot engraving of Capitano Babbeo and Cucuba.

◆ *Lazzo of Spilling No Wine*   Startled, Arlecchino, holding a full glass of wine, executes a complete backward somersault without spilling a drop.

Gordon also lists scatological and sexual *lazzi*, reporting them "among the most popular" of the repertoire:

◆ *Lazzo of Vomit*   After drinking some of the Dottore's medicine, Arlecchino mimes vomiting.

◆ *Lazzo of the Rising Dagger*   Hearing about the physical perfection of a certain woman, Pantalone's dagger begins to rise between his legs.

Performing such *lazzi* is a matter of carefully elaborating the mime, and often improvising dialog to go with it. In teams of two or more people, develop routines of such *lazzi* that could be inserted into a typical *commedia* plot.

◆ S C E N E   11-1

Nicomaco and Sofronia

What follows is an abridged version of a scene in *Clizia* between Nicomaco and his wife, Sofronia. Nicomaco is plotting to have his stupid and ineffectual servant Pirro marry Clizia, so that he can keep Clizia in his house and make her his mistress; Sofronia, naturally, is plotting to stop him.

NICOMACO: Uh-oh, here she comes: Pirro, get out of here fast!

SOFRONIA: I've had to lock Clizia in her room: My son's after her; my husband's after her; the servants are after her—my house is becoming a den of iniquity, for God's sake!

NICOMACO: Where're you going?

SOFRONIA: To church.

NICOMACO: To church? What on earth for? It's not Lent! It's not even Sunday!

SOFRONIA: It's a day in the life of the wicked, all of whom need our prayers. Including you!

NICOMACO: Me? What's wrong with me?

SOFRONIA: Here we've raised this lovely young girl, for which everyone in town admires us, and now you're trying to marry her off to this brainless idiot Pirro! Who can't even support the fleas in his beard! We'll be the laughingstock of Florence.

NICOMACO: Sofronia, darling, you're dead wrong as usual. Pirro's young, he's good-looking, and he loves her. These are the three things a husband should have: youth, looks, and . . . *amore*; who could ask for anything "ahhhh . . . more, eh"?

SOFRONIA: That's not funny! I could like something more! Like more *lire!*

NICOMACO: I know he's not rich, but you know money, it goes from boom to bust, bust to boom, and Pirro's a boomer if I've ever seen one! Indeed, I'm thinking of setting him up.

SOFRONIA: Ha ha ha!

NICOMACO: You're laughing?

SOFRONIA: Who wouldn't? And what are you "setting him up" in?

NICOMACO: What do you mean "in"? In business, of course!

SOFRONIA: In monkey business, I bet! You're going to take the girl away from your son and give her to your steward, right? Something's fishy here, Nicomaco!

NICOMACO: Monkey? Fishy? What are you saying, monkey-fishy?

SOFRONIA: You already know, so I won't tell you.

NICOMACO: What . . . what . . . what do I know?

SOFRONIA: Forget it! Why are you so eager to marry Clizia to Pirro? She's got no dowry, and he's got no prospects! Right?

NICOMACO: Right . . . I guess . . . But I love them both so much, I raised them both; they're both so very . . . so very . . . so very ME! I know they'll be happy together.

SOFRONIA: Happy! Pirro spends all his time drinking and gambling. He would starve to death in the Garden of Eden!

NICOMACO: I told you, I'll set him up!

SOFRONIA: And I told you, you'd just be throwing good money after bad! And you'd convert all our good work into a public scandal! Listen, Nicomaco, we're both involved here: You may have paid the bills for raising Clizia, but I'm the one who brought her up, and I'll have my say about what happens to her! Or else there'll be hell to pay all over town: I'll make sure of that!

NICOMACO: Are you crazy? What are you trying to say? I'm telling you they're getting married tonight, no matter what you do!

SOFRONIA: Maybe yes and maybe no.

NICOMACO: Oho, you're threatening to slander me. Watch out, woman, two can play at that game! You're not all that innocent, you know, helping your dear Cleandro out in his little adventures . . . !

SOFRONIA: What adventures? What are you talking about?

NICOMACO: Oh ho ho! Don't make me say it, dear wife: You know, and I know, and I know that you know, and you know that I know that you know . . . that I . . . that uh . . . that . . . Arghhhh! We're becoming idiots here! Let's make a deal before we make a public spectacle of ourselves.

SOFRONIA: A spectacle, yes, *commedia dell'arte*! And you: old Pantalone! All Florence will be rolling in the aisles!

NICOMACO: Arghhhh! Arghhhh! *[sings]* Sofronia! Sofronia! You're so full of macaronia!*

SOFRONIA: God forgive you, husband. I'm going to church; I'll see you later!

Read the scene aloud with a partner three or four times.

---

* In the original, Machiavelli rhymes *Sofronia* with *soffiona*—a wind machine.

Remember, as with the speeches in the preceding exercise, that the scene takes place in public and that you have a twofold job: first, to convince your spouse to accommodate your interests, and second, to convince any curious passersby that your values are the worthier ones. As with Noah and his wife, Nicomaco should particularly try to get the male passersby on his side, and Sofronia the Florentine wives. So, while seeking to win your argument with your spouse, you should also develop some presentation techniques that will entertain your potential supporters in the town—and therefore in the audience. Humiliate your spouse in public: Make him or her reverse course!

With that in mind, prepare and rehearse the same scene with your partner using the stage directions that follow, which include standard *commedia lazzi* and universal comic business. *Entertain* the audience of passersby, not to prove that you're a comic but to "capture their attention"—to your cause. With the rest of the class on and around the street where this scene is set (some standing, some strolling in the distance, some seated on several sides), play it for all it's worth. Impress your potential supporters both with your truths and with your wit, and try openly, brutally if need be, to win over the Florentine public. Remember, your public and private honor (represented by Nicomaco's lust and Sofronia's marriage) is at stake; lose, and you will be disgraced for the rest of your life!

NICOMACO: *[talking to Pirro]* Uh-oh, here she comes: Pirro, get out of here fast! *[He shoves Pirro, who falls, gets up, falls again, gets up, limps around in a circle until Nicomaco chases him around the stage, as Sofronia enters from the other direction.]*

SOFRONIA: *[speaking to the audience]* I've had to lock Clizia in her room: My son's after her; *[pointing to Nicomaco]* my husband's after her; *[Pirro walks in front of her as he leaves the stage; she points at him]* the servants are after her—my house is becoming a den of iniquity, for God's sake! *[She snarls at her husband and starts off.]*

NICOMACO: Where're you going?

SOFRONIA: To church.

NICOMACO: To church? What on earth for? It's not Lent! It's not even Sunday!

SOFRONIA: It's a day in the life of the wicked, all of whom need our prayers. Including you! *[She falls to her knees and starts to pray vigorously.]*

NICOMACO: Me? *[He too falls to his knees, loudly mocking her praying and making her stop.]* What's wrong with me?

SOFRONIA: *[rising and confronting him directly]* Here we've raised this lovely young girl, for which everyone in town admires us, and now you're trying to marry her off to   *[pointing to where Pirro left the stage]*   this brainless idiot Pirro! Who can't even support the fleas in his beard!   *[Imitates a man trying to pick fleas from his beard. Nicomaco starts to rise; she knocks him down. He starts to rise again; she knocks him down again.]*   We'll be the laughingstock of Florence.

NICOMACO: Sofronia, darling, you're dead wrong as usual.   *[He starts to rise a third time; she raises her hand, he falls down on his own. She walks away.]*   Pirro's young, he's good-looking, and he loves her.   *[As she has moved away, Nicomaco slowly rises to his feet during the following.]*   These are the three things a husband should have: youth, looks, and   *[searching for the Italian word for "love"]* . . . amore; who could ask for anything "ahhhh . . . more, eh"?   *[laughs wildly at his pun]*

SOFRONIA: That's not funny! I could like something more! Like more lire!   *[which she pronounces "leer, eh!" and then echoes his wild laughter]*

NICOMACO: *[in a rage]*   I know he's not rich   *[she snorts]*   but you know money, it goes from boom to bust, bust to boom, and Pirro's a boomer if I've ever seen one!   *[she "booms"—farts—around the stage in protest, saying "boom" with each fart.]*   Indeed, I'm thinking of setting him up.

SOFRONIA: *[laughs uproariously]*   Ha ha ha!

NICOMACO: *[scandalized]*   You're laughing?

SOFRONIA: Who wouldn't?   *[more laughter]*   And what are you "setting him up" IN?

NICOMACO: What do you mean "in"? In business, of course!

SOFRONIA: In monkey business, I bet!   *[prancing about like a monkey]*   You're going to take the girl away from your son and give her to your steward, right?   *[sniffing loudly]*   Something's fishy here, Nicomaco!

NICOMACO: *[He sniffs too, taking her literally.]*   Monkey? Fishy? What are you saying, monkey-fishy?

SOFRONIA: *[coyly, walking away]*   You already know, so I won't tell you.

NICOMACO: *[frightened, following her]*   What . . . what . . . what do I know?

SOFRONIA: *[She stops and turns suddenly; he bumps into her and falls.)*   Forget it! Why are you so eager to marry Clizia to Pirro? She's got no dowry, and he's got no prospects! Right?

NICOMACO: Right . . . I guess . . .   *[He gets up, she again walks away until he restrains her.]*   But I love them both so much, I raised them both;

they're both so very . . . so very . . . so very ME! I know they'll be happy together.

SOFRONIA: Happy! Pirro spends all his time drinking and gambling. He would starve to death in the Garden of Eden!

NICOMACO: I told you, I'll set him up!

SOFRONIA: And I told you, you'd just be throwing good money after bad! And you'd convert all our good work into a public scandal!   *[She points to the audience. Nicomaco, turning to the audience at her gesture, suddenly panics at the thought of creating a scandal. Sofronia turns back to him.]*   Listen, Nicomaco, we're both involved here: You may have paid the bills for raising Clizia, but I'm the one who brought her up, and I'll have my say about what happens to her!   *[looking out at the audience once again to solicit their approval]*   Or else there'll be hell to pay all over town: I'll make sure of that!

NICOMACO: *[Still looking at the audience, he tries to calm them with hand gestures—but then, suddenly panicking more at the thought of losing Clizia, he turns back to Sofronia.]*   Are you crazy? What are you trying to say? I'm telling you they're getting married tonight, no matter what you do!   *[He turns and starts to leave.]*

SOFRONIA: Maybe yes and maybe no.   *[She turns to leave in the opposite direction.]*

NICOMACO: *[His bluff called, he stops and speaks.]*   Oho, you're threatening to slander me.   *[She stops for a second, then sets out again. He again calls to her—as forcefully as he can.]*   Watch out, woman, two can play at that game!   *[same business; he shouts at her]*   You're not all that innocent, you know, helping your dear Cleandro out in his little adventures . . . !

SOFRONIA: *[stopping for real: She has reason to feel some guilt as well.]*   What adventures? What are you talking about?

NICOMACO: *[feeling, for the first time, that he's on a winning track]*   Oh ho ho! Don't make me say it, dear wife: You know, and I know, and I know that you know, and you know that I know that you know . . .   *[loses his thought]*   that I . . . that uh . . . that . . .   *[breaks down in self-rage]*   Arghhhh! We're becoming idiots here! Let's make a deal before we make a public spectacle of ourselves.

SOFRONIA: A spectacle, yes, *commedia dell'arte*! And you: old Pantalone!   *[gesturing to the audience of Florentines]*   All Florence will be rolling in the aisles!

NICOMACO: Arghhhh! Arghhhh!   *[sings]*   Sofronia! Sofronia! You're so full of macaronia!   *[imitates a fart: Pfffffffffffffffffffffft!]*

SOFRONIA: *[He keeps singing wordlessly, and Sofronia, speaking half to him and half to the audience, feels she has gotten as much from him as she can expect at this time.]*   God forgive you, husband. I'm going to church; I'll see you later!   *[She storms off, knocking him down in the process.]*

Stock Characters

Commedia characters are ordinary people—not royalty, like Oedipus and Jocasta, nor biblical figures with divine connections, like Noah and his wife. Nicomaco and Sofronia go to work, cook meals, raise children, gossip with their neighbors, struggle with their finances, go to church, and die known only to their immediate circle of family and friends. They're like us, in other words, and don't present the challenges of a larger-than-life reality you will find in, say, Teiresias or Lucifer.

But they're also *not* like us, for they lack the complexity of thinking and feeling, and the trail of history, that have gone into the making of our personalities. This is somewhat true for all dramatic figures but particularly for those we call "stock characters," who are used by dramatists to indicate not a specific real-life person but a class of like-minded and like-behaving individuals. So, while they may be presumed to cook meals, pay bills, and go to work, we don't see them doing this in the play—unless it is part of the stereotypical behavior of the part. Neither do we know any of their history. Nicomaco is a "dirty old man" conniving to win the sexual favors of a young woman, but Machiavelli gives us no clues as to how he got that way. Sofronia is a "suffering wife" (*soffrire* is Italian for "to suffer"), but we have no idea how or why she came to that role or what earlier options she may have discarded. These considerations, and the acting questions they provoke, are for another sort of drama. Rather, the character "type" precedes and determines the parameters of the role. The "wily servant" will be a wily servant, regardless of his name—which is why *commedia dell'arte* simply dispensed with individual names and called him Arlecchino, and gave him a mask to boot, thus subordinating the actor's individual face to the stock characteristics of the role.

Indeed, stock characters, invented by the Greeks in their New Comedy, were all masked and remained masked in Roman times. And the mask, in all these plays, *is* in a certain sense the character.* Consequently, there is little

---

* The Latin word for "mask" is *persona* and is the root of our words *person* and *personality*.

if any subtle psychology in any *commedia* role. The characters are driven by universal instinct (Nicomaco's lust, Sofronia's jealousy) rather than psychological developments unique to themselves.

This does not mean, however, that stock characters must be played uniformly. Quite to the contrary: The playing of stock characters can be as brilliantly innovative and individual as the actor's imagination allows. One need only remember (if we have seen them) the *commedia* performances of Jim Dale, Bill Irwin, or David Shiner, or imagine those of Jim Carrey, Robin Williams, or Whoopi Goldberg, to realize how brilliantly unique these roles can be in performance. Stock characters demand, above all, outrageously energetic and creative performers, making radical choices in playing—and exaggerating—the aspects of the stereotypical behavior the dramatist was hoping to poke fun at.

Playing stock characters, therefore, is fundamentally a *theatrical* act, dependent not so much on investigations revealing the real-life background of the character but preparations based on an understanding of the author's use (and abuse) of the character's stock urges and behavior and how they intermingle with others in a theatrical construct. Though with this necessary caveat: Stock characters are based on real life, but on the *collective* behaviors of real life, rather than on those of individual men and women.

(And a further caveat: "Nicomaco," had you not guessed, is a shorthand version of "Niccolò Machiavelli," who was known to consort with young prostitutes and actresses, including one who performed in the premiere of this play. The stock characters herein, therefore, while abstractions of individuals, are filled with the breath of real human life.)

More *Commedia* Scenes

Scenes in this genre are hard to find because *commedia dell'arte* is largely improvised and unscripted and *commedia erudita* scripts are rare. But you can look at additional scenes in *Clizia* and in Machiavelli's even better known *Mandragola* (*The Mandrake*), and also at the partly scripted plays of two eighteenth-century Venetians with *commedia* roots: Carlo Gozzi (*The King Stag; The Snake Woman*) and Carlo Goldoni (*Arlecchino: The Servant of Two Masters,* which Goldoni adapted from an original *commedia dell'arte* version; *The Cunning Widow; The Mistress of the Inn; The Venetian Twins; The Fan*).

And you can *improvise* your own *commedia dell'arte* as well! Using the skeleton of any scene in these plays, or from any Roman comedy, or traditional folk tale from any culture, and mixing in comic *lazzi* and physical and verbal high jinks of your own making, create your own *commedia dell'arte* plot, outlining the main events and character entrances and exits, and, with one or more fellow actors improvising the plot's dialog with you as you go along, preparing, rehearsing, and staging your mini-masterpiece.

LESSON

12

Shakespeare and the Elizabethan Theatre

From Italy, the Renaissance spread north, bringing with it a revival of long-lost plays and theatrical insights from ancient Greece and Rome, which soon were merged with the popular folk dance, song, storytelling, mime, and acrobatic entertainment of medieval Europe. Nowhere was this combination more thrilling and vigorous than in England, chiefly during the reigns of Queen Elizabeth (1558–1603) and subsequently King James I (1603–25). Dozens of playwrights became immensely popular during these decades, including John Lyly, Christopher Marlowe, Thomas Kyd, John Webster, Ben Jonson, Thomas Dekker, and of course William Shakespeare, now considered the greatest dramatist not only of his time but of all time.

Like its classical and *commedia* predecessors, Elizabethan drama was largely played in a public theatre, usually outdoors.* The first theatres were trestle stages set up in streets and innyards; by the 1570s, grand open-air public theatres were erected in suburbs north and south of London (playgoing having been outlawed within the city itself). These public theatres seated upwards of 3,000 spectators, ranged around the actors on at least three sides (some scholars say all four), where they sat in three galleries above the stage, stood on the earthen "pit" at the actors' feet, or, if they could afford it (and the theatre permitted it on that date), were seated right on the stage itself.

---

* Technically, the term "Elizabethan" refers only to the period of Elizabeth's reign; dramas—including some of Shakespeare's—from the time of King James are more properly called "Jacobean." But "Elizabethan" can also be used in a general sense to cover both periods and, for the sake of simplicity, is so here.

Some Elizabethan stage characters This well-known engraving, made about fifty years after Shakespeare's death, shows costumes and postures of various popular Elizabethan characters, including two of Shakespeare's (Falstaff and Mistress Quickly—here labeled "Hoftes," or Hostess), and probably indicates current costuming of those characters and others.

Basic Elizabethan male attire   The doublet (a vestlike jacket, ending in a short skirt) and hose (tights) were basic attire for young men in the Elizabethan era, often with breeches (short pants, often padded) bridging the two. A long-sleeved blouse was usually underneath, and boots, belts, hats, capes, and accessories completed the picture. Stylistic variations, however, were enormous. Pictured is Iris Brooke's reconstruction of a basic male attire for 1595.

Surrounded by their audience, Elizabethan actors were, therefore, necessarily virtuoso artists—skilled at holding an audience on all sides with their great skills at singing, dancing, fencing, storytelling, verse and prose speaking, and milking the dramatic styles of both comedy and tragedy to maximum effect. And they were adept at playing characters of both sexes—despite the fact that throughout the entire period, all professional actors, by law, were male. But make no mistake: The Elizabethan actors were emotionally expressive (and impressive) actors as well, engaging their own and the audience's feelings, and, unquestionably, crying real tears on stage when the text demanded it, as it very often did.*

Like their Italian Renaissance counterparts, Elizabethan dramatists often began by revising ancient Roman plays. For example, one of Shakespeare's first plays, *The Comedy of Errors,* was an adaptation of Plautus's *Menaechmi,* eighteen centuries old at the time. Indeed, most Elizabethan plays were adaptations of older plays or of historical chronicles, including Greek and Roman history as well as British. But Elizabethan drama diverged from

---

* See my "Be Your Tears Wet: Tears (and Acting) in Shakespeare," *Journal of Dramatic Theory and Criticism,* Winter 1996, and for a general discussion of acting in the plays of Shakespeare, my *Acting in Shakespeare* (Mayfield, 1992).

Elizabethan ladies, in representative attire as drawn by Iris Brooke.

the Italian by dispensing quickly with stock characters, and the plays of Shakespeare, in particular, have given us dramatic roles of extraordinary complexity, individuality, and profoundly credible humanity.

Early in his own time, Shakespeare was identified as a great dramatic poet—equal to the ancients—in both comedy and tragedy. But he also virtually invented, and remains the sole true master of, a new genre of drama: the history play, inspired by events in English history from the time of King John. For our first exploration of the genius of his age, we turn to one of Shakespeare's earliest and, in his own time, most successful history plays, *Richard III,* first published in 1597.

◆ S c e n e 12-1

The Past Made Vivid: Richard and Anne

This exchange, from Act 1, Scene 2 of *Richard III,* takes place between Richard, Duke of Gloucester (who when crowned will become King Richard III), and Lady Anne, whose husband Richard has just murdered. To heighten the drama, Shakespeare, counter to the historical record, sets his scene next to the corpse of King Henry VI, Anne's father-in-law, whom Richard has also murdered. The dialog mixes grief, fury, and sexual adventurism—all in verse—in the brilliant theatricality we have come to associate with the world's most celebrated playwright.

RICHARD: I did not kill your husband.

ANNE: Why, then he is alive.

Marco Barricelli plays the crook-backed King Richard in the Oregon Shakespeare Festival's 1993 production of *Richard III*. (Courtesy Oregon Shakespeare Festival; photo by Christopher Briscoe)

RICHARD: Nay, he is dead; and slain by Edward's hand.

ANNE: In thy foul throat thou liest: Queen Margaret saw
Thy murderous falchion° smoking in his blood;   °*sword*
The which thou once didst bend against her breast,
But that thy brothers beat aside the point.

RICHARD: I was provoked by her sland'rous tongue,
That laid their guilt upon my guiltless shoulders.

ANNE: Thou wast provoked by thy bloody mind,
That never dreamt on aught but butcheries.
Didst thou not kill this king?

RICHARD: I grant ye.

ANNE: Dost grant me, hedgehog? Then, God grant me too
Thou mayst be damned for that wicked deed!
O! he was gentle, mild, and virtuous!

RICHARD: The better for the King of heaven, that hath him.

David Troughton plays the title role and Jennifer Ehle plays Lady Anne in this Royal Shakespeare Company 1995 production of *Richard III*. (© Clive Barda/ Performing Arts Library)

ANNE: He is in heaven, where thou shalt never come.

RICHARD: Let him thank me, that holp° to send   °*helped*
  him thither;
  For he was fitter for that place than earth.

ANNE: And thou unfit for any place but hell.

RICHARD: Yes, one place else, if you will hear me name it.

ANNE: Some dungeon.

RICHARD: Your bed chamber.

ANNE: Ill rest betide° the chamber where thou liest!   °*come to*

RICHARD: So will it, madam, till I lie with you.

The characters' goals are both simple and complex. At the simple level, Richard seeks a sexual encounter with Lady Anne—to "lie with" her. Lady Anne, on the other hand, seeks to make Richard suffer ("God grant . . . thou mayst be damned") for murdering her husband and her father-in-law; she wants to get him to confess to those crimes if she can and, at the very least, shame him into a numbing guilt. As these simple goals rely on basic instincts, lust (for Richard) and revenge (for Lady Anne), this scene can develop a ferocious interpersonal intensity.

But there are subtler goals as well. Richard's drive is at least as political as sexual—as a royal prince, he surely would have no trouble acquiring mere sexual gratification, and Lady Anne represents a crucial stepping stone to his winning the crown: Marrying her could make his claim to the throne appear almost legitimate. Nor is Lady Anne, recently widowed, without political desire; in those times, ousted royals were more likely to be executed than retired to a country estate. Unmarried, Anne would be vulnerable to whoever came to power; married to Richard, she might at least have a protector and access to the royal way of life to which she had surely become accustomed.

So this scene, with a few minor modifications, would be a striking dramatic interchange in any theatrical form: contemporary cinema, TV soap opera, opera, or modern urban drama. But the particular style of Shakespeare's language poses rare—even unprecedented—opportunities for suspenseful, sensual, and emotionally thrilling performances.

Learn, rehearse, and play the scene with a partner before proceeding to the following discussions of the text elements.

Scansion

This is a verse text, which means the language has a definable pattern of accented syllables and sometimes a rhyme pattern as well.

The basic elements of dramatic verse are very simple to understand: It is language composed in *lines* of a regular length, and each line can be subdivided into a repeating series of *feet,* which are units of a fixed length, and with a recognizable and repeated pattern of accented syllables.

And just what is an accented syllable? Generally, it is one spoken with a bit more force and, particularly in dramatic verse, with a slightly raised pitch.

Reading the pattern of the line lengths and accented syllables is called *scansion,* or a scanning of the verse. Thus, for example, scanning Anne's line "And thou unfit for any place but hell" shows a natural speaking rhythm of five paired syllables, each with the second syllable slightly accented: something like "duh DUM, duh DUM, duh DUM, duh DUM, duh DUM." The line could be spoken as something like this (with the accented syllables shown in capitals): "And THOU un-FIT for A-ny PLACE but HELL."

Now, in fact, very few good actors would stress all five of the syllables equally in that (or any) blank-verse line. Some wouldn't stress more than two or three of them—at least as far as the untrained ear could tell. You would hear such actors say something like "And THOU unfit for A-ny place but HELL," thus giving *thou* (the person she's angry at) and *hell* (the place she wants him to go) the strongest emphases and the *a* in *any* a light or moderate stress just to punch up the middle of the line.

But if you listen very closely, you might hear that *fit* and *place* are at least micro-stressed, given an emphasis that is barely perceptible but that still lends added flavor and sharper distinction to the text.

The "duh DUM" is, in this case, the *verse foot.* This particular type of two-syllable foot, with the second syllable accented, is called *iambic.* Iambic feet are the most common in Elizabethan verse drama, and in most other verse dramas as well—including ancient Greek, neoclassic French, and modern English. Repeated iambic feet are also often employed in ritualized prose, as in the first eight syllables of the Pledge of Allegiance ("i PLEDGE al-LEgiance TO the FLAG").

A verse scheme that uses lines with five feet is called *pentameter,* from the Greek word for "five." Pentameter is the most common line length in English verse drama.

Iambic pentameter is thus the most common verse form employed by Shakespeare and other Elizabethan dramatists, and it is the form of Anne's quoted line. When iambic pentameter is not rhymed, it is (and was in Shakespeare's day) more popularly known as *blank verse.* In fact, the first reference to Shakespeare in print was a rival playwright complaining to his friends in 1592 that the young Shakespeare "supposes he is as well able to bombast out blank verse as the best of you." And he was.

There are other verse forms used in Elizabethan drama, of course. As to feet: While iambs are the most common, *trochees* (trochaic feet), which also contain two syllables but with the first accented, also appear, often as the first foot of a line. There are also three-syllable feet: *anapests,* which have the last syllable accented (as in the word *underneath*), and *dactyls,* in which the first syllable bears the accent (as in *broccoli*).

As to line length: A four-foot line is called *tetrameter;* a three-foot line *trimeter,* a two-foot line *dimeter,* and a six-foot line (which is the verse form for most French drama) *hexameter.*

As to rhyme: Shakespeare often uses rhyming pentameter couplets, where the last two syllables of two consecutive lines rhyme. And he uses rhymes in more complex ways as well.

While blank verse is the most common form of versification in Shakespeare, it is not the only one. Later in the same scene between Richard and Anne we have a section of iambic trimeter:

ANNE: I would I knew thy heart.

RICHARD: 'Tis figur'd in my tongue.

ANNE: I fear me both are false.

RICHARD: Then never man was true.

ANNE: Well, well, put up your sword.

RICHARD: Say, then, my peace is made.

ANNE: That shalt thou know hereafter.

RICHARD: But shall I live in hope?

ANNE: All men, I hope, live so.

And the play concludes, as do most Shakespearean dramas, with a rhyming couplet:

> Now civil wounds are stopp'd, Peace lives again;
> That she may long live here, God say amen!

SWORDS, STAFFS, AND WALKING STICKS

Notice that Anne asks Richard to "put up" his sword. From medieval times until the eighteenth century, men from about fifteen to fifty commonly wore swords, even in urban settings. One reason was for protection in an era when public safety was not yet secured; another was to establish an image of bravado and manly sophistication. In Shakespeare, young men are continually drawing swords upon each other at the slightest provocation (as in the famous opening scene of *Romeo and Juliet*). The sword was worn on the left hip, in a holder or scabbard, and the wearer's left hand commonly rested on the hilt, with the right hand always ready to move to the hilt immediately at the suggestion of an affront or attack.

And when the sword itself became unnecessary, either because of improved public safety or the age and infirmity of the man who might carry it, a staff or walking stick was often substituted. The staff, a tall and sometimes decorated pole normally higher than the man himself, implied an official position (as with a "staff of office") and normally conveyed authority; it dates from ancient times, and one often sees the blind and holy Teiresias employing one in productions of *Oedipus*. The walking stick, generally about waist-high, give or take a few inches, conveyed a dapper urbanity. Staff and walking stick alike were useful in negotiating rough cobblestones and unpaved pathways, and for batting

(continued)

(continued)

Walking sticks and swords   Notice the swords (held by the man at the lower right) and the walking sticks employed by gentlemen in this Flemish street scene by Jean le Tavernier dating from about 1460. At the upper right, a book is being presented by a kneeling servant to Philip the Good of Burgundy.

away stray dogs and, on occasion, purse-snatchers and pickpockets. They were nearly ubiquitous as accessories to male attire in Europe for several hundred years, as the Flemish street scene of 1460 above shows.

Actors playing male roles in period dramas, therefore, can spend useful time experimenting with and practicing the carrying and employment of swords, staffs, and walking sticks.

Verse Variations

Blank verse used in a play is not always regular. While the earliest dramatic blank verse in English was uniform in its iambic pentameters, as can be seen in the first English play employing this form, Thomas Sackville and Thomas Norton's *Gorboduc* (1561), most later plays, and all of Shakespeare's, have a richer poetic texture, one that admits abundant variations or irregularities of both line length and accents. In Scene 12-1, for example, we find:

1. Lines with an extra (eleventh), unaccented syllable. This is called a "feminine ending":* "That laid their guilt upon my guiltless shoulders" and "Let him thank me, that holp to send him thither."

2. Lines with just three feet: "Why, then he is alive" and "Didst thou not kill this king?"

3. Lines in which the pentameter is maintained only by accenting normally unaccented *-ed* endings (as we sometimes do today when pronouncing the word *blessed* as *bless-ed*): "Thou wast provokèd by thy bloody mind." In these cases, the speaking accent is often noted by modern editors with a downward accent over the *e*, as above.

4. A line in which the pentameter rhythm is maintained by accenting the *-ed* ending of one word and shortening a three-syllable word (*slanderous*) into a two-syllable one: "I was provokèd by her sland'rous tongue."

5. Lines simply of prose: "I grant ye" and "Some dungeon."

6. A line of twelve syllables (eleven if *heaven* is pronounced "heav'n") that is best considered prose as well: "The better for the King of heaven that hath him."

7. Lines that would never be spoken as five consecutive iambs, such as "Nay, he is dead; and slain by Edward's hands." The first foot is probably best read as trochaic ("NAY, he"), with the four following feet iambic ("is DEAD and SLAIN by ED-ward's HAND").

Thus Shakespeare's verse, though it is underlaid by a "standard" pattern, deviates from that pattern almost as often as it follows it.

It isn't, of course, essential to know all the verse forms by their formal names to speak them effectively; there are surely many professional Shakespearean actors who could not define iambic trimeter if you paid them, and perhaps some of Shakespeare's own actors couldn't define it either, learning verse rhythms by experience rather than by instruction. Nonetheless, a deep understanding, as much visceral as cognitive, of the inherent cadences of

---

* So called because it follows the pattern of French lines that end with feminine nouns, such as *chambre* and *monde*, which often have an unstressed final syllable.

verse is crucial to conveying the power, sensuality, delicacy, and intellectual complexity of Elizabethan dramatic language.

Playing the Verse

Playing verse is not easily or quickly learned—it is not simply a matter of slavishly studying or rigidly following the scansion, which would produce mere singsong. But neither can the metrical patterns be flagrantly overridden by pumped-up feeling without sacrificing the text's dramatic power and sensuality. Blank verse, when skillfully handled, matches meter and meaning, rhythm and emotion, in dynamic tension, with each played off the other, affording multiple nuances at every turn. It is also a steady pulse under the dialog (the iambic rhythm, "duh *DUM,*" is the same pulse as a heartbeat), which creates the sense of a living presence in the text and becomes an agitated living presence when, like a heart monitor on an overexcited patient, the once-regular iambic measures start going awry.

Let's see how the verse works in Scene 12-1.

RICHARD: I did not kill your husband.

ANNE: Why, then he is alive.

These first two lines are iambic trimeter fragments, with Richard softening his with a feminine ending, and the masculine ending of Anne's consequently providing a sarcastic jab ("Come off it," the clipped rhythm says)—for they both know that her husband is dead.

RICHARD: Nay, he is dead; and slain by Edward's hand.

Richard's reply, in blank verse but with a trochee instead of an iamb for the first foot, cuts Anne off and brings her back to reality.

ANNE: In thy foul throat thou liest: Queen Margaret saw . . .

This line begins in an iambic pattern (through "liest"), which provides a smooth denunciation of Richard; she then shifts essentially to prose for three words ("Queen Margaret saw") to introduce a story, which is her version of what Margaret saw. Anne goes on:

Thy murderous falchion smoking in his blood;
The which thou once didst bend against her breast,
But that thy brothers beat aside the point.

The story, horrific in its imagery, is contained in three lines of iambic pentameter that recount two separate events: the discovery of Richard assassinating

Anne's husband, and his earlier attack on Margaret, Anne's mother-in-law, with the same sword. But there's a substituted trochee here, too—in the last foot of the second line, which, for sense, would have to read "didst BEND a-GAINST HER breast," with the word *her* lifted in pitch to point up the distinction between *her* (Margaret's) breast and *his* (Anne's husband's) blood. A slavish adherence to the iambic rhythm at that point ("didst BEND a-GAINST her BREAST") would obscure the meaning of the line.

RICHARD: I was provokèd by her sland'rous tongue,
That laid their guilt upon my guiltless shoulders.

ANNE: Thou wast provokèd by thy bloody mind,
That never dreamt on aught but butcheries.

Here Richard forces the scansion of a line into blank verse and completes the idea with a second line that adds a final unstressed syllable to make a feminine ending, again softening his villainy. Anne, not to be intimidated, parallels his first line, picking up and repudiating his exact words ("I can beat you at this fancy-talk 'provokèd' game!"), then completing her sentence with a searing accusation, with the masculine ending on *butcheries*. The parallel phrasing shows her jockeying not only for political power but literary dominance. History, it is said, is written by the winners: Both are fighting for the right to define history (in words), so that they can create a better future for themselves (in actions).

ANNE: Didst thou not kill this king?

RICHARD: I grant ye.

Anne starts a line of blank verse, but Richard responds in terse prose, mocking her attempt to versify.

ANNE: Dost grant me, hedgehog? Then, God grant me too
Thou mayst be damnèd for that wicked deed!
O! he was gentle, mild, and virtuous!

RICHARD: The better for the King of heav'n, that hath him.

ANNE: He is in heav'n, where thou shalt never come.

RICHARD: Let him thank me, that holp to send him thither;
For he was fitter for that place than earth.

ANNE: And thou unfit for any place but hell.

RICHARD: Yes, one place else, if you will hear me name it.

Anne denounces Richard in five reasonably regular verse lines (presuming she expands *damned* to two syllables and contracts *heaven* to one), to which Richard responds in four lines, only one of which can be read as regular blank verse (three have at least eleven syllables), thus continuing to rudely mock her regularity of style. Then his mockery becomes savage:

ANNE: Some dungeon.

RICHARD: Your bed chamber.

Anne, flustered, tries to continue her verbal assault, but her ferocity is slightly undercut by the feminine ending of her response. And Richard, sensing his opportunity, nails the masculine closure:

ANNE: Ill rest betide the chamber where thou liest!

RICHARD: So will it, madam, till I lie with you.

Three lines later, Richard will invite Anne to "leave this keen encounter of our wits, / And fall something into a slower method," and the verse will shift to a more regular pattern. And he will sleep with her, marry her, and eventually have her executed.

Rhetoric

Playing the verse is only a first step toward meeting the dramatic challenge of Elizabethan dramatists, who were also, by and large, dazzling rhetoricians. Rhetoric, the art of persuasive speech, is fundamental to any theatre that encompasses political or legal debate, as so many plays do—Shakespeare, indeed, was such a master of rhetoric that many scholars believe he must have spent part of his youth working in a lawyer's office.* He was certainly well versed in the language of the courts, both judicial ones (he engaged in numerous lawsuits, as did his father) and the royal courts of Queen Elizabeth and King James, where he and his company often performed.

Effective rhetoric—in politics, courts, or on the stage—is largely dependent on well-turned verbal constructions. These include

◆ *words repeated to build a crescendo*: "government of the people, by the people, for the people"—Abraham Lincoln

◆ *words repeated to contrast antithetical ends*: "ask not what your country can do for you; ask what you can do for your country"—John F. Kennedy

◆ *poised antonyms*: "give me liberty or give me death"—Patrick Henry

---

* See the controversial Eric Sams, *The Real Shakespeare* (Yale University Press, 1995).

◆ *parallel phrasing,* sometimes underlined by alliteration: "not be judged by the color of their skin, but by the content of their character"
—Martin Luther King, Jr.

◆ *building* of words or phrases, each more potent than the last: "victory at all costs, victory in spite of all terror; victory however long and hard the road may be"—Winston Churchill

In Scene 12-1 we can see repeated words (*heaven, provoked, grant*), building lists of adjectives (*gentle, mild, virtuous*), poised antonyms (*alive/dead, guilt/ guiltless, heaven/hell, fitter/unfit*), and parallel phrasings ("I was provoked by her sland'rous tongue"..."Thou wast provoked by thy bloody mind"). These rhetorical ingredients can be combined into powerfully persuasive arguments when pointed and accented with great specificity.

Playing and Building the Rhetoric

How do actors do this pointing and accenting, or accentuating? Mainly (but not solely) by sharply turned inflections, or pitch changes. For example:

RICHARD: I grant ye.

ANNE: Dost ^grant me, ^hedgehog? Then, God ^grant ^me ^too
Thou mayst be ^^^damnèd for that wicked deed!

The upward inflections, marked by one or more carets (^) before the syllables to be lifted and pointed, here make a pattern of the two repetitions of the word *grant* which Anne appropriates from Richard's callous admission of murder, pointedly reusing them to seek a grant in return. Anne's first reuse ("Dost grant me"), sharply pointed, has the edge of sarcasm, tacitly criticizing Richard's casual dismissal of his crime; and her second, attached by alliteration as well as proximity to God ("God grant me"), seeks divine help to overpower that contempt. Anne's second *me* in that line is precisely matched to Richard's previous "I grant ye," making the *me* a direct, and rhyming, appropriation of Richard's *ye,* betokening a strong accent as well.
    The trading of matched alternatives in the short line exchange

ANNE: Some dungeon.

RICHARD: Your ^bed chamber.

is a shocking and effective rhetorical ploy, particularly as it leads the stunned Lady Anne to walk into a verbal trap:

ANNE: Ill rest betide the chamber where thou liest!

RICHARD: So will it, madam, till I lie with ^you.

Richard's manipulation has forced Anne back into echoing her earlier invective, "In thy foul throat thou liest" (employing a different meaning of *liest*), and has set him up to turn his evildoing into sexual seduction: When Richard says "I lie . . ." he is simultaneously confessing deceit and proposing an affair!

ANNE: O, he was ˆgentle, ˜mild, and ˜˜˜virtuous!

Describing her dead father-in-law, Henry VI, Anne uses three adjectives. *Gentle* basically refers to his rank (he was a gentleman, with the implication of perfect breeding and manners), *mild* to his demeanor, and *virtuous* to his moral integrity. In this order, the words increasingly indicate the difference between Henry and Richard, Henry being roughly equal in gentility (both men are of royal blood), quite a bit milder (Richard is cruel), but *vastly* more virtuous—and moral virtue is the critical issue of this scene. Say the words in any other order and the sentence is weaker: Neither "O, he was gentle, virtuous, and mild!" nor "O, he was virtuous, mild, and gentle!" works. The accusations that Richard is merely low-born (non-gentle) and a hothead (non-mild) are effective only as stepping stones to the real attack: that he is utterly immoral (non-virtuous).

Therefore, if you say these words flatly, with each adjective having equal emotional importance (as if you were saying "The flag is red, white, and blue"), your comparison lacks bite; it is a description rather than an attack. So try to *build* these words with ascending authority and passion in your voice; combined with the build that Shakespeare has created in the word order, you will achieve a commanding rhetorical flourish that urges your hearers (not just Richard but the pallbearers standing by) to remember Henry's goodness.

O, he was ˆgentle, ˜mild, and ˜˜˜VIRtuous!

Good rhetoric is concise, controlled, and forceful, the result of precise word choice, word placement, pointed inflection, and sonic momentum. Seeming dispassionate, even playful, it can be devastating in propounding an argument, winning an election, moving troops into life-and-death battle. It is one of the particular glories of the human mind—and of Elizabethan drama.

The Public Environment

The action of Elizabethan drama takes place in an environment as public as those theatres that preceded it, with the bulk of the scenes unfolding in streets, plazas, taverns, battlefields, courts, parties, trials, weddings, or ceremonies. Lots of people are to be found hanging around the Elizabethan stage;

even in scenes set in a desert (*Timon of Athens*), a deserted island (*The Tempest*), a forest (*A Midsummer Night's Dream*), or the battlements of a castle at midnight (*Hamlet*), there is always the possibility of passersby, including those from both the human and the spirit realm.

And when Hamlet says "Now I am alone," he is "alone" with a Globe Theatre audience of up to 3,000 persons, all equally lit by the same sun he is, surrounding him a full 300 degrees from right to left and 90 degrees bottom to top; there is simply no place Richard Burbage, the actor playing Hamlet, could have looked without seeing the packed theatre audience around him. It is no wonder these outdoor theatres, which were the dominant performance spaces of Elizabethan times, were called "public" theatres.*

Scene 12-1 takes place not just between Richard and Anne but also in front of the guards who are carrying the late king's corpse. And while these are nonspeaking characters, they are not to be presumed nonhearing ones, and everyone in the audience would recognize that the support of such armed forces would prove crucial to any power-seeker in a royal court.

Therefore Richard, though he will presumably never look at them nor acknowledge their presence, will certainly be trying to impress the guards with his intelligence and authority. He will also make clear to them, his secondary audience, that he is not a man to be crossed lightly. Richard will want them on his side when the time comes for his assault on the crown.

And so, of course, will Lady Anne. Neither of these characters can completely forget that their conversation is taking place in public and that the public (which includes the guards, plus anyone who might happen by) may eventually play a role in their political success or failure.

There's a tertiary audience for this scene as well. As the apostrophe, *O*, indicates, the scene also takes place, in Anne's eyes at least, within the view of God, the "King of heaven" (as Richard mockingly calls him) whom she hopes will eventually support her quest. And Richard, too, we will later find, has at least an unconscious awareness of a God who might oversee his adventures: "Have mercy, Jesu!" Richard cries, in a dream, at the end of the play. These characters, at least in some part of their minds, clearly imagine they are acting within the context of a divine universe, and their goals are consequently tuned to garner support from a godly as well as a human audience.

Besides God and Jesus, there are a host of spirit or spiritual characters in the universe of Elizabethan drama, or at least in the minds of Elizabethan dramatic characters. Shakespeare's plays are filled with supernatural figures:

---

* There were also a few smaller "private" theatres in London late in the period, located indoors and lit by candles. Shakespeare's company owned and performed in one of these, the Blackfriars Theatre, from about 1608 until the end of the era.

Ghosts appear on stage (*Hamlet, Macbeth, Richard III*), as do fairies (*A Midsummer Night's Dream, The Tempest*), witches (*Macbeth*), soothsayers (*Julius Caesar, Antony and Cleopatra*), prophets (*Troilus and Cressida*), Greek and Roman goddesses (*As You Like It, The Tempest, Pericles*), fiends (*Henry VI*), apparitions (*Cymbeline*), and the allegorical figure of Time (*The Winter's Tale*). Most of these beings speak, and all become audiences to the human characters in the plays; their presence must be imagined and played to, even when they are not on stage, by actors playing such characters.

Playing to a spirit audience often means the actor must try (in imagination, of course!) to connect to an unseen world. When Lady Macbeth cries "Come, thick night," or King Lear says "Blow, winds!," these are not—on stage at least—mere literary metaphors; the actors playing the roles must attempt to command the spirits of night and the wind.

And when Anne in *Richard III* says "O, he was gentle . . . ," the actor must seek the ear of a divine spirit (God) who, she feels, would be compassionate toward her distress at the injustice she is experiencing.

Does volume help in summoning spirits? Rarely. The most effective way of reaching such audiences (God in Anne's case) is to find the voice that spirit audiences, were they to exist, would listen to and respect. And that's where an actor's imagination, and understanding of human nature, proves essential.

Extending yourself into an Elizabethan text, therefore, means to extend yourself into a spiritual world you probably don't yourself dwell in during your offstage hours, a world that your rational self probably regards as superstitious or fantastical. But theatre means bringing that superstition or fantasy into the reality of a character's belief. And this transfer results in making it an audience's belief, as when Peter Pan, in James M. Barrie's great play of that name, gets the audience to demonstrate, by their applause, that they, too, "believe in fairies." They don't, of course, outside the theatre—but they will for the dramatic moment if the actors so extend themselves as to *live* in a world where fairies fly.

Try Scene 12-1 one more time (I won't say one "final" time, as these scenes can be worked on for a lifetime), bringing as much from these discussions, and your previous work, to the exchange as you can. Have classmates play the pallbearers silently standing behind, not looking directly at you but perhaps stealing an occasional glimpse. Try to win all your character's goals.

These discussions won't immediately make you the world's greatest Elizabethan actor (it probably took the Elizabethans ten to twenty years of day-to-day acting experience to be able to satisfy audiences in these roles),* but play and replay the Richard–Anne scene several times, trying to implement

---

*   François Talma, the great eighteenth-century French actor, insisted it took twenty years of apprenticeship to master the craft.

the cleverness of the verse, the power of the rhetoric, and the appeal to the secondary and tertiary audiences in this scene.

◆ SCENE 12-2

A Merry War: Beatrice and Benedick

Let's move to something on the lighter side. Beatrice and Benedick are also a warring couple, but in their case it is, as described by her uncle in the opening scene of *Much Ado About Nothing,* "a kind of a merry war," in which the pair engage in "a skirmish of wit" every time they meet. A few lines later in the same scene, Benedick and his companions, returning uninjured from a victorious military engagement, are greeted by Beatrice and her family and friends, including various gentlemen and young ladies. After a round of joyous greetings for the men, Beatrice fires the opening salvo in the "merry war" by commenting on a lame joke Benedick has just uttered:

BEATRICE: I wonder that you will still be talking, Signior Benedick: nobody marks° you.   °*listens to*

BENEDICK: What! my dear Lady Disdain, are you yet living?

BEATRICE: Is it possible Disdain should die while she hath such meet° food to feed it as Signior Benedick? Courtesy   °*appropriate* itself must convert to disdain, if you come in her presence.

BENEDICK: Then is courtesy a turncoat. But it is certain I am loved of all ladies, only you excepted; and I would I could find in my heart that I had not a hard heart; for, truly, I love none.

BEATRICE: A dear happiness° to women: they would   °*rare good fortune* else have been troubled with a pernicious suitor. I thank God and my cold blood, I am of your humor° for that: I had rather   °*disposition* hear my dog bark at a crow than a man swear he loves me.

BENEDICK: God keep your ladyship still in that mind; so some gentleman or other shall 'scape a predestinate° scratched face.   °*preordained*

BEATRICE: Scratching could not make it worse, an 'twere°   °*if it were* such a face as yours were.

BENEDICK: Well, you are a rare parrot-teacher.°   °*one who, like a parrot, scratches with words instead of claws*

BEATRICE: A bird of my tongue is better than a beast of yours.°   °*I, though a parrot, am better than you, a brute animal.*

Nike Doukas as Beatrice and Douglas Sills as Benedick banter with each other, while still trying to put on a good face for their friends, in the first scene of the 2001 South Coast Repertory production of *Much Ado About Nothing*, directed by Mark Rucker and set in the 1930s. (Courtesy South Coast Repertory; photo by Ken Howard)

BENEDICK: I would my horse had the speed of your tongue, and so good a
  continuer.° But keep your way, i' God's name;   °*so able to keep going*
  I have done.

BEATRICE: You always end with a jade's trick.°   °*horse's trick, such as slipping*
  I know you of old.   *out of the bridle*

Even with the glosses, this dialog is not, on its surface, easy to understand.
Nor are you likely to find the "jokes" funny. But the meaning of this scene is
not to be found on its surface, nor are the jokes even remotely funny—out
of context. In context, however, the scene is potentially both touching and
humorous. Let's explore it.

The first thing actors approaching this scene must realize is (once again!)
that it takes place in public: amid a crowd of young, glamorous, and unattached men and women, meeting on a particularly celebratory occasion.
Romance, one might quickly conclude, is in the air.

Yet the second thing a reading of the entire script reveals is a deeply
personal note: that Beatrice and Benedick love, but do not trust, each other.
Beatrice seems to feel that Benedick once betrayed her ("He wears his faith
but as the fashion of his hat," she complains just before his entrance), and
Benedick distrusts all women as unfaithful to the men who commit to
them. What lies beneath this wariness? Shakespeare provides no details,
but anyone who has been wounded in love can come up with a thousand
possibilities—those you choose (and Shakespeare does provide some starting
points) will determine the specific sort of Beatrice or Benedick you will play.

We're not looking for a definitive "interpretation" of the scene here in this
exercise, however. Just learn and rehearse the lines, with a partner, and perform it *in the midst of a crowd of young men and women roughly your age.*

The primary goal for each of you in this opening scene of the play is to
impress the *crowd* with your wittiness, attractiveness, friskiness, and bold-
ness. Circulate among them as you speak, getting them on your side in this
eternal (but, to you, very particular) battle of the sexes. Impressing the crowd
is how you will impress—and silence—the acting partner with whom you
are fighting your "merry war." For this is war, no matter how merry, and you
must do everything you can to win it!

So impress those of your own sex with how well you represent your side's
goals and values. Make them cheer you on and laugh at your bon mots and
ripostes. (And, crowd, please *do* cheer on and laugh with your gender representative! As you do so, let the men drift toward the other men, and the
women toward the other women, thus becoming two camps, each rooting
for their flag-bearer.)

And impress on those of the opposite sex how right your own gender's
values are, and how a very special person of the opposite sex will ultimately
realize this and come over to your side. In this anti-flirting dialog, flirt outrageously. Be the sexiest "anti-sex warrior" imaginable.

Try to show not your anger, nor your hurt feelings, but your pride, your wit, your charm, your sexual power, and the rightness of your position.

Of course, your hurt feelings will show before the scene is completed. And, possibly, so will your anger. They will probably come from your partner's being cheered by his backers, and your inevitable sense of failure. So try all the harder *not* to let them show—and not to admit failure. *Try to win the merry war!*

Now you see why the jokes weren't very good when you read them and why it took a dozen glosses to explain the scene—which is, at the level of content, about nothing of consequence. Shakespeare shows you flailing about, trying to best someone you secretly adore, someone you can't bear to be humiliated by, someone who makes you nervous just to look at. In your nervousness, in your failure to achieve any but the hollowest victory, lies the success of the scene.

In a class situation, let everyone play the scene in turn, mixing partners arbitrarily, and let the "crowd" respond as fully as they wish. Try to win— even if you don't. Try again to win again, even if you continue to fail. "Failure" is built into the scene—Shakespeare knows what he's doing with these lame jokes—but you must never try to fail! Shakespeare doesn't need any help from you on that score; he needs you to try desperately to entertain everyone and let everyone come to their own conclusions as to what's happening.

Introduce props suggesting a party. Set a table with glasses of (imaginary!) champagne that Beatrice and Benedick can lift as toasts before downing their drinks at appropriate moments.

Move around freely and interact with your partner as well as with the crowd. Let Benedick demonstrate that he is "loved of all ladies" by embracing one or two in the crowd; let Beatrice show how ugly she thinks Benedick is by boldly pinching his cheeks on "such a face as yours were." Come up with your own, spontaneous business as you run through this scene.

Shakespeare and *Commedia*

We should point out a huge difference between Shakespeare and the *commedia* dramatists that preceded (and in some cases influenced) him. Benedick and Beatrice are not stock characters. They are unique personages, as individually defined as anyone who ever lived; we even feel that we know them as real people, as we never would with Sofronia or Nicomaco. While Shakespeare's couple are part of an identifiable class of characters (the shy but witty bachelor; the brilliant, awkward, older, and unmarried niece), even these categorizations are more complex than traditional stock, and the categorizations fall pathetically short of a complete description. You can read *Much Ado About Nothing* twenty times, and you will learn more about these characters—their past, their families, their hopes, their fears, their passions—on every reading. With *Clizia,* your twenty readings may afford you new ideas on how to play the roles, but 99 percent of the characters' inner lives will be evident the first time through.

And so, though there are places for it later in the play, adapting *lazzi* or inventing slapstick business would be worse than useless in Scene 12-2, where we are getting to know the characters as people, not simply as theatrical figures set out for our entertainment. This is not to rate Shakespearean drama over *commedia,* although you are welcome to do that on your own, but merely to make crystal clear that these are very different sorts of plays.*

More Elizabethan Scenes

There are four encounters between these two characters: this one from Act 1, Scene 1; more banter (with Beatrice this time pulling the jade's trick) during a dance in Act 2, Scene 1; a mutual declaration of love (but also a discovery of further conflict) in Act 4, Scene 1; and a resolved sharing of goals and desires in Act 5. With one or more partners, rehearse and perform any or all of these scenes.

In *Richard III* the entire scene between Richard and Anne in Act 1, Scene 2 bears consideration, as does the long scene (suitable for cutting) between Richard and Elizabeth in Act 4, Scene 4.

But there are hundreds, if not thousands, of great scenes in Shakespeare, as well as in Jonson, Marlowe, and Webster, easily available at any library, that will provide material for years of acting classes.

---

* Shakespeare's early comedies owe much to *commedia* techniques, particularly *The Comedy of Errors,* which was directly adapted from Plautus's comedy *Menaechmi,* and *The Taming of the Shrew.* But *Much Ado About Nothing* is a somewhat later play, with much more complexly conceived characters.

The Theatre of Molière

The French drama of the seventeenth century, often termed "neoclassic" (*neo* = "new") because it sought to follow the rules of the Greek philosopher Aristotle and his *Poetics* of the fourth century B.C., is the first Western drama for which we have rich and authoritative documentation: not only of plays but of costumes, scenery, staging plans, and acting styles. This was also an era when theatrical staging had largely moved indoors, with the stage placed behind a proscenium opening. In short, it was a theatre whose external aspects were, more than any predecessors', most like our own. But the differences were enormous as well.

Jean-Baptiste Poquelin, known as Molière, is to the French national theatre what Shakespeare is to the English. Flourishing both at the court of King Louis XIV and in the public theatre of Paris during the middle decades of the seventeenth century, Molière wrote, directed, produced, and starred in more than thirty plays, most of which remain in the repertories of theatres around the world today. His company, renamed the Comédie Française in 1680, seven years after his death, is the premiere classical theatre in France to this day, and his drama criticism, generally imbedded in plays about the theatre (*The Versailles Rehearsals, The Critique of the School for Wives*), remains among the world's wisest.

And while his works are largely in the genre of comedy (including farces, comedy-ballets, and courtly diversions), he dealt in these plays with some of the most serious, and dangerously controversial, issues of his day, including religious hypocrisy (in *Tartuffe*), freethinking liberalism (*Dom Juan*), incapacitating jealousy (*The Misanthrope*), and embittered avarice (*The Miser*).

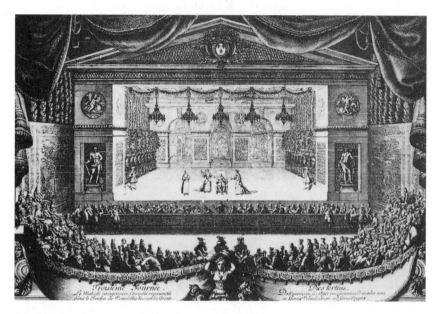

Presentational staging   The highly presentational staging, with the four actors arranged in a straight line, the title character seated squarely in the middle and facing the audience, and the orchestra in plain view, is from a 1674 production of Molière's *The Imaginary Invalid* at the palace of Versailles; note the long trains of the dresses, the magnificence of the surrounding decor and chandeliers. It was in a performance of this same play a year earlier that Molière, playing the title role, collapsed onstage and died later in the evening.

He also attempted tragedy-ballet (*Psyché*) and, notably, served as the producer of France's two greatest classical tragedians: Pierre Corneille, with whom he collaborated, and Jean Racine, whom he virtually discovered. He was truly what the French call *un homme du théâtre,* a man of the stage.

Molière's theatre combines many elements. For Louis XIV, he provided the music and dance entertainments that the king loved to see, and frequently participate in; for the court scholars, he supplied the neoclassic verse that French poets had refined from Aristotle's precepts and also court-comforting satire punctuating bourgeois foibles; for his public audiences, first as a traveling showman in the countryside and subsequently as a royal favorite in Paris, he offered great farcical performances with dull-witted characters and rollicking slapstick humor derived from his associations with *commedia dell'arte,* which crowds love everywhere.* Thus he provided both high com-

---

* When Molière was given a theatre in Paris, he was at first forced to share it on alternate nights with Louis XIV's favorite *commedia dell'arte* troupe.

Brisart d.   J. Sauvé f.

L'IMPOSTEUR

Hand gestures   In *Tartuffe,* Molière's most serious play, the title character, a religious impostor, is shown hiding under the table. Trying to seduce Elmire, he has been caught by her outraged husband, Orgon, who, still in his hat and cape, has just returned home. Hand gestures underline both actions and reactions. From the frontispiece to the 1682 edition of the play.

edy (witty repartee) and low comedy (buffoons and pratfalls), and what is more significant, he often provided them in a virtually seamless combination.

Molière wrote plays in both prose and verse; we'll begin with one of his farcical prose masterpieces, *The Bourgeois Gentleman,* a play so indebted to *commedia dell'arte* that one of its characters, the wily servant Covielle, is named after his Italian *commedia* predecessor, Coviello.

LE BOURGEOIS GENTILHŌME

Molière as Monsieur Jourdain   The playwright here appears in the title role of *The Bourgeois Gentleman*, surrounded by pretend "Turks." From the frontispiece to the 1682 edition of the play.

The play, written on direct command from King Louis XIV for performance at the royal court of Chambord in 1600, mocks Monsieur Jourdain, a wealthy member of the bourgeois class (that is, a middle-class craftsman or shop owner) who aspires to be elevated to the social rank of gentleman so as to, among other things, attract a young countess for amorous adventures; he thus hires instructors to teach him the social graces of aristocrats. The play is, then, a comic satire on the theme of social climbing, and Molière, in the title role, proved a great success in both court and public performances of the play.

◆ SCENE 13-1

Physical Comedy: Jourdain and the Philosopher

In one of the classic scenes in *The Bourgeois Gentleman,* from Act 2, a philosopher is trying to teach Jourdain the rudiments of speech. I've provided stage directions (not in the original but implied by the text) to help you visualize the action. The translation is my own.

PHILOSOPHER: What would you like me to teach you?

JOURDAIN: Everything! I adore learning! I am furious at my parents—they never made me study when I was young.

PHILOSOPHER: Yes, I see. *Nam sine doctrina vita est quasi mortis imago.* Of course you know Latin—

JOURDAIN: *[lying through his teeth]*   Of course! But pretend I don't— explain it to me.

PHILOSOPHER: Without knowledge, life is the reflection of death.

JOURDAIN: *[beaming beatifically]*   Latin is always right.

PHILOSOPHER: Then where shall we begin? With logic?

JOURDAIN: What's that?

PHILOSOPHER: It's what organizes the mind into its three functions.

JOURDAIN: Three functions? What are they?

PHILOSOPHER: The first, the second, and the third.

JOURDAIN: *[confused]*   Oh . . .

PHILOSOPHER: The first is to conceptualize, through universal understandings, the second is to evaluate, through categorical reasoning, and the third is to draw conclusions, through identifications and syllogisms.

JOURDAIN: Oh, no. Too hard. I'm afraid logic doesn't suit me very well. Do you have anything jollier?

PHILOSOPHER: Physics, then?

JOURDAIN: What's that?

Charles Hallahan is Monsieur Jourdain, with Barbara Dirickson as his servant
Nicole, in an American Conservatory Theatre production of Molière's *Bourgeois
Gentleman*. (Courtesy American Conservatory Theatre; photo by William Canslen)

PHILOSOPHER: Physics is the science of natural order, of the properties
of matter: the elements, the metals, the minerals, the stones, the plants
and animals; the causes of meteors, the rainbow, the northern lights,
the comets, lightning, thunder, thunderclaps, rain, snow, hail, winds,
tornadoes . . .

JOURDAIN: *[becoming truly frightened]*   A lot of hullabaloo, if you ask
me.

PHILOSOPHER: What then?

JOURDAIN: How about spelling?

PHILOSOPHER: Marvelous.

JOURDAIN: And then the almanac, so I can tell when the moon is out and when it's not.

PHILOSOPHER: Very good. But to learn spelling philosophically, we must begin at the beginning, by an understanding of the nature of letters and their various pronunciations.   *[making this up as he goes along]*   Now first, there are the vowels, so named because they *avow* the voice. And then there are the consonants, so called because they *consonate* the vowels, and mark the many measures of vowelization. There are five vowels: ah, eh, ee, aw, oo.*   *[He pronounces these in the French manner.]*

JOURDAIN: Yes, I know.

PHILOSOPHER: The sound "ah" is formed by opening the mouth wide— *[he does so, saying]*   "ah."

JOURDAIN: *[imitating]*   "Ah" . . . "ah"   *[nodding vigorously; very pleased with himself]*   Yes!

PHILOSOPHER: The sound "eh" is made by closing the jaws.   *[opening his mouth wide]*   "Ah."   *[closing it]*   "Eh."

JOURDAIN: *[opening and closing his mouth mechanically as instructed]*   "ah"—"eh," "ah"—"eh." My God! You're right! How wonderful learning is!

PHILOSOPHER: And to make an "ee" you close your jaws even further, and spread your cheeks to your ears— *[which he does]*   "ah"—"eh"—"ee."

JOURDAIN: *[with exaggerated movements]*   "Ah"—"eh"—"ee." "Ee!"   *[spreads his cheeks as wide as he can with his fingers]*   "Ee!" "Ee!" It's true! Magnificent! Long live philosophy!

PHILOSOPHER: To make an "oh" you must open your jaw and bring together the corners of your lips: "oh."

JOURDAIN: "Oh!" "Oh!" Nothing could be more wonderful than this!   *[moving his face in absurdly exaggerated configurations]*   "Ah"—"eh"— "ee"—"oh." "Ee"—"oh!" Splendid!   *[sounding like a donkey's hee-haw]*   "Ee"—"oh!" "Ee—oh!" Wonderful!

---

* The pronunciation of the French *u*—here spelled *oo*—has no exact equivalent in English spelling. It is basically formed by speaking the *u* in *puke* but with the lips pushed forward and the tongue extended upward so that it nearly touches the hard palate.

PHILOSOPHER: *[nastily, making a circle with his fingers]*   The shape of your mouth, you see, is a little round "o."   *[which he now pronounces like "oh"]*

JOURDAIN: *[astounded, making the same circle with his finger and tracing his lips in an "o"]*   "Oh"—"oh"—"oh"—you're sooooh right. Sooooh! Ah, what a beautiful thing to knooooh something.

PHILOSOPHER: The sound of the French "u" is made by bringing the teeth together, then spreading the lips, then making them come together without quite touching: "oo."

JOURDAIN: "Oo." "Oo." Nothing could be truer: "Oo!"

PHILOSOPHER: *[suddenly makes a grotesque face at Jourdain, who recoils in shock]*   It's like making a face at someone: If you want to make fun of somebody, just say "oo" at him and watch him jump!   *[He practices this on Jourdain, who finally "gets" it and tries it on the philosopher.]*

JOURDAIN: "Oo!" "Oo!" Oh, it's truuuuuuuuuue! Oh, why didn't I take up education earlier. I would have known all this!

Rehearse and perform this scene with a partner. Follow the stage directions if you wish but augment them with others of your own. Wrap yourself in absurdly elegant and colorful fabrics; cloak, hat, scarf, high-button or high-heeled shoes. Find an ornate walking stick and practice using it.

Try, as Monsieur (or Madame, if you wish to transgender the role) Jourdain, to impress the Philosopher with your learning, and with your clothing, and with your brilliance, and to also impress *anybody* who might peer into the room—including the audience of your classmates. Try, as the Philosopher, to make Jourdain feel he (or she) is brilliantly succeeding in learning something vitally important, so that you will get a suitable reward. And try at the same time to make him look foolish to anyone peering into the room—including the audience of your classmates—so that no one would mistake you for an admirer of his. Though this scene is largely set in a home interior, it is a large house where servants, guests, and resident family and their friends and lovers continuously come and go, so it is as public a dramatic environment as any.

Molière and *Commedia*

One of the dramaturgical devices Molière adapted from his classical and *commedia* predecessors is the stock character, which results in many of his plays' being named not after their principal characters (like Shakespeare's *Othello, Macbeth,* and *Hamlet,* for example) but the specific character *types* portrayed (*The Misanthrope, The Miser, The Blunderer, The Affected Ladies, The Bores, The Sicilian, The Imaginary Invalid, The Bourgeois Gentleman*). And in this scene, the Philosopher has no personal name; he is just a representative of his profession.

Other devices, common to *commedia* and low comedy in general, include the broad physical gags that end up with Monsieur Jourdain tricked into literally making a hee-hawing ass out of himself. The comic success of this scene depends, in large measure, on the actors' confident skill at rubber-faced mimicry; at the absurd configurations that the Philosopher, by encouragement, threats, description, and personal use of himself as an example, persuades Jourdain to adopt: ridiculous pursings of his lips and mouth in order to utter incomprehensible sounds. Henri Bergson, a French philosopher of the early twentieth century, declared that comedy was essentially an "encrustation of the mechanical upon the living," or portraying a living person as being as rigid as a machine, and the comedies of Molière—as in scenes such as this—were among Bergson's primary examples.

Yet the literary skill and obvious intelligence of Molière's dramaturgy, and the intellectual sophistication of his audiences in the burgeoning scientific era that was soon to develop into a full-fledged Age of Enlightenment, move this material far beyond the single-minded slapstick of *commedia.* While there are elements of a Dottore in Molière's Philosopher, and of a Pantalone beneath Jourdain, a font of wisdom and irony underlies the Philosopher's puffed-up imbecilities, and a whimsical tenderness can be found in the social-climbing Jourdain, whose character, after all, bears a clear resemblance to Molière and his father—both of them from the bourgeoisie (Molière's father was an upholsterer) but who had attained positions in the court of King Louis XIV.

Costume and Deportment

Every age has its wardrobe, but the age of Louis XIV (and of the English Restoration which followed close upon it—see Lesson 14) was a period of exceptionally glamorous and elaborate costumes and accessories throughout Western Europe. Clothing design had become a fully professional craft, and fashion plates (illustrations) of the latest styles were widely circulated. Silks, satins, brocades, lace, ribbons, and pearls were abundant in the clothing of both sexes, with men often wearing tricornes (cocked hats), fancy doublets, petticoat breeches, colorful neck cravats, and flounced shirt cuffs under elaborately constructed flared coats or capes, while balancing themselves atop high-heeled, front-buttoned shoes; women sported elongated bodices (stiffened by wooden or ivory busks to induce an erect posture), bell-shaped skirts, richly embroidered petticoats under open gowns, bosom-revealing décolleté necklines, and richly colored makeup. Wildly exaggerated perukes (periwigs) were common for male court dandies, and tall lace headdresses, known as commodes, encased women's upswept hairstyles.* "Showing off" one's costume was an expected social grace in late-seventeenth-century French aristocratic circles, and costume becomes a subject of, not merely an adjunct to, many of the dramas of the day. (In fact, a hilarious scene in which Monsieur Jourdain is fitted into a new court costume, which he is talked into accepting even though the embroidered flowers were mistakenly sewn in upside-down, immediately follows this one.) So your standing, walking, sitting, rising, and gesturing are all opportunities to show how fashionable (that is, how witty, how attractive, how rich, how much in royal favor) your character is.

Try it. Climb to the top of the seventeenth-century social ladder by showing off your brilliance, your taste, your style, your poise, and your complete consonance with the world of the Sun King himself.

French Verse

To truly understand the art of Molière, and the plays of his time, it is necessary to study the intricacy of classical French verse. Not all—or even most—of Molière's plays were written in verse, but those that were, which include his most serious and celebrated works, among them *Tartuffe, The Misanthrope,* and *The School for Wives,* followed the model for all neoclassic French dramatists, comic and tragic: the Alexandrine couplet.

The Alexandrine couplet, based on a hexameter, or six-foot, line, is maddeningly complicated, but fortunately you won't have to learn it in English; the hexameter is both too long and too choppy to be effectively rendered into our language, as Alexander Pope noted in his "Essay on Criticism":

A needless Alexandrine ends the song,
That, like a wounded snake, drags its slow length along.†

---

* I am indebted to Blanche Payne, Geitel Winakor, and Jane Farrell-Beck, *The History of Costume,* 2nd ed. (HarperCollins, 1992) for these descriptions.

† The Alexandrine line is a six-foot, twelve-syllable iambic line (iambic hexameter), with a momentary pause, known as a *caesura,* after the third foot. In the Alexandrine couplet, each pair of lines rhyme; moreover, the rhymes alternate between *masculine* rhymes of one syllable ("bait" and "date"), and *feminine* rhymes of two syllables ("parted" and "started"), which add an unstressed syllable to each line's concluding foot. But that's not all: The half-lines on

Virtually all modern English verse translations of Molière's verse plays, and of those by Racine and Corneille for that matter, are in rhymed iambic pentameters, not hexameters, as in Scene 13-2 (see also the box at the end of this lesson).

That you won't have to grapple with the complexity of the Alexandrine, however, does not mean you shouldn't pause to marvel at it, and at the classic French writers' ability to deploy it while writing plays that are masterpieces of logic, credibility, speakability, dramatic momentum, poetic flow, atmospheric texture, and even figurative (if not literal) verisimilitude. Moreover, those playwrights were restrained by many other limitations on their creativity, since royally honored neoclassic critics dictated other "rules" supposedly (though not actually) drawn from Aristotle, including demands that a play represent only one day's action, take place in a single locale, be divided into five acts with the stage cleared after each act, and report rather than show acts of physical violence. This is almost like writing a play that is at the same time a crossword puzzle. Nonetheless, it was the achievement not only of Molière but of Corneille, Racine, and, indeed, all the great playwrights and poets of the glorious era of Louis XIV to transcend these dictated parameters of art into a glorious drama of comedy, wit, intelligence, and passion;

---

either side of the caesura, called *hemistiches,* must be spoken in precisely equal time durations; moreover, the hemistiches themselves are divided into two *measures,* which must also be spoken in equal time durations. However, the hemistiches need not be divided into equal numbers of syllables; they can be divided three and three, two and four, or one and five syllables, which means that, in the last case, a one-syllable measure must be slowed down in speech to equal the duration of the matching five-syllable one. Have I lost you yet? It is the accelerating and decelerating of speaking velocity during the measures, in contrast to the rigid time divisions of the measures within the hemistiches, and the hemistiches within the lines, that create the near-infinite variety of rhythm in the Alexandrine couplet (or, more properly, the Alexandrine quatrain, since the pattern extends over four full lines). It is little wonder that traditionally trained French actors take many years to perfect their mastery of this staggeringly complex verse form—which, by the way, is unvarying for every single line in a play. See Maurice Grammont, *Petit traité de versification Française* (Armand Colin, 1965 [1908]).

I am indebted to Edgar Schell for bringing the line from Pope to my attention. Of course, the Alexandrine sounds terrific in French, which is a less percussive and more assonant language. For those who can read it, here's the original French opening of Alceste's long speech ("It's not a stick, Madame . . .") in Scene 13-2. The first couplet ends in feminine rhymes, the second in masculine.

Non, ce n'est pas, Madame, un bâton qu'il faut prendre,
Mais un coeur à leurs vœux moins facile et moins tendre.
Je sais que vos appas vous suivent en tous lieux;
Mais votre accueil retient ceux qu'attirent vos yeux.

perhaps it was the very discipline of writing under such impossible con-
straints that sharpened their wits to genius level.

Thus the first challenge for the actor in Molière's verse plays is to handle
the formality of the outward structure with a feeling for the passion, creativity, and variety within. We will examine this challenge in a scene from
Molière's masterpiece, *The Misanthrope*.

♦ SCENE 13-2

Quarreling in Couplets: Alceste and Célimène

Study the following scene. Alceste (pronounced all-SEST) is a youngish man,
proud of his integrity and intellectual brilliance; he is in love with Célimène
(pronounced SAY-lee-MEN), a pretty and still-unattached young socialite.
This is the first scene between them in the play, and as you will quickly see,
they are having a fight. The translation is my own.

ALCESTE: Well, Lady Célimène! May I be frank?
   The way you acted yesterday? It stank!
   I must say that I'm totally disgusted.
   Your actions demonstrate you can't be trusted;
   In fact, I've come today to tell you
   Our liaison is off! You—Jezebel, you!
   No matter if I promised otherwise:
   Your conduct leaves no room for compromise!

CÉLIMÈNE: Is that why you came here, to start a fight?
   I thought we talked this all out—just last night!

ALCESTE: I'll say no more! But you're insatiably driven
   To mass flirtations! They can't be forgiven!
   You bring the whole world into your salon
   Where troops of lovers seek to carry on!

CÉLIMÈNE: You're angry that they find me—affable?
   You think I'm wrong; I think you're laughable!
   What should I do, then, hit them with a stick?
   Drive them from my home? Why are you so thick?

ALCESTE: It's not a stick, Madame,° that you should   °*mah-DAHM*
      brandish,
   You must be hard-hearted! Less outlandish!
   They're drawn to you, because you're beautiful,

But your response goes far beyond what's dutiful!
Your racy words, and cooing affectations,
Lead them to elevated aspirations!
And you adore them! They're your panting harem;
This bunch of lisping fops; God, I can't bear 'em!
Ah, Célimène! I don't know what to do!
You LIKE to have these phonies chasing you?
Explain, my dear, what idiotic pleasure
You take in old Clitandre.° What a treasure!   °clee-TAN-druh
You like the curling fingernail he's grown?
Perhaps the horrid wigs he calls his own,
With cannon curls that fall down to the floor
Which all the demoiselles° at court adore!   °deh-mwah-ZELZ : young ladies
Perhaps the codpiece sewn into his hose!
Those ribboned sleeves on which he wipes his nose!*
Or maybe it's his phony, flat falsetto?
Or else his scent: two dabs of Amaretto?

CÉLIMÈNE: You're so infuriatingly UNJUST!
You know I have him here because I MUST!
It's for my lawsuit: You know his support—
His and his friends'—can win my case at court!

ALCESTE: Forget your case! I'd just as soon you lost!
To have Clitandre's help—you'll pay the cost!

CÉLIMÈNE: Well, you're just jealous, all the world knows that.

ALCESTE: Who's "all the world"? Those you make passes at?

CÉLIMÈNE: I don't see why this makes you so distressed!
You should be pleased I love them ALL, Alceste!
By not identifying any one as best,
I love, but don't become BY love possessed!

ALCESTE: Well, that's just fine, my dear, but tell me—say:
Just what from you do I get more than they?

CÉLIMÈNE: The happiness of knowing that you're loved!

ALCESTE: I won't know that—till OUT THE DOOR THEY'RE
SHOVED!

---

* These lines give a marvelous picture of the accoutrements of the court dandy
in the time of Molière. The separate leg hosiery with an open crotch, the
privates encased in a neomedieval codpiece, was very fashionable courtly
male attire in the late 1660s.

CÉLIMÈNE: How selfish of you! No, Alceste, you've heard
All I can say! And that's my final word!

ALCESTE: To me—and to the others too! You love—MANKIND!
For you, dear Célimène, love's REALLY blind!

CÉLIMÈNE: Why, how romantic! Darling, I'm delighted!
You sure can make a girl get all excited!
And just so you won't fret your little head—
I TAKE BACK EVERY SINGLE WORD I SAID!
Oof! What an imbecilic fool you are!
Is this your wish?

ALCESTE: This isn't love: It's war!

Several questions naturally come to mind with this material, the most immediate being: How should the rhymes be played? Should they be emphasized, or simply tossed away, or something in-between? And what do the dramatist's rhymes have to do with the character's situation? While blank verse can almost pass as everyday speech (for example, "I'll have the ham and eggs with toast today"), rhyming couplets blatantly call attention to themselves and to the artificial contrivance of the form that contains them.

In this case, Alceste and Célimène are using their rhymes to *show off*, with the ultimate goal of gaining the upper hand in a battle of wits.

For it is an explosion of wit—the sparkling wordplay that asserts intellectual superiority, lightness of spirit, and carefree invulnerability—that is particularly characteristic of high comedy in the time of Molière, and nothing displays seventeenth-century wit so well as rival characters in a verbal joust. The delightful French film *Ridicule* (1996) portrays French courtiers in the time of King Louis XVI playing wicked rhyming games at dinner parties, ridiculing into social disgrace those failing to instantly improvise a clever rhyming couplet on a specified topic.

So when Alceste says

Well, Lady Célimène! May I be frank?
The way you acted yesterday? It stank!

he is, while stating something quite plain and unpleasant (emphasized by the slangy word *stank*), packaging his message in a rhymed couplet that, he hopes, will argue his authority to do so.

Of course, Célimène will answer him in kind. Thus the incessant rhymings become weapons in a continual battle between these two wits, each trying to outdo the other. Thus the rhymes should not then be swallowed or buried as though these speeches were written in prose. If Molière had wanted to write the play in prose, he would have done so—he did so on many other occasions. No, Molière wants the rhymes to stand out: He has designed the characters to be jockeying for superiority by showing off their verbal dexterity—and hence their brilliance.

On the other hand, showing off with *every* rhyme would clearly be excessive, since every line in this entire play rhymes with its predecessor or successor. So lines like

I must say that I'm totally disgusted.
Your actions demonstrate you can't be trusted

need little underlining of their rhyme. Indeed, as with blank verse, the versifying features (rhythm and rhyme) assert themselves simply as part of a pattern, registering with the audience—and the characters spoken to—as ideas rather than as words. The "showing off" in this case conveys itself through the entire speech, its structure and momentum, rather than the singularity of a single rhyme.

However, when a particularly important line is accompanied by an unusually contrived rhyme, as with

In fact, I've come today to tell you
Our liaison is off! You—Jezebel, you!

a pointing of the rhyme could be effective.* Alceste is making a formal pronouncement—ending his affair—followed by an accusation: that Célimène is, like the biblical queen Jezebel, a woman of low morals. Of course, the accusation is overblown, and Alceste will come panting back, hence the wit is forced, and the tension between the playful verse and the maddening quarrel it contains becomes the dynamic pulse of the drama as acted and staged.

This is the point of Molière's style in *The Misanthrope,* and of many other formally contrived dramatic scripts as well: The outward style may be precisely measured and controlled, but the inner action must be passionate and chaotic. It is like a boxing match: That the boxers are required to wear padded gloves, avoid hitting below the belt, and stop fighting every time the referee speaks or the bell rings does not mean they aren't, at the same time, trying to pulverize each other. The tension between outer form and inner drive sets up the very vibrations of stylized drama.

And another kind of tension is at work here: between the types of characters represented. Célimène and Alceste do not fight with the same

---

* Of course, all the rhymes in this scene were created by the translator. You are, of course, welcome to analyze and present the scene in the original French if you are able, and the instructor approves, for the identical principles will apply.

tactics. Célimène responds calmly, as a peacemaker, rebuking Alceste for his unseemly behavior:

> Is that why you came here, to start a fight?
> I thought we talked this all out—just last night!

while Alceste can only bluster:

> I'll say no more! But you're insatiably driven
> To mass flirtations! They can't be forgiven!

Having declared he'll speak no more, Alceste then speaks some more. And he persists in what has already been demonstrated to be a useless argument—a mere repetition of the one they had last night:

> You bring the whole world into your salon
> Where troops of lovers seek to carry on!

Whereupon Célimène simply refuses to join the debate, declaring it—in a fine metatheatrical comment within this comedy—comical.

> You're angry that they find me—affable?
> You think I'm wrong; I think you're laughable!

And then, with wonderfully teasing seductiveness, she reduces Alceste's argument—and Alceste himself—to absurdity:

> What should I do, then, hit them with a stick?
> Drive them from my home? Why are you so thick?

The fact that two people are fighting—even in equally rhyming iambic pentameter—doesn't mean they must use the same weapons. Alceste attacks, Célimène coos; Alceste accuses, Célimène mocks; Alceste denounces Célimène for flirting, Célimène responds by flirting with him.

As noted earlier, characters in Molière have their origins in stock figures, but they transcend them. Alceste, though he says he's going off to be a hermit by play's end, is not really a misanthrope; what he truly hates is not human-kind but the intellectual pretension, malicious gossip, and dishonesty he finds within his social circle. Active and extreme in his predilections, he feels compelled to attack directly what he despises. Though there is something undeniably foolish about Alceste, there is much about him with which we invariably identify: his integrity, his forthrightness, his hatred of pretense, even if overwrought. This play is sometimes called "the French *Hamlet*" for these reasons. Célimène, on the other hand, while she courts all men's favor, giving each what they desire and offending none—at least to their faces—is no mere empty-headed flirt. She has a brilliant wit, a profound understanding of practical psychology (particularly with regard to men), a need for strong allies (she is presented as a recent widow, with no apparent family support), and the ability to maintain a splendid and serene composure. So, as furious as Alceste becomes, he is completely overmatched by Célimène's laughing dismissals of his escalating ire. She doesn't rebut him, she ridicules him with his own desire. Imagine, for example, Célimène imitating Marilyn Monroe in a 1950s film—pouty and wispy and crawling all over him—as she delivers her line, "Why are you so thick?" It's enough to make a misanthrope explode, as Célimène well knows.

These parts were originally played by Molière himself and his famously unfaithful (and very much younger) wife, Armande Béjart.* As the battles between the playwright and his bride were known throughout French society, Molière's audiences could easily see the real-life lovers' quarrel underneath the staged drama, Alexandrine couplets and matched hemistiches notwithstanding.

Alceste's speech that begins "It's not a stick" is what French drama scholars call a *tirade* (pronounced tee-RAHD), which, while similar to the English word, also connotes a long speech that, with exquisite logic and intellectual momentum, persuasively argues a single theme. In the hands of anyone but a great master, of course, it would be not just a long but an overlong speech; fashioned by Molière, however, it has a structure that builds each idea upon its predecessor and makes each detail consequently more hilarious than the one before. Alceste's tirade begins with a brutal instruction:

> It's not a stick, Madame, that you should brandish,
> You must be hard-hearted! Less outlandish!

then quiets down with a finding of facts that support that instruction:

> They're drawn to you, because you're beautiful,
> But your response goes far beyond what's dutiful!
> Your racy words, and cooing affectations,
> Lead them to elevated aspirations!

and then completes the first beat with a conclusion:

> And you adore them! They're your panting harem;
> This bunch of lisping fops;

followed by Alceste's emotional, reaction to that conclusion:

> God, I can't bear 'em!

---

* The gossip goes further than that: Armande was widely believed to be the daughter of Molière's fellow actor and longtime mistress Madeleine Béjart, and therefore said by many to be the playwright's own daughter.

Beginning the second beat, Alceste pretends confusion—"Ah, Célimène! I don't know what to do!"—in order to propose a rhetorical question (one for which no answer is expected) by which he urges Célimène to rethink her priorities: "You LIKE to have these phonies chasing you?"

The rhetorical question is a ploy: Célimène cannot respond (to say either yes or no implies she accepts the definition of her suitors as phonies), which gives the almost-crafty Alceste the opportunity to follow with correlated rhetorical questions about one of her suitors, the pretentious aristocrat Clitandre, with an eye to driving his point home with increasing ferocity as, one by one, he enumerates Clitandre's absurdly foppish grooming, attire, and behavior:

> Explain, my dear, what idiotic pleasure
> You take in old Clitandre. What a treasure!
> You like the curling fingernail he's grown?
> Perhaps the horrid wigs he calls his own,
> With cannon curls that fall down to the floor
> Which all the demoiselles at court adore!
> Perhaps the codpiece sewn into his hose!
> Those ribboned sleeves on which he wipes his nose!
> Or maybe it's his phony, flat falsetto?
> Or else his scent: two dabs of Amaretto?

A *tirade* must be sustained by the structuring of its parts: the neutral introduction of its topic, the accumulation of evidence, the careful assembling of "proofs," and the clinching windup. Molière was trained as a lawyer, and his speeches are often crafted as versified legal writs, where the verdict is expected to come through the jury's response to the attorney's accumulation, organizing, and focusing of myriad details.* For an actor to get intellectually lost in such a speech, or to simply slog through it line by line (to "roll it out like a string of sausages" is the term for it at one celebrated classical North American theatre), is to make both argument and character tedious.

Alceste's windup, however, is hardly a clincher; "two dabs of Amaretto" is just a lame joke (again, in the translator's version), not a convincing explanation: It's by phrases like this we recognize that, for all its seriousness and importance, *The Misanthrope* remains a comedy, and Alceste is essentially a fool—if a noble one. So it's no wonder that Célimène can simply undermine his *tirade* by changing the subject entirely and adding a new piece of information, possibly true and possibly not:

> You're so infuriatingly UNJUST!
> You know I have him here because I MUST!

---

* He received a law degree from the University of Orléans but never practiced.

It's for my lawsuit: You know his support—
His and his friends'—can win my case at court!

Alceste is suddenly thrown on the defensive; this lawsuit is clearly something he has not considered. But he doesn't have time to think (owing to the unstoppable momentum of the Alexandrines, and the battle of wits, in which pausing means total defeat), so he is forced to gamely argue on—despite his obviously unwinnable position.

Forget your case! I'd just as soon you lost!
To have Clitandre's help—you'll pay the cost!

And now Célimène is back in charge, which she takes full advantage of by making an accusation of her own: "Well, you're just jealous, all the world knows that." The hapless Clitandre has now been taken off the table, and the subject of derision is now none other than Alceste, who can only weakly defend himself by the vaguest of counteraccusations: "Who's 'all the world'? Those you make passes at?"

Célimène the peacemaker now moves in for the kill, promoting as her philosophy a generosity of spirit that seems (to everyone but Alceste) profound, just, and even spiritual, capping her argument with a line that (in this translation) creates closure with literary overtones.

I don't see why this makes you so distressed!
You should be pleased I love them ALL, Alceste!
By not identifying any one as best,
I love, but don't become BY love possessed!

Alceste is completely flummoxed. It is total defeat; Célimène has seized the apparent high ground, and he knows that no one in Paris—other than himself—is clever enough to see through her argument. Unable to debate successfully against such evident beatitude (and knowing a darker secret—that only he is possessed by love), he retreats, hoping, perhaps, to lull Célimène into overconfidence.

Well, that's just fine, my dear, but tell me—say:
Just what from you do I get more than they?

But Célimène has the perfect rejoinder and presses it lovingly on him with the very "cooing affection" that he has earlier accused her of: "The happiness of knowing that you're loved!"

In the agony of defeat, Alceste tries to terrify her with a shout, certainly accompanied by some would-be-manly strutting: "I won't know that—till OUT THE DOOR THEY'RE SHOVED!"

Alceste has completely and abjectly failed. He began this scene telling Célimène "our liaison is off"; by now he is only demonstrating his undying infatuation. He began by framing his argument rationally and by crafting a skillful *tirade* about his rivals; he is now braying at her like a petulant child. He began with a show of authority; he is now unmasked as impotent and driveling. It's now Célimène's turn to issue an ultimatum, and she does:

> How selfish of you! No, Alceste, you've heard
> All I can say! And that's my final word!

And, unlike Alceste, who said he would speak no more but then continued, Célimène leaves it at that, and probably starts to make her exit. Alceste's position is hopeless. He has come (he said) to end the liaison, and now Célimène is the one ending it. He calls after her in desperation:

> To me—and to the others too! You love—MANKIND!
> For you, dear Célimène, love's REALLY blind!

And Célimène, far from taking the bait, moves them one giant step further. Turning, smiling, and at first pretending to have changed her mind, she coos to him, "Why, how romantic! Darling, I'm delighted!"

But it is almost immediately evident that this cooing is pure irony. With savagely seductive pouts she advances on him, building on his unquenchable desire: "You sure can make a girl get all excited!" Then, having set him up, she brays right back at him with the full force of a woman scorned: "I TAKE BACK EVERY SINGLE WORD I SAID!" Next she stabs him where it hurts most: his intelligence: "Oof! What an imbecilic fool you are!" and concludes by inquiring, "Is this your wish?," seeking closure by blaming the entire argument on him. To which Alceste responds, completing her half-line but addressing it to the audience more than to her: "This isn't love: It's war!"

Taking this discussion of the structure and momentum of the *Misanthrope* scene into consideration, rehearse it with a partner. Devise movements and business for each of you that will carry the verbal tactics into the physical realm.

Let the rhymes create, as discussed in Lesson 3, a "playing environment" for each of you, in both the sense of "playfulness" ("to play") and "dramatic" ("a play"). Entertain each other with your rhymes, even as you're fighting, and let each other know that you're an entertaining sort of social person—able to amuse others if not each other. Use your rhymes to make yourself irresistible; make your lover *hate* to lose such a magnificent partner!

How might you dress the parts? An engraving of Molière in the role survives; despite his vaunted unpretentiousness, his Alceste wears a reasonably typical male costume of the period (see illustration on page 191): loose breeches gathered right below the knee, and, peering from an open, richly embroidered coat, billowing and ruffled sleeves; hose into his ribboned, high-heeled shoes; and a simple round-brimmed hat, front cocked up, holding down his peruke that flows beyond his shoulders. Célimène would have worn something on the order of a long flowing gown with a plunging neck-

LE MISANTROPE

Molière as Alceste   The playwright (right) performs the title role in *The Misanthrope*. Half-seated, perhaps sinking evasively into his chair, he is probably in conversation with the obnoxiously foppish poet, Oronte. Notice the high heels, ruffled cuffs, elaborately brocaded gowns, and the cascading cannon curls of the wigs; no matter how much the misanthrope rails against society, he is a part of it, and dresses (and must move) accordingly. From the frontispiece to the 1682 edition of the play.

line, and a high headdress; she may well have carried (and used) a folding fan. You may find these garments hard to come by in your contemporary wardrobes, but do come up with ways to capture the shapes and volumes of this period costuming, for it will provide you with dozens of opportunities to match fabric with rhetoric, and sartorial elegance with semantic sophistication. Pivoting sharply in a flowing gown, or harrumphing off in a frock coat and high heels, conveys a seventeenth-century energy—the furious tension between inward rage and outward formality—that cannot be fully realized in jeans and sneakers.

Stage yourselves. Furniture is written into this play. One or two chairs would be useful; adding a pouf (circular couch or ottoman, permitting reclining) would be even better. Fan gestures—which can be sharply pointed, coyly seductive, fiercely aggressive, and demure by turns (see page 196)—can be usefully employed by Célimène; Alceste's manner of sitting, standing, striding, and collapsing will say as much as Molière's words (as nobody understood better than the actor-dramatist himself).

Go ahead. Have a ball. Rhyme each other into submission.

PLAYING TRANSLATIONS

Molière's plays were adapted for the English-speaking stage during his own lifetime, and of course increasingly thereafter, and acting in them—or in any translated plays, for that matter—presents actors and directors with a broad set of options. With an author of Molière's repute, you may have multiple translations to choose from: *The Misanthrope,* for example, is published in several dozen English versions, both in prose and in verse. Which one is the "best"? That depends on the reader, and in this case perhaps on the actor as well; no translation can ever be definitive. The art of translation is subjective, and languages do not pair up precisely with regard to meaning, tone, rhythm, or rhyme: "Translator? Traitor!" says a euphonious Italian proverb. For *The Misanthrope,* the American poet Richard Wilbur's 1954 translation is certainly the best known today, but there are more contemporary as well as more antique ones available, presenting their own challenges and opportunities. You might, as an added exercise, try reading with a partner the following lines from the play's first scene as they appear in a variety of published versions. In the scene, Alceste is arguing with his friend Philinte (pronounced Phil-ANT) about the latter's recent public flattery of and friendliness toward a man they both dislike.

Anonymous, 1716

ALCESTE: I'm your friend no longer—No—I'll have no share in a Corrupt Heart.

PHILINTE: Then you think, Alceste, that I am much to blame?

ALCESTE: To blame? You ought to blush to Death. Such an Action admits no Excuse; and every honest Man must be Scandalized at it.

Waldo Frank, 1926

ALCESTE: After what I have just seen of you, I tell you candidly that I am no longer your friend. I have no wish to occupy a place in a corrupt heart.

PHILINTE: I am then very much to be blamed from your point of view, Alceste?

ALCESTE: To be blamed? You ought to die from very shame; there is no excuse for such behaviour, and every man of honor must be disgusted at it.

Richard Wilbur, 1954

ALCESTE: I tell you flatly that our ways must part
I wish no place in a dishonest heart.

PHILINTE: Why, what have I done, Alceste? Is this quite just?

ALCESTE: My God, you ought to die of self-disgust.
I call your conduct inexcusable, Sir,
And every man of honor will concur.

Robert Cohen, 1997

ALCESTE: This morning, sir, our friendship was destroyed
When you pretended to be overjoyed.

PHILINTE: Just when did I do that? Why'm I to blame?

ALCESTE: How can you ask that and not die of shame?
Your honesty's been permanently bruised,
And what you did can NEVER be excused!

Martin Crimp, 1996

ALCESTE: And when I see you talking such total shit
I realise I'm dealing with just one more hypocrite.

"JOHN":   Alceste, don't tell me you're upset.

ALCESTE: Upset? That's the best understatement yet.
To do that to a man with no coercion
is a form of social perversion.

Restoration Comedy

English comedy during the Restoration—a four-decade period beginning in 1660, when the English royal family was restored to the throne after a long civil war and a Puritan government—owes far more to the French Molière than to the English Shakespeare, for the English aristocracy, including King Charles II, lived mostly in Paris during the twenty-eight years of Puritan rule. There they acquired not only French manners but a taste for the brilliant theatre of Molière at the court of King Louis XIV. And so Restoration comedies, like Molière's, were staged indoors and normally concerned contemporary characters in contemporary settings, most often the same city where they were performed. It was, also like Molière's, a generally aristocratic theatre, even when performed in public houses, and both courtiers and courtesans (elegant prostitutes), often masked, circulated in the audience seeking romantic assignations as much as dramatic entertainment. Caustic wit, amorous adventurism, and the unflagging satire of pretentious fops characterized these English plays, which also featured extravagant costumes, elaborate stage scenery such as had never been seen in England outside of a palace masque, and elegantly turned language. Verse remained the proper language for tragedy, but Restoration comedy was mostly written in very carefully crafted prose.

This was also the era when women made their first appearance as actors on the professional English stage—aided by an official edict of King Charles II, who counted the actress Nell Gwyn among his mistresses—and the backstage liaisons between courtiers and actresses was the stuff of winking London gossip.

The costumes and manners of English Restoration drama are close enough to those of Molière's time and clime to be treated in the same way in a

FRENCH AND RESTORATION ACCESSORIES:
THE FAN AND THE HANDKERCHIEF

The decorated fan (for women) and the elegant handkerchief (for men) are essential props for certain courtly characters in the plays of Molière and the English Restoration; indeed, most English women who considered themselves refined carried fans well into the beginning of the twentieth century. When open, fans could be coquettishly employed to cool the overly amorous body—or to hide the blushingly embarrassed face; when closed, they could rap a naughtily overreaching suitor's knuckles, or indignantly indicate, to an unwelcome visitor, the nearest door. The handkerchief, originally employed to capture the toxic snuff sneezed out the nose by Restoration gentlemen, could be flourished (when held by its center) to show off its expensive lace embroidery, as well as the gracefulness of its bearer's wrists, fingers, and jewelry. The repertoire of fan and handkerchief gestures is almost limitless, and actors specializing in roles from this period often spend years researching and (for the most part) inventing such movements and flourishes.

study of acting styles—with, perhaps, the exception that the sniffing of tobacco (snuff) was a habit more to the taste of seventeenth-century English fops than to that of French *galants* of the same era, and the English cavalier preferred a slightly more casual coiffure than the cascading French peruke.

There is one major difference between Restoration comedy and Molière's, however: Restoration comedy is always about sex. Moreover, it is frankly, openly, and almost solely about sex; it is more graphically sexual, in fact, than any mainstream theatre in world drama between the time of Aristophanes (fifth century B.C.) and the late 1960s.

Aphra Behn, one of the finest dramatists of the Restoration, was the first woman in history to make a living as a playwright. Behn's 1677 comedy, *The Rover,* concerns several young Englishmen visiting the Italian city of Naples, where, as the title character rhapsodizes, "the kind sun has its godlike power still over the wine and woman." Love (generally meaning sex) is in the air in *The Rover,* as it is in all Restoration comedies.

◆ EXERCISE 14-1

Restoration Speeches

Let's look first at a couple of individual speeches from different scenes in *The Rover.*

Elegant Restoration attire   Notice the full gowns, bustles, and headdresses of the ladies, and the huge cuffs, extravagant cravats, feathered hats, high-heeled and high-collared shoes, and (usually) powdered periwigs of the gentlemen. The low-hung sword position of the one gentleman, being essentially useless for combat, indicates his urbane gentility.

HELLENA: *[a young woman, preparing to be a nun but still interested in finding a love, to her sister who has already taken a lover]*   Now you have provided yourself with a man, you take no care for poor me— prithee tell me, what dost thou see about me that is unfit for love—have I not a world of youth? a humor gay? a beauty passable? a vigor desirable? well shaped? clean limbed? sweet breath'd? and sense enough to know how all these ought to be employed to the best advantage? Yes, I do and will.

. . .

WILLMORE: *[The Rover himself, a young English cavalier, newly in town and seeking a lover, as Hellena asks him if he likes her face]*   Like it! By Heaven, I never saw so much beauty. Oh the charms of those sprightly black eyes, that strangely fair face, full of smiles and dimples! Those soft round melting cherry lips! And small even white teeth! Not to be expressed, but silently adored!—Oh, one look more and strike me dumb, or I shall repeat nothing else till I am mad!

These speeches share the characteristics of the French *tirade* (see Lesson 13); though not as long, they are syntactically complex and rich in detail, and they spin a single, relatively simple idea into rhetorical gold. But the complexity and richness of the language are employed not so much to explore the intellectual ramifications of the speaker's argument as to show off the speaker's splendid wit—and thereby her or his romantic charm.

The tone of superficial understatement overlaying an exuberant boastfulness is characteristic of the entire era. Hellena's speech begins with a mock self-deprecation of her appeal ("poor me"), which is only an excuse to then list seven of her most attractive and sexy qualities, concluding with an eighth: the sense to use them to get a man.

But of course it is not sufficient for Hellena merely to enumerate her charms, she (meaning, of course, the actress playing her) must also *demonstrate* them, and do so convincingly. Hellena is not trying to seduce her sister, of course, but she is trying to convince her that, though she is in training to become a nun, she nonetheless has made a commitment to romance. Only if her sister believes her will she aid in Hellena's quest.

Hellena is also using her sister to *rehearse* her seductive ploys. When a man comes into view, as one surely will, Hellena will have some experience in sexual badinage that surpasses any she might have practiced at the convent.

Women in the class: Learn, rehearse, and perform Hellena's speech.

In your long gown and stiffened bodice, practice movements and expressions that will convince your sister that you have the requisite confidence in your sexual attractiveness to take this holiday from your religious training. Show her that you are—or can quickly become—a temptress. As you become comfortable with the language, flounce around the room, exhibiting your charms along with your petticoats. Use an inexpensive folding fan to point out your various gifts, as well as to fan the heat of your escalating passion, and to coyly hide behind when the opportunity presents itself.

Rehearse, as the Restoration temptress you wish to become, the seduction of a Restoration man—employing fabric, prop, and text with equal relish.

Imagine a group of attractive young men hiding behind a bush near you, spying on you; pretending to be unaware of them, try to encourage *their* romantic interest with this speech—which is now only superficially addressed to your sister.

Willmore's speech also begins with a topic phrase ("I never saw so much beauty"), which is also followed by a list: in this case, an enumeration of Hellena's attractions. Is Willmore's list a sincere appraisal? Hardly, nor is it meant to be: Willmore's eloquent flattery, in the Restoration era, is itself seductive; the light tone of mockery shows that he is taking great pains to exaggerate and, therefore, shows his witty refinement along with his appreciation and desire.

When Willmore describes Hellena's teeth as "not to be expressed, but silently adored," and then expresses this thought in anything but silent adoration, his self-contradiction sharply announces the fierceness of his ardor, which is further proclaimed by his wish to be stricken dumb—at the risk of going totally insane for love. No right-minded woman (as Hellena surely is) could possibly be fooled by Willmore's literal declaration, but any Restoration lady, and perhaps many contemporary ones as well, would be impressed with the energy, imagination, and linguistic dexterity of his over-the-top

A court dandy   An extravagant court fop, from a 1687 engraving by J.D. de St. Jean. Billowing cuffs, a wig to the waist, and lavish waistcoat decoration—with ample lace and fringe—typify male flamboyance of the era. (© Corbis)

proposal—particularly if he underlines it with a dashing doff of his hat and an accompanying toss of his long, curling locks.

And to whom does Willmore address "Oh, one more look and strike me dumb"? This is clearly an apostrophe (a phrase directed to a person or personified deity or object not physically present) directed either to God or some supernatural spirit, even if tongue-in-cheek. It could, however, be directed right to Hellena, as though she were the Goddess of Beauty, or at least a stand-in for such a presence.

Men in the class: Learn, rehearse, and perform Willmore's speech. Choose movements and expressions that will convince Hellena you truly adore her features (eyes, face, lips, teeth), and build them, one upon the other, as increasingly aphrodisiac incentives, so that the splendor of her lips throws

FRENCH AND RESTORATION GREETINGS

Salutations in the time of Molière, which also became the salutations of the French-influenced English Restoration, elaborated the bows and curtsies of Elizabethan England.

Bows for Men

The simple: The left foot is swept back as in the Elizabethan bow, though less boldly, the body is inclined and the head cocked slightly to one side, and the right hand is brought upward and palm inward to the heart, as if to say "You have my heart."

The elaborate: The hat is removed with the right hand and tucked under the left arm, as the left foot is swept back (or the right one is advanced) until the feet are perpendicular, the left behind the right, in the dancer's fourth position. At the same time, the body is inclined forward, and the right hand is swept from the left hip in a broad upward circle toward the person being greeted. The hand is then returned, palm inward, to the left hip. On rising, the greeter may continue this circling movement of the right hand and bring the back side of his inwardly curled fingers to his lips, pretending to kiss them, and then continue the arm circle to present the person being greeted with his thusly kissed fingers, palm-side up, before retaking the hat in the left hand.

Curtsies for Women

Essentially the same as the Elizabethan but usually preceded with a small step to one side and a head nod in the same direction.

---

you into uncontrollable desire and her teeth, for reasons you do not need to explain, send you into an absolute paroxysm of ecstasy. Then, with a look up to the divine presence, beg for the muteness that can "cure" you of this unbearable infatuation. And top even that with the explanation, looking at Hellena this time, that otherwise you will go utterly insane. Overwhelm *her* with the desire that overwhelms *you*.

As you become comfortable with the language, dress yourself (to the extent possible) in the getup of a Restoration gallant, using any of the following you can find or create: an overlong-sleeved shirt, a fitted vest and tight pants, dress shoes with a visible heel, a floppy hat, a sword in your belt loop, and a long, curly wig. Practice the speech while circling Hellena, doffing your hat to her, holding it close to you (on "never saw such beauty," for example), and then raising it as a challenge to God when invoking him to silence you.

Molière bows   The actor-playwright demonstrates, in the role of Sganarelle, a seventeenth-century bow. Notice the out-turned feet, the elevated heels, the cocked head and smile, and the ingratiatingly submissive bent arms and curved fingers. (© The Granger Collection, New York)

Rehearse, as the gallant you would like the ladies to see, the seduction of a seventeenth-century lady with this speech.

Imagine a group of attractive young women hiding behind a bush near the two of you; imagine that they are spying on you. Pretending to be unaware of them, try to encourage *their* romantic interest with this speech as well—in case Hellena spurns your approach. Don't worry that they will be jealous of your interest in Hellena—it will only get them more excited (since you are really showing off not your love for any one particular woman, but your ability to speak brilliantly about feminine beauty).

◆ Scene 14-1

Sexual Banter: Willmore and Hellena

Rehearse and present this first encounter between Willmore and Hellena from Act 1, Scene 2 of *The Rover*. Willmore has just arrived in Naples, and almost immediately encounters Hellena, who is masked as a gypsy for a carnival masquerade.

WILLMORE: Dear pretty (and I hope) young devil, will you tell an amorous stranger what luck he's like to have?

HELLENA: Have a care how you venture with me, sir, lest I pick your pocket,* which will more vex° your English humour°   °*irritate* °*disposition* than an Italian fortune will please you.

WILLMORE: How the devil cam'st thou to know my country and humour?

HELLENA: The first I guess by a certain forward impudence, which does not displease me at this time; and the loss of your money will vex you because I hope° you have but very little to lose.   °*expect*

WILLMORE: Egad,° child, thou'rt i'th'right;   °*oh God (a common Restoration oath)* it is so little, I dare not offer it thee for a kindness—But cannot you divine what other things of more value I have about me, that I would more willingly part with?

HELLENA: Indeed no, that's the business of a witch and I am but a gypsy yet°—Yet, without looking in your hand, I have a   °*still* parlous° guess, 'tis some foolish heart you mean, an   °*dangerous* inconstant English heart, as little worth stealing as your purse.

WILLMORE: Nay, then thou dost deal with the devil, that's certain— thou hast guessed as right as if thou hadst been one of that number it° has languished for—I find you'll be better acquainted   °*his heart*

---

* Gypsies were then believed to be pickpockets.

with it; nor can you take it in a better time, for I am come from sea, child;
and Venus not being propitious to me in her own element,* I have a
world of love in store—would° you would be good-   °*I wish*
natured and take some on't° off my hands?   °*of it*

HELLENA: Why—I could be inclined that way—but for a foolish vow
I am going to make—to die a maid.°   °*virgin*

WILLMORE: Then thou art damned without redemption; and as I am a
good Christian, I ought in charity to divert so wicked a design—therefore prithee, dear creature, let me know quickly when and where I shall
begin to set a helping hand to so good a work.

HELLENA: If you should prevail with my tender heart (as I begin to fear
you will, for you have horrible loving eyes) there will be difficulty in't
that you'll hardly undergo for my sake.

WILLMORE: Faith, child, I have been bred in dangers, and wear a sword that
has been employed in a worse cause than for a handsome kind woman—
name the danger—let it be anything but a long siege, and I'll undertake it.

HELLENA: Can you storm?

WILLMORE: Oh, most furiously.

HELLENA: What think you of a nunnery-wall? For he that wins me must
gain that first.

WILLMORE: A nun! Oh how I love thee for't! There's no sinner like a
young saint. . . . Oh, I'm impatient. Thy lodging, sweetheart, thy lodging, or I'm a dead man.

HELLENA: Why must we be either guilty of fornication or murder, if
we converse with you men? And is there no difference between
leave° to love me, and leave to lie with me?   °*permission*

WILLMORE: Faith, child, they were made to go together.

This is a witty wooing scene, not entirely unlike that of Beatrice and
Benedick in Scene 12-3; here, however, the emphasis is not on the ambiguity
and fragility of human relationships but more simply on the particularities
of flirting and sexual conquest. Restoration comedy is not known for exploring the multisided complexities of human emotion, but rather for the
delightful ploys of sexual adventurism, mainly expressed through linguistic

---

* Venus, the goddess of love, was born in the sea; Willmore arrived in Naples
from the sea.

A Restorating staging   A scene from the original staging in 1707 of Restoration dramatist George Farquhar's *The Beaux' Stratagem,* according to the frontispiece of the 1733 edition.

wit and extravagant behavior; *The Rover,* like other Restoration comedies, is a virtuoso presentation of style and manners.

Moreover, the style and manners are *publicly* deployed. This scene takes place at a masquerade, amid a crowd of revelers. Willmore and Hellena are not merely flirting with each other, they are flirting with the crowd. And, in the larger arena of the Dorset Garden Theatre where the play premiered, they were flirting with the royal and aristocratic audience as well: For an appealing and ambitious actress, a dalliance with the king himself (and a royal income in the bargain) was not outside the realm of possibility.

Willmore begins by setting the topic in a single sentence filled with no less than seven eternal parameters of sexual adventure: beauty, hopefulness, youth, deviltry, desire, novelty, and opportunity: "Dear pretty (and I hope) young devil, will you tell an amorous stranger what luck he's like to have?"

Hellena's riposte, "Have a care how you venture with me, sir, lest I pick your pocket, which will more vex your English humour than an Italian fortune will please you," is not to abjure the adventure but to take full charge of what will clearly become a romp: "Pick your pocket" carries the express suggestion that she will penetrate his garments—rather than the other way around! By identifying his country and his interest in (and lack of) money, she gains the immediate upper hand. She will surely be no passive victim to this would-be Petruchio (the wooing character in Shakespeare's *Taming of the Shrew*, to which Behn's play is openly indebted).

WILLMORE: How the devil cam'st thou to know my country and humour?

HELLENA: The first I guess by a certain forward impudence, which does not displease me at this time; and the loss of your money will vex you because I hope you have but very little to lose.

Hellena extends her advantage by an apparently simple but actually complex response to Willmore's question: identifying his country by his manner (for which she gives him a temporary break) and, then, without giving the "second" explanation to pair with the first, adding a gratuitous dig at his obvious (despite his elegant cavalier costume) poverty.

Willmore comes off the floor with his counter-riposte, employing a Shakespearean allusion as he refuses to be torpedoed by Hellena's wit: "Egad, child, thou'rt i'th'right; it is so little, I dare not offer it thee for a kindness— But cannot you divine what other things of more value I have about me, that I would more willingly part with?" These last four words are an allusion to Hamlet's reply to Polonius's leave-taking in Act 2, Scene 2: "You cannot, sir, take from me anything that I will more willingly part withal," Hamlet says, then slyly adds, "except my life, except my life, except my life." Willmore is slyly offering his "life," in the form of his heart, to Hellena in return for a taste of her sexual favors.

Hellena responds with a riff on Willmore's heart, first framed by locating herself somewhere between witch and gypsy: "Indeed no, that's the business of a witch and I am but a gypsy yet—" and then by repeating the word *yet*, but with the contrary meaning of "but": "Yet, without looking in your hand, I have a parlous guess, 'tis some foolish heart you mean, an inconstant English heart, as little worth stealing as your purse." "Who steals my purse steals trash," Iago says in Shakespeare's *Othello*, so Hellena matches Willmore's literary allusion with one of her own.

This only makes Willmore more confident that she has devilish qualities: "Nay, then thou dost deal with the devil, that's certain—thou hast guessed

Michael Pennington as Mirabell courts Judi Dench as Millamant, while Beryl Reid, as the seated Lady Wishfort, gazes at them nostalgically in a Royal Shakespeare Company production of William Congreve's Restoration comedy *The Way of the World*. (Courtesy Royal Shakespeare Company; photo by Donald Cooper)

as right as if thou hadst been one of that number it has languished for—" A two-fold assault: Willmore suggests she must be devilish to know his inconstancy so well, and that, Benedick-like, he's not at all attracted to her. But he will be, he goes on to suggest, in the more pagan Neapolitan world in which they now cavort.

Willmore now identifies himself with the Mediterranean Sea, from which he has just come ashore, and the Roman goddess of love who was born there—but whose fruits cannot be enjoyed in that element (that is, on shipboard, with presumably an all-male crew). Then he proclaims: "I have a world of love in store—would you would be good-natured and take some on't off my hands?" The "world of love in store" is a (literally) seminal metaphor; he has earlier said he would not offer his purse for a kindness, but he now offers his love juices were Hellena to be "good-natured" and "take some." One hears few sexual proposals in such politely euphemistic terms in the twenty-first century, but the gist of the offer is no less potent than it would be today.

Hellena has no problem understanding what Willmore intends: "Why—I could be inclined that way—but for a foolish vow I am going to make—to die a maid." She does not decline his offer—and indeed shows some interest in it—but points out a particular obstacle: her "foolish vow" to remain a virgin. This is virtually a thrown-down gauntlet: Any Restoration cavalier would eagerly take up the challenge of seducing her from her "foolish" morality. Willmore is clearly up to the task. Turning Christian theology on its head, he argues that chastity is tantamount to damnation, and it is only his religion and his charity, not his lust, that will force him to "divert so wicked a design" as to violate it. To that end he invites Hellena to quickly explain just "when and where" (on her body, presumably) he may set his "helping hand" so as to undermine her vow.

Hellena's response, "If you should prevail with my tender heart (as I begin to fear you will, for you have horrible loving eyes) there will be difficulty in't that you'll hardly undergo for my sake," with its wonderful opposites ("horrible loving") showing her intertwined fear and desire, encourages Willmore's pursuit while at the same time warning him how difficult it will be. To the Restoration gallant and his desired lady—as well as to the Restoration audience—the greater the challenge, the more powerful the aphrodisiac effect.

In their last two speeches, Willmore and Hellena have named three parts of the body—hand, heart, eyes—that are predominant in romantic lovemaking; Willmore will now refer to, and perhaps symbolically produce, the phallic symbol that will take the scene to its next, more explicit level: "Faith, child, I have been bred in dangers, and wear a sword that has been employed in a worse cause than for a handsome kind woman—name the danger—let it be anything but a long siege, and I'll undertake it."

What follows is pure symbolic copulation, with "Can you storm?" referring to his lovemaking abilities, the "nunnery-wall" to the female hymen, and "thy lodging" representing Hellena's home, her bed, and her private parts.

Willmore's paradoxical "There's no sinner like a young saint" (that is, there's no lover like a virgin) builds on the earlier opposites of the scene—"pretty devil" and "horrible loving"—and the repetition of "thy lodging" becomes sonic representations of Willmore's phallic thrusts; having earlier offered Hellena his "life," he now assures her that any denial means his death.

Now spent by the virtually orgasmic ferocity of the wooing, Hellena coolly reflects, with rhetorical questions (half-addressed to the audience, the women who are incorporated in her two uses of the word we), on what has just passed: "Why must we be either guilty of fornication or murder, if we converse with you men?"

And then, directly to Willmore, the central issue of the scene, expressed alliteratively: "And is there no difference between leave to love me, and leave to lie with me?" Can there be love without sex? she asks plaintively.

Willmore's reply, beginning with its religious invocation, represents the moral credo of the Restoration: "Faith, child, they were made to go together."

Katherine Ferrand, as Amanda, sneaks a smile behind her fan at the ludicrously vain Lord Foppington, as played by Bernard Behrens, in a Guthrie Theatre production of John Vanbrugh's Restoration comedy *The Relapse*. (Courtesy Guthrie Theatre)

As you rehearse and play this scene with a partner, remember: You are flirting with the audience as well as each other, so flaunt your wit, your education (those Shakespearean allusions!), your good looks, your terrific clothes, and your above-it-all recklessness to the entire crowd.

Dress yourselves in some fashion as described above or illustrated in this or the preceding lesson. Willmore should have a sword (a makeshift broom handle will do) in his belt and a cap in his hand, and Hellena a full, flowing skirt and a folding fan (which can also be stored in her belt).

And do remember, this is not a scene of groping each other. The sex in Restoration comedy is a matter of conversational charm, not physical assault; it is the *control* of sexual passion, and its channeling into the brilliance of banter and reproach, sashay and glance, tantalizing double entendres (words with two meanings) and sly, knowing winks that characterizes the ideal Restoration foreplay—with the "real action" occurring, as it does in virtually all drama, safely offstage.

So flirt *outrageously*—with passion, imagination, and delicacy—as you play the scene. And take a cold shower afterward.

15

The Belle Epoque

The Belle Epoque (French for "beautiful era") is the period of European culture from 1890 to 1914: from the final decade of Queen Victoria's rule to the beginning of the First World War. It is the last great age before what we generally think of as modern, and a full century before what we think of as contemporary: an age before radio, television, recorded music, interstate highways, and commercial air travel; one when film, still silent, was in its infancy.

In Europe, it was also an immensely rich era of drama, encompassing major plays by Oscar Wilde, James M. Barrie, and George Bernard Shaw in England; Anton Chekhov, Maksim Gorky, and Lev Tolstoy in Russia; August Strindberg in Sweden; Edmond Rostand and Alfred Jarry in France; and Ferenc Molnár in Hungary. It was also the era when directors rose to prominence in the theatre establishment, creating, blending, and unifying theatrical styles from a wide variety of sources rarely explored by playwrights or implemented by theatre companies before. For the first time in history, plays were not simply mounted by their authors, or by their leading actors, in accepted and traditional fashion but were rather—certainly in the case of revivals—reconceived by independent artists eager to make the texts freshly relevant, surprising, revelatory, and sometimes shocking. Perhaps for this reason, this is the first era in which plays were published with extensive stage and acting directions.

Though best known in art circles for the distinctive Art Nouveau style in painting, sculpture, and architecture, the Belle Epoque was not dominated by a single theatrical style: Indeed, it was an era of multiple "isms," including expressionism, theatricalism, surrealism, and, yes, naturalism. All had their

SALUTATIONS OF THE BELLE EPOQUE

While handshakes between men and between women (but not between men and women) became common in elegant urban nineteenth-century society, men continued to bow and women to curtsy throughout the Belle Epoque. The male bow was a simple inclination from the waist, with the feet turned out (heels together) and the head cocked deferentially to one side. Hands could be clasped behind the back or below the belly button, and the body could be angled a full quarter-turn in either direction to give a more dashing profile. A more formal male bow, associated with Prussia (and carried elsewhere), began with the heels apart so that they could be smartly clicked together during the descent of the upper torso.

Women might bow as well during this era, or they could curtsy by first taking a step (to either side) and pointing the foot outward, then bringing the other foot behind the first, bending the knees, and inclining the head forward in the direction of the pointed foot—while at the same time raising both hands toward the heart.

A simple nod of acknowledgment, with the head briefly raised and then inclined downward and to the side, was even more common than full bows or curtsies for both men and women. And a maidservant's curtsy would be a mere bob: a quick bend of the knees and incline of the head, and straight up again to do the mistress's bidding.

The kiss on the hand—"quite continental," as the song says—became common between European men and women at this time: the man bowing slightly and lifting, with the back of his own right hand, the lady's right hand to his slightly pinched (nonmoistened!) lips. Should the lady's hand inadvertently touch the gentleman's nose, mortification would result for both parties.

---

heyday, and all have lasted to the present. But it was an era that can be defined by some common characteristics:

- It was the last general era of strictly enforced class divisions, which were shattered by the First World War and were never to dominate Europe's cultural life to the extent they had done in the age of Queen Victoria and Kaiser Wilhelm II.

- It was the last era when the capacity for lively, intelligent conversation, being the world's main form of entertainment as well as its means for determining wise public policy, was considered a crucial social skill, something to be conscientiously, not randomly, acquired.

◆ It was an age of genteel manners, modeled on court behavior (or at least the public perception of it), which still set the tone of social gatherings in every major European country but the France of the Third Republic—which itself possessed an aristocratic and cultural elite (the very word is French), regal all but for an actual crown.

Drama had moved indoors in the age of Molière and the English Restoration; it had largely dropped its verse in the age of Romanticism that followed in the eighteenth and early nineteenth centuries; and it had been toned down from its Romantic exoticisms and grotesqueries by Henrik Ibsen and his followers in the last decades of the nineteenth century. Much of Belle Epoque drama, then, is living-room talk. But what talk!

We'll concern ourselves with two of the greatest dramatists of the era, radically different on the surface but with underlying similarities that bespeak their commonality.

George Bernard Shaw

George Bernard Shaw is one of the finest prose writers in the English language, the author of some of the world's finest music criticism and drama reviews, as well as hundreds of novels, essays, political speeches, published letters, and plays—most of which are accompanied by long prefaces, afterwords, dedicatory epistles, or ancillary documents. As a dramatist, he is ranked second in English only to Shakespeare by some (and Shaw—hardly a modest man—ranked himself well *above* Shakespeare).

Shaw was a thinker, an "advanced thinker" in his own terms; he was, in his early life, a soapbox orator at London's Hyde Park Corner and, for all of his life, an impassioned speaker at political gatherings. His thoughts ranged from politics (he was an avowed socialist and pacifist) to women's rights (the final scene of Shakespeare's *Taming of the Shrew,* he said, was "altogether disgusting to modern sensibility"), eating habits (he was a devout vegetarian and teetotaler), modern drama (he championed the plays of Ibsen), sexual relations (though married, he claimed to be abstinent), and a system of reformed spelling that, among other things, dispensed with most apostrophes. A consummate stylist, Shaw insisted that "effectiveness of assertion," not literary decoration, was the essence of style, and his plays, therefore, are formed around vigorous debates covering a wide range of subjects. In the flash and fire of conflicting assertions lies the Shavian (the adjectival form of his name, pronounced SHAY-vee-un) style, and, as virtually all his ideas retain their provocative edge, we are still fascinated—and can still learn from—the arguments Shaw put on the stage a century ago.

Richard Bauer and Gail Grate are Henry Higgins and Eliza Doolittle in a Yale Repertory Theatre production of Shaw's *Pygmalion*. (Courtesy Bil Schneider, Yale Repertory Theatre; photo © Gerry Goldstein)

◆ EXERCISE 15-1

Shaw's Political Speeches

Here are two speeches, each slightly edited, from the final scene of Shaw's *Major Barbara* (1905). The first is by Andrew Undershaft, the owner of a

In this production of *Major Barbara* at London's Picadilly Theatre in 1998, Gemma Redgrave plays Barbara and Peter Bowles appears as her father, Andrew Undershaft. (© Ben Christopher/Performing Arts Library)

cannon factory; the second is by Barbara, his daughter and the play's title character, a major in the Salvation Army. They are obviously at odds. Undershaft is speaking to Barbara, trying to convince her and her fiancé, Adolphus Cusins (known as "Dolly"), to leave the Salvation Army and join him in the cannon business. In the second speech, Barbara has agreed but, standing in her father's gun factory, she is seeking to convince Cusins to consider this apparent reversal as an extension of her idealism rather than a mere sellout.

UNDERSHAFT: *[speaking of his cannon factory]*   I see no darkness here, no dreadfulness. In your Salvation shelter I saw poverty, misery, cold and hunger. You give them bread and treacle and dreams of heaven. I give from thirty shillings a week to twelve thousand a year. They find their own dreams; but I look after the drainage. And their souls! I save their souls just as I saved yours. Oh, yes, I saved your soul; I fed you and clothed you and housed you. I took care that you should have money enough to live handsomely—more than enough; so that you could be wasteful, careless, generous. That saved your soul from the seven deadly sins. Yes, the deadly seven.   *[Counting on his fingers]*   Food, clothing, firing,° rent, taxes, respectability and children. Nothing can   °*firewood* lift those seven millstones from Man's neck but money; and the spirit

cannot soar until the millstones are lifted. I lifted them from your spirit. I
enabled Barbara to become Major Barbara; and I saved her from the
crime of poverty. Yes, I call poverty a crime! The worst of crimes. All the
other crimes are virtues beside it: all the other dishonors are chivalry
itself by comparison. Poverty blights whole cities; spreads horrible pestilences; strikes dead the very souls of all who come within sight, sound, or
smell of it. What you call crime is nothing: a murder here and a theft
there, a blow now and a curse then: what do they matter? they are only
the accidents and illnesses of life: there are not fifty genuine professional
criminals in London. But there are millions of poor people, abject people, dirty people, ill fed, ill clothed people. They poison us morally and
physically: they kill the happiness of society: they force us to do away
with our own liberties and to organize unnatural cruelties for fear they
should rise against us and drag us down into their abyss. Only fools fear
crime: we all fear poverty!

. . .

BARBARA: [speaking of her father and Bodger, the liquor distiller]
Undershaft and Bodger: their hands stretch everywhere: when we feed a
starving fellow creature, it is with their bread, because there is no other
bread; when we tend the sick, it is in the hospitals they endow; if we turn
from the churches they build, we must kneel on the stones of the streets
they pave. As long as that lasts, there is no getting away from them.
Turning our backs on Bodger and Undershaft is turning our backs on
life. Oh, Dolly, you thought I was determined to turn my back on the
wicked side of life, but there is no wicked side: life is all one. And I never
wanted to shirk my share in whatever evil must be endured, whether it
be sin or suffering. Oh, I wish I could cure you of middle-class ideas,
Dolly. I have no class: I come straight out of the heart of the whole people. If I were middle-class I should turn my back on my father's business;
and we should both live in an artistic drawing room, with you reading
the reviews in one corner, and I in the other at the piano, playing Schumann: both very superior persons, and neither of us a bit of use. Sooner
than that, I would sweep out the guncotton shed, or be one of Bodger's
barmaids. Do you know what would have happened if you had refused
Papa's offer? I should have given you up and married the man who accepted it. After all, my dear old mother has more sense than any of you. I
felt like her when I saw this place—felt that I must have it—that never,
never, never could I let it go. Only she thought it was the houses and the
kitchen ranges and the linen and china, when it was really all the human
souls to be saved: not weak souls in starved bodies, sobbing with gratitude for a scrap of bread and treacle, but full-fed, quarrelsome, snobbish,
uppish creatures, all standing on their little rights and dignities, and
thinking that my father ought to be greatly obliged to them for making

so much money for him—and so he ought. That is where salvation is really wanted. My father shall never throw it in my teeth again that my converts were bribed with bread. *[She is transfigured.]* I have got rid of the bribe of bread. I have got rid of the bribe of heaven. Let God's work be done for its own sake: the work he had to create us to do because it cannot be done except by living men and women. When I die, let him be in my debt, not I in his; and let me forgive him as becomes a woman of my rank. Yes, Dolly, the way of life lies through the factory of death. Through the raising of hell to heaven and of man to God, through the unveiling of an eternal light in the Valley of the Shadow. *[Seizing Dolly with both hands]* Oh, did you think my courage would never come back? did you believe that I was a deserter? that I, who have stood in the streets, and taken my people to my heart, and talked of the holiest and greatest things with them, could ever turn back and chatter foolishly to fashionable people about nothing in a drawing room? Never, never, never, never: Major Barbara will die with the colors.° °*with military flags flying*

As you see immediately, these are both long speeches*—but they can be absolutely captivating with the necessary understanding and work, as they are masterpieces of clear thinking and dramatic momentum. There is a reason for this: Shaw's characters are essentially political orators—as Shaw was himself—and they can argue their points with great clarity and immense rhetorical skill. It is "effectiveness of assertion" that creates the galvanizing theatrical appeal of Shavian rhetoric: It declares, it is persuasive, and, far from droning on, it commands increasing attention—perhaps even leading to action.

Regarding the length of these speeches, we should also recall that in the days before television, people spoke (and listened!) for far longer stretches than they do today. Church sermons, from Shakespeare's day until Shaw's, could last two hours or more. In the famous Lincoln–Douglas debates of 1858, each candidate was given *ninety minutes* for his opening statement, compared to two minutes today, then thirty minutes (versus today's thirty seconds) to rebut his opponent. One of the great challenges of playing Shaw is to recapture the sheer magnitude of conversational rhetoric, capable of addressing a complex issue in rich detail, and to develop the soaring momentum that reaches a rousing, inspiring conclusion.

Try one of these speeches. Memorize it carefully (allow plenty of time for this) and perfectly: exact word for exact word.

---

* In the original, the characters are momentarily interrupted with three or four interjections—single lines or words—by the addressed characters, which I have incorporated into their monologues.

The battle of the sexes A would-be courtier seeks to charm a 1903 feminist at tea. The original caption: "But although you are all known as men-haters, aren't there now and again occasions when you find it *very* hard to live up to your reputation?"

Understand the basic architecture of each speech and how transitions link its structural units. See how each speech begins with a general statement, then moves to its particulars, which build in an ascending order of emotionally laden incidents and details, and finally culminates with the speaker's preordained but decidedly passionate conclusion.

There can be no mistake about this last aspect: Shaw's speeches are passionate in their advocacy. That they have structural integrity—assembled as they are from sequentially interrelated ideas, rather than a patchwork of shouting and name-calling—does not in any way diminish the emotional fire of their expression; rather, the sturdy rhetorical architecture should enhance your conviction and confidence—and hence, your righteous fervor.

Consider the following guidelines to the organization and rhetorical ploys of each speech, set in **boldface**. Important upglide inflections (pitch-lifted syllables), used to build lists of words or phrases, are indicated by carets (ˆ), with the number of carets indicating the relative extent of the upward shift. Important downward pitch shifts, indicative of argument closure, are marked with a downslash (\). (See Lesson 12 for a fuller explanation of inflections and builds.)

UNDERSHAFT: *[speaking of his cannon factory]* **[seize the stage with a bold attack]**   I see no darkness here, no dreadfulness.

[Announce your topic notion]   In your Salvation shelter I saw   **[build the following four nouns]**   poverty, misery, cold and hunger.

[Lift the following "You" to announce the beginning of a comparison]   ˆYou give them   **[build the following three nouns]**   bread and treacle and dreams of heaven.   **[Lift even more the following "I" as an antithesis to the preceding "You"]**   ˆˆI give from thirty shillings a week to twelve thousand a year.

[Conclude the topic idea with an arresting metaphor/image, and once again lightly contrast the pronouns]   ˆThey find their own dreams; but ˆˆI look after the drainage.

[Expand the topic idea into a theology, so as to match Barbara's soul-saving Salvation Army creed]   And their souls! I save their souls just as I saved yours.

[Then turn theology on its head, redefining Christianity into economic bounty]   Oh, yes,   **[build these next three clauses beginning with the word "I"]**   I saved your soul; I   **[build these three verbs, each followed by the object "you"]**   fed you and clothed you and housed you. I took care that you should have money enough to live handsomely—more than enough; so that you could be   **[build these three adjectives]**   wasteful, careless, generous.

[Conclude your new theology with a provocative statement, one that asks "which seven deadly sins"]   That saved your soul from the seven deadly sins.

[Seeing the quizzical looks around you, enumerate the "new" seven deadly sins of your iconoclastic theology]   Yes, the deadly seven.   **[build the following seven nouns, counting on your fingers—as Shaw requests—to vigorously emphasize the build]**   *[Counting on his fingers]*   Food, clothing, firing, rent, taxes, respectability and children.

[Putting "children" at the end of that list, implying that having children is the worst sin of all, is a deliberate shock. Take advantage of the shock to make your major point, which answers your topic notion at the opening.]   Nothing can lift those seven millstones from Man's neck but money; and the spirit cannot soar until the millstones are lifted.

[The pointed antithesis of "money" and "spirit"—set up by the repeated notion of lifted millstones—has proven successful; no one now contests your right to go on. Build the following three clauses beginning with the word "I," thus identifying yourself as one who acts—successfully—on the basis of this philosophy.]   ˆI lifted them from your spirit. ˜I enabled Barbara to become Major Barbara; and ˜˜˜I saved her from the crime of poverty.

[You've shocked them again: Money is not the root of all evil, but the source of salvation! Having proved that, now prove the opposite: that poverty—the opposite of money—is not sainted but evil.]   Yes, I call poverty a crime! The worst of crimes. All the other crimes are virtues beside it: all the other dishonors are chivalry itself by comparison.

[Build the following three verb clauses, beginning with "blights," "spreads," "strikes"]   Poverty blights whole cities; spreads horrible pestilences; strikes dead the very souls of all who come within   [build the following three nouns]   sight, sound, or smell of it. What you call crime is nothing:

[Build downward the following four nouns, dismissing each as more insignificant than the one preceding]   a ˜˜˜murder here and a ˜˜theft there, a ˜˜blow now and a ˆcurse then: what do they matter? they are only the ˜˜accidents and ˆillnesses of life:

[matter of fact: the baseline from which you are going into your major build of the speech]   there are not fifty genuine professional criminals in London.

[And here it comes]   But there are millions of   [start building, first with the following five adjectives]   ˆpoor people, ˜˜abject people, ˜˜˜dirty people, ill-˜˜˜fed, ill-˜˜˜˜clothed people.   [Build further on the six clauses defined by the verbs "poison," "kill," "force," "organize," "rise," "drag," culminating in the emotion-laden noun, "abyss"]   They ˆpoison us morally and physically: they ˜˜kill the happiness of society: they ˜˜˜force us to do away with our own liberties and to ˜˜˜˜organize unnatural cruelties for fear they should ˜˜rise against us and ˜˜˜drag us down into their ab˜˜˜yss.

[Conclude with the new maxim, worthy of inscribing in the Undershaft Bible]   Only ˜˜˜fools fear crime: we ˜˜˜˜all fear poverty! \

Students of rhetoric will be able to identify the devices used by Undershaft in this speech: *anaphora,* a series of phrases that begin identically ("I lifted . . . I enabled . . . I saved"; "they poison . . . they kill . . . they force"); *epistrophe,* a series of phrases that end identically ("poor people, abject people, dirty people"); and *ploce,* a patterned and emphatic repetition of the same word or words in a single sentence ("nothing can lift those seven millstones from Man's neck but money; and the spirit cannot soar until the millstones are lifted").

But you don't need to know these terms to recognize that a very skillful argumentative hand has shaped Undershaft's speech for maximum effectiveness. Effectiveness of assertion, once again, is the beginning and end of style in the Shaw dramatic canon.

Let us do the same sort of rhetorical analysis for Barbara's speech.

BARBARA: *[speaking of her father and Bodger, the liquor distiller]* [**Seize the stage with your topic sentence: Industrial might is pervasive; we can't solve the world's problems simply by ignoring them.**] Undershaft and Bodger: their hands stretch everywhere:

[**Illustrate the topic sentence with details, building the three clauses beginning with "when," "when," and "if"**] ^when we feed a starving fellow ^creature, it is with their bread, because there is no other bread; ^when we tend the ^^^sick, it is in the hospitals they endow; ^if we turn from the ^^^^churches they build, we must kneel on the stones of the streets they pave.

[**Conclude by elaborating, on the basis of this evidence, your topic sentence**] As long as that lasts, there is no getting away from them.\

[**Draw Dolly's attention to the major implication—in your lives—of this theme**] Turning our backs on ^Bodger and ^Undershaft is turning our backs on ^life.

[**Contrast past with present**] Oh, Dolly, ^you thought I was determined to turn my back on the wicked side of life, but there   [**lift the preferred alternative**] ^^is no wicked side: life is all one. And ^^I [**lift negation of "never"—to be picked up again at speech's end**] ^never wanted to shirk my share in whatever evil must be endured, whether it be ^sin or ^^^suffering.

[**Build on your "life is all one" to a repudiation of the limitations of class consciousness, building these three sentences that employ the word "class"**] Oh, I wish I could ^cure you of middle-class ideas, Dolly. I ^have no class: I come straight out of the heart of the whole people. If I were ^^^middle-class I should [**build on your refusal to "turn my back" in the last section**] "turn my back" on my father's business; and we should both live in an artistic drawing room,   [build the following four clauses, playing on the antitheses "you," "I," "both," and "neither of us"]   with ^you reading the reviews in one corner, and ^I in the other at the piano, playing Schumann; ^^^both very superior persons, and ^^^^nei-ther of us a bit of   [strongly punctuate your conclusion of this idea, but without giving up the floor]   ^^^^^use.

[Move to the positive: from what you won't to what you will do, refer-ring to the two industrialists mentioned in your topic sentence]   Sooner than that, I would ^sweep out the guncotton shed, or be one of Bodger's ^barmaids.

[Pose a rhetorical question]   Do you know what would have happened if you had refused Papa's offer?

[And answer it]   I should have given you up and married the man who accepted it.

[And explain your answer]   After all, my dear old mother has more sense than any of you.

[Build the repetition of "felt . . . felt" and then the repetition of "never, never, never"]   I felt like her when I saw this place—felt that I must have it—that never, never, never could I let it go. Only she thought it was the . . .

[build the following four nouns/noun phrases describing your mother's concerns]   houses and the kitchen ranges and the linen and china, when it was really all the   [top the previous build with your single concern]   human souls to be saved:

[Explain by setting up an antithesis]   not ^weak souls in   [build the words starting with "s"]   ^starved bodies, ^^sobbing with gratitude for a ^^^scrap of bread and treacle,   [nail the antithesis]   but   [build the fol-lowing four adjectives to a great peak on "uppish"—which even suggests the top of a build]   ^full-fed, ^^quarrelsome, ^^^snobbish, ^^^^uppish creatures, all   [enjoy the irony of "standing" vis-à-vis "little"]   standing on their little rights and dignities,

[diminish this—and them—by racing through the text here, making light of their concerns]   and-thinking-that-my-father-ought- to-be-greatly-obliged-to-them-for-making-so-much-money-for-him   [a mid-sentence reversal of tone ending with a preliminary downshift: you're now headed back to your final build]   and so he ought.\

[Return to your life-theme: Lay out the premise]   That is where salva-tion is really wanted.

[Get personal]   My father shall never throw it in my teeth again that my converts were bribed with bread.   *[She is transfigured.]*

[The ideas begin to speak through you, as in Shaw's description of transfiguration. Build the escalating phrases beginning with the same words by lifting the repeated verb, "rid"]   I have got ^rid of the bribe of bread. I have got ^~rid of the bribe of heaven.

[Move, as your father did, into a new theology]   Let God's work be done for its own sake: the work he had to create us to do because it cannot be done except by living men and women.

[In this all-but-heretical theology, emphasize your antitheses in the contrasting personal pronouns for yourself and God—"I" and "him;" "me" and "him"]   When ʼI die, let ^him be in my debt, not I in his; and let ^~~me forgive ^~~~him as becomes a woman of my rank.

[Announce your conclusion]   Yes, Dolly, the way of life lies through the factory of death.

[Elaborate your conclusion in theological terms]   Through the raising of hell to heaven and of man to God, through the unveiling of an eternal light in the Valley of the Shadow.

[Get personal with your fiancé, building your three rhetorical questions] *[Seizing Dolly with both hands]*   Oh, did you think my courage would never come ^back? did you believe that I was a des^erter? that I,   [build the three clauses employing the verbs "stood," "taken," and "talked"] who have ^stood in the streets, and ^taken my people to my heart, and ^~~talked of the   [build the following two adjectives]   ^holiest and ^~~greatest things with them, could ever ^~~~turn back and chatter   [build the alliterative and multisyllabic "foolishly" and "fashionable"] ^foolishly to ^fashionable people about ^~~~nothing in a ^~~~drawing room?   [Explode into the final epizeuxis (immediate word repetition) of "nevers"]   ^~~~Never, ^~~~never, ^~~~never, ^~~~never:

[Conclude with a radical, emotion-laden image]   Major Barbara will die with the colors.

The rhetorical architecture has only one reason for existence: It's not to convince us that you're a good actor, or a good Undershaft or Barbara, but simply to convince us that *you're right!* That you have the all-time solution for world happiness, ethics, and prosperity!

Don't just play these characters, *be* them, in the sense that you are trying to convince us of the rightness of their arguments, points of view, and values. And, of course, the best way to convince us of your arguments is to show us that you're *passionate* about them. Shaw's theatre is not a seminar of ideas: It is a struggle to revolutionize the world.

As Shaw was a charismatic and compelling speaker on almost every cultural topic, so are his characters. Mastering a single Shaw speech will raise your persuasive capacity and rhetorical skill in almost every verbal act you undertake for the rest of your life.

Work on either of these speeches. Play them to a partner with your classmates gathered around, with the goal of using all of Shaw's words and rhetorical devices, and your own passion for your character's ideas, to captivate and convert all those around you.

Anton Chekhov

We met Anton Chekhov and *Three Sisters* briefly in Lesson 9. The play was written in 1901, only four years before Shaw's *Major Barbara*, but the styles of these two plays (and their respective playwrights) could hardly be more different.

Whereas Shaw portrayed witty, confident, cogent debaters, eager to express themselves on the vital issues of their time, Chekhov, a doctor by training, studied (and reported on) human malaise: the awkwardness of social behavior, including confusion, indecision, and the bewildering clumsiness of verbal communication, particularly between the sexes. There are few topic sentences or rhetorical flourishes in Chekhov's dialog but rather an unerring depiction of the deeper meanings that lie buried below language itself, a dramatic communication that we call, after Stanislavsky, *subtext*. Subtext is the text that is thought rather than spoken; it is implicit rather than explicit. It is a combination of hinting, soliciting, wondering, proposing, and shading; it is attractive because it is, if need be, deniable: If your hints are rejected, you cannot be accused of intrusion; if confronted, you can simply say, "I never meant *that!*"

A nineteenth-century Russian, Chekhov was also imbued with the ambient Slavic sentimentality of the era—nostalgia, compassion, and brooding rumination—as well as a wary distrust of smug intellectuality and of clinical, scientific objectivity. Indeed, this is one of the reasons Chekhov spurned the practice of medicine in favor of writing short stories and plays.

It is sometimes convenient, but entirely misleading, to think that Chekhov doesn't have a style but simply "writes the way people speak." It is true that Chekhov's dialog sounds conversational and lifelike, particularly in its starts and stops, non sequiturs, and misplaced or broken-off expressions—very few of which would ever be found in a Shaw play, much less in a play by Sophocles, Shakespeare, Machiavelli, or Molière. But there is a precise architecture to these seeming conversations, which, though we call them

Chekhovian realism   The three sisters huddle at a side door of their provincial home as one of the officers prepares to leave town, in the final scene of *Three Sisters*, as sketched by its original stage designer, V. Simov, for the Moscow Art Theatre in 1901.

"realistic" or "naturalistic," are crafted with great care. They are, in the first place, refined, the interchanges of a society in which conversing is still regarded as a social grace—particularly the conversations of people in or around the professions: teaching, medicine, and, in *Three Sisters*, the military. Secondly, they are composed by Chekhov in an elegant impressionistic score that alternates and blends argument with romance, philosophy with jokiness, and laughter with tears—an immensely satisfying symphony of feeling, ideas, and action.

And the action of Chekhov, though generally inner and subtextual rather than blatant and overt, provides powerful storytelling. When performed well (not a common occurrence), Chekhov's plays are as mesmerizing as any in the dramatic canon. Chekhov's characters seek to win their battles with the same passion and intensity as Shaw's do, and though their battles are more ambiguously defined, and their victories fewer and farther between, they nonetheless struggle to meet life's challenges. That they are defeated on most occasions is Chekhov's genius; that they *try* to win, however, is his—and his actors'—glory. Through all the hemming and hawing of a Chekhov masterpiece, the apparent verbal (and often physical) clumsiness, audiences recognize the lively efforts to impress, the stabs at rhetoric from the less-than-skilled, and the vital passions that cannot be fully expressed.

One might indeed think of Chekhov's characters as trying hard to be Shavian characters but getting distracted, often by their sexual urge (always present in Chekhov, and generally absent in Shaw), or by their overwhelming sensations of loss, dread, and failure.

◆ Scene 15-1

Chekhov's Symphony of Feeling

Study the following scene from *Three Sisters*. Lieutenant-Colonel Vershinin, recently arrived at a new, provincial garrison from his former posting in Moscow, is visiting with Masha, the eldest of the three Prozorov sisters whom he had met years ago when they lived in Moscow. They are both married now (Masha to Kuligin, a portion of whose earlier scene with her you may have worked on in Lesson 9), but they are also infatuated with each other. In this scene from Act 2, Vershinin and Masha are seen entering a quiet but not entirely walled-off corner of the Prozorov family living room; in mid-conversation as they enter, they sit, while servants can be seen or heard at a distance around them. All stage directions, dashes (—), and ellipses (. . .) are in the original.

MASHA: I don't know. Of course habit does a great deal. After Father's death, for instance, it was a long time before we could get used to having no orderlies in the house. But apart from habit, I think it's a feeling of justice makes me say so. Perhaps it is not so in other places, but in our town the most decent, honorable, and well-bred people are all in the army.

VERSHININ: I am thirsty. I should like some tea.

MASHA: *[glancing at the clock]*   They will soon be bringing it. I was married when I was eighteen, and I was afraid of my husband because he was a teacher, and I had only just left school. In those days I thought him an awfully learned, clever, and important person. And now it is not the same, unfortunately. . . .

VERSHININ: Yes. . . . I see. . . .

MASHA: I am not speaking of my husband—I am used to him; but among civilians generally there are so many rude, ill-mannered, badly-brought-up people. Rudeness upsets and distresses me: I am unhappy when I see that a man is not refined, not gentle, not polite enough. When I have to be among the teachers, my husband's colleagues, it makes me quite miserable.

VERSHININ: Yes. . . . But to my mind, it makes no difference whether they are civilians or military men—they are equally uninteresting, in this

town, anyway. It's all the same! If one listens to a man of the educated
class here, civilian or military, he is worried to death by his wife, worried
to death by his house, worried to death by his estate, worried to death by
his horses. . . . A Russian is peculiarly given to exalted ideas, but why is
it he always falls so short in his life? Why?

MASHA: Why?

VERSHININ: Why is he worried to death by his children and by his wife?
And why are his wife and children worried to death by him?

MASHA: You are rather depressed this evening.

VERSHININ: Perhaps. . . . I've had no dinner today, and had nothing to eat
since the morning. My daughter is not quite well, and when my little
girls are ill I am consumed by anxiety; my conscience reproaches me for
having given them such a mother. Oh, if you could have seen her today!
She is a wretched creature! We began quarreling at seven o'clock in the
morning, and at nine I slammed the door and went away. *[a pause]*   I
never talk about it. Strange, it's only to you I complain. *[kisses her
hand]*   Don't be angry with me. . . . Except for you I have no one—no
one . . . *[a pause]*

MASHA: What a noise in the stove! Before Father died there was a howling in the chimney. There, just like that.

VERSHININ: Are you superstitious?

MASHA: Yes.

VERSHININ: That's strange. *[kisses her hand]*   You are a splendid, wonderful woman. Splendid! Wonderful! It's dark, but I see the light in your
eyes.

MASHA: *[moves to another chair]*   It's lighter here.

VERSHININ: I love you—love, love . . . I love your eyes, your movements, I
see them in my dreams. . . . Splendid, wonderful woman!

MASHA: *[laughing softly]*   When you talk to me like that, for some reason I laugh, though I am frightened. . . . Please don't do it again. . . .
[in an undertone]   You may say it, though; I don't mind. . . . *[covers
her face with her hands]*   I don't mind. . . . Someone is coming. Talk of
something else.

The scene begins with a characteristic Chekhovian demurral: "I don't
know." We haven't heard the exact question Masha is responding to (it is
presumably something about why the sisters like to invite military officers to

their home), but the specifics don't really matter: What we soon realize is that Masha doesn't know what to do about Vershinin, her husband, or her life; she's in a quandary and fearful of making the wrong move—in any direction. "I don't know," in fact, is perhaps the commonest expression in Chekhov—just as it is virtually unknown in the plays of Shaw (whose characters *always* know whatever needs to be known).

But quandary or no, Masha wants to look her best and sound her best. And so does Vershinin, whose basic life-confusion is similar, though different in its specifics.

Let's explore a possible subtext—that which the characters are thinking and hoping, though not saying—for this scene. Such a subtext is also often called the character's *inner monologue*. It will be noted here in **bold** type. It represents a nonspoken text, the "inner voice" of the characters, not of the author of the play or this textbook. And since the inner voice of the character must be created by a contemporary actor, the inner monologue will necessarily be in the actor's, not the character's, normal "thinking" language.

MASHA: I don't know.   [**I should come up with some sort of eloquent, even philosophical, response here, dammit! And smile, Masha! Let him see your sparkling eyes!**]   Of course habit does a great deal.   [**What a stupid thing to say! Oh, gosh, he's bored already. Let me play "abandoned orphan" again; let him see how well-off we used to be.**]   After Father's death, for instance, it was a long time before we could get used to having no orderlies in the house.   [**Uh-oh; he must think I've been spoiled with servants. I'll show him the righteousness of my motives.**] But apart from habit, I think it's a feeling of justice makes me say so. [**He's listening! I should say something nice to him. A compliment?**] Perhaps it is not so in other places, but in our town the most decent, [**Oh, hell, let's go all the way**]   honorable, and well-bred people are all in the army.   [**Oh, please let him say something nice to me in return!**]

VERSHININ: [**Does she mean me? What the hell can I say? I'll tell her I love her, yes! But how?**]   I am thirsty.   [**What's the matter with me?! Why can't I just . . . Well, I can't just keep sitting here grinning like an imbecile!**]   I should like some tea.   [**Argh! Coward!**]

MASHA: [**He hates me!**]   *[glancing at the clock]*   [**But how can I get him tea without leaving his side? If I get up, I may never have a chance to talk to him alone again. Then it will be all over.**]   They will soon be bringing it.   [**He's looking at me funny, though. Maybe he's just afraid to talk to me because I'm married. How can he know how unhappy I am? Can't he take a hint? I've been trying to show him what a jerk my husband is for the last two weeks. Well, what have I got to lose?**]   I was married when I was eighteen, and I was afraid of my husband because he was a teacher, and I had only just left school. In those days I thought him an awfully learned, clever, and important person. [I'll laugh, and see if he laughs too. . . . Well, he chuckled a bit! Maybe I'd better lay it out for him.] And now it is not the same, unfortunately. . . .

VERSHININ: [Whew, she's pushing. I guess we're going there, yes. Wow, her eyes are beautiful. But it's still early for this, this step. . . . I don't know if I can . . . But I've got to say something! She'll think I'm an idiot! I *am* an idiot! IDIOT!] Yes. . . . I see. . . .

MASHA: [Oh hell, I've frightened him! I'll take it back.] I am not speaking of my husband— [uh-oh, that's too far back. . . . It's not that I find my husband stupid, just boring] I am used to him; but among civilians generally [no, I'll show Vershinin how much I hate people *exactly* like my husband; he'll get it!] there are so many rude, ill-mannered, [I'm on a roll: I hate all men but him!] badly-brought-up people. [He's excited! He loves this! I'll really show him how much I love him—by showing how much I hate my moronic husband and all his loathsome, disgusting friends!] Rudeness upsets and distresses me: I am unhappy when I see that a man is not [make sure Vershinin realizes I'm really talking about him] refined, not gentle, not polite enough. [I love you, Vershinin! I love you, and I'm miserable when I'm with anybody in the world but you!!!] When I have to be among the teachers, my husband's colleagues, it makes me quite miserable.

VERSHININ: [Boy, Masha is hot! When her eyes flash like that, and the blood comes up in her cheeks, I want to hold her, I want to touch her, I want to . . . But do I really want to go down this path? Now? There are so many people here today. And my children . . .] Yes. . . . [Come on, Vershinin, shit or get off the pot! Agree with her, at least.] But to my mind, it makes no difference whether they are civilians or military men— they are equally uninteresting, in this town, anyway. [Yes, this excites her. I'll build on this.] It's all the same! If one listens to a man of the educated class here, civilian or military, he is worried to death by his wife, worried to death by his house, [hey, this is great! It's better than sex! I'll keep building] worried to death by his estate, [uhhhh, where do I go from here?] worried to death by his horses. . . . [No, it isn't better than sex. It's just stupid rhetoric. I'm just a big phony. I'll never have the courage to make love to this woman. Well, I'll smile.] A Russian is peculiarly given to exalted ideas, but why is it he always falls so short in his life? [I've completely lost her. Why do I get so intellectual? Dammit! She isn't answering. Come on, Masha, take me off the hook here!] Why?

MASHA: [God, he's fantastic. But what is he talking about? And what the hell does he want me to say? I've got to say SOMETHING!] Why?

VERSHININ: [She won't answer! She wants me to answer! I've forgotten
the question! Something about . . . Yeah, that's it.]   Why is he worried
to death by his children and by his wife?   [No! That wasn't it! She
doesn't know what I'm talking about, does she?]   And why are his wife
and children worried to death by him?   [Oh, God, I've completely lost
her now! STUPID!]

MASHA: [He's so deep. And so miserable. But I'm making him miserable,
aren't I? Let me see if I can lighten his mood. Smile, Masha!]   You are
rather depressed this evening.   [Did I just say that? What an idiot!]

VERSHININ: [Thank God, she's let me off the hook!]   Perhaps. . . .   [Well,
a second chance. I'll just blame everything on my wife; that's what we
have in common: Blame the spouse! But I can't seem depressed—that
will make her blame herself. I'll laugh! Ha! Ha!]   I've had no dinner
today, and had nothing to eat since the morning.   [Ha! Ha! Good, she's
laughing with me! I'll try to laugh this off as well; we're just two old
married folk, complaining about our spouses! Ha! Ha! Haha!]   My
daughter is not quite well, and when my little girls are ill I am consumed
by anxiety; my conscience reproaches me for having given them such a
mother.   [Hahahah! Oh, well said, Vershinin! This is a lot better than
blaming yourself. Pour it on, boy!]   Oh, if you could have seen her today!   [This is really funny!]   She is a wretched creature!   [And this is
even funnier.]   We began quarreling at seven o'clock in the morning,
[and now I'll show her what a hero I was in meeting this challenge!]
and at nine I slammed the door and went away.   *[a pause]*   [Masha's
not laughing anymore, but this is exhilarating . . . she's moved. I think
she loves me. I've never seen a woman look at me like this before.]   I
never talk about it.   [Oh, hell, let her know.]   Strange, it's only to you I
complain.   [Go for it, guy! On the hand. Formal. She can't complain
about this. It only means what she makes of it.]   *[kisses her hand]*
Don't be angry with me. . . .   [She's not angry at all. She's crying! Tell
her! Tell her! You'll never have another chance! It's now or never!]
Except for you I have no one—   [TELL HER AGAIN!]   no one . . .
[a pause]

MASHA: [I've waited all my life for this, but what . . . SMILE, BABE!
What do I do now? I'm not going to have an affair, am I? Or am I? What
am I supposed to do? KEEP SMILING! Does he pick me up and carry
me away now? Am I supposed to kiss his hand? Why doesn't he DO
something? He's just staring into my eyes, waiting, waiting, for, for
what? I can't just sit silently here smiling like an idiot! I'm starting to cry,
dammit! . . . Ah, thank God, something to talk about.]   What a noise
in the stove!   [He must think I'm crazy, changing the subject like that!
I'd better explain why it's important. But it's not important! Well, I'll
lie, what the hell.]   Before Father died there was a howling in the chim-

ney. [He bought it. Why not? There's the sound again . . .]   There, just
like that.

VERSHININ: [All right, the cat's out of the bag, there's no stopping now.
But what should I say? Damn the noise in the chimney; she probably
made it up.]   Are you superstitious? [Why did I ask her that?]

MASHA: [I think he's hoping that I say "yes"]   Yes.

VERSHININ: [Pure instinct to ask her that! Yes: howling, chimney, father
dying . . . It's fate, isn't it? We're fated. She's a creature of fate, not bound
by conventional morality. I'll test her.]   That's strange! [She's smiling
again! She agrees; she's strange! I'm strange too! So let's throw caution to
that strange wind engulfing us! Her father's dead, we're both strange,
and the winds of fate are blowing us away! I'll kiss her hand again. Her
beautiful hand!] [kisses her hand]   You are a splendid, wonderful
woman. [Elaborate, Vershinin!]   Splendid! [Come on, dammit, elaborate!]   Wonderful! [Well, I'm not Cyrano, but she seems to be buying
it anyway. I'll think of something real cool to tell her.]   It's dark, but I
see the light in your eyes.

MASHA: [I'm completely paralyzed. I can't move. But does this mean we
have to have sex now? He's beautiful. This is funny. This is like in a play.
Let me see if I can get up.] [moves to another chair]   [I have to explain
why I just did that. I know.]   It's lighter here.

VERSHININ: [God, I haven't done this in ten years.]   I love you— [Elab-
orate, idiot!]   love, love . . . I love your eyes, your movements, [now
I'm on track]   I see them in my dreams. . . .   [Does this mean we have to
sleep together?]   Splendid, wonderful woman! [Didn't I just say that?]

MASHA: [God, he's better at this than I thought! If he thinks I'm helpless, I
could be ruined. Show control, Masha, show you're a woman of the
world. Laugh a little . . .] [laughing softly]   [That was too much! Let
him know you LOVE this.]   When you talk to me like that, for some
reason I laugh, though   ["be gentle, baby, I've never done this"]   I am
frightened. . . .   [What does he think: I'm a loose woman?]   Please
don't do it again . . .   [Oh God, he's taking me seriously! He's moving
away. NO! COME BACK!] [in an undertone]   You may say it, though;
I don't mind. . . .   [I'll submit; it's all his doing; I had nothing to do with
this. I'm simply blown by fate; it was the howling in the chimney; IT'S
NOT MY FAULT!] [covers her face with her hands]   I don't mind. . . .
[A NOISE! And it IS my fault! Shut up! I'm a fallen woman!]   Someone
is coming. Talk of something else.

It is clear, even if an entirely different subtext were to elicit these lines, that
the action of *Three Sisters* takes place largely *in the minds of the characters*—
though such inner action is of course exemplified by the behavior (body

language, expression, movement, gesture, inflection, tone of voice) of the actors in performance. The ideal of naturalistic acting is simply to vigorously use a character's tactics in pursuit of his or her goals, but you must also enter into the specific world of the characters to see how those goals, and more specifically the tactics, have evolved. Masha's and Vershinin's tactics are probably different from yours and those of your fellow classmates. They may include:

- Expressed gentility of spirit and refinement of manners appropriate among the professional and landowning classes in late tsarist Russia

- Regular entertaining of many visitors, for extended afternoons and evenings, and without set programs or activities, in the country homes of these classes

- Formal clothing and formal modes of behavior and conversation, expected when entertaining visitors in such homes

- Appreciation of the art of philosophizing: generalizing principles out of daily life occurrences

- Fascination with "the Russian character," an enduring topic of profound conversation

- Unquestioned acceptance (by the majority of the professional and landowning class) of the inborn superiority of the upper classes

- Admiration of military officers, selected from aristocratic and gentleman ranks: generally well-traveled and educated

- A polite disdain for working and servant classes; exceptions are rare but noteworthy when they occur

The direct contrast of this formal and refined code of conduct with the internal confusion—bordering on chaos—of the human souls Chekhov depicts creates the paralyzing ambivalence of the typical Chekhov character, whose aspirations run directly counter to his or her fears and feelings of inadequacy. The fears and feelings contribute, to Chekhov's (and thereby the actor's) work, a profound sadness, but the social refinement, and the will to transcend despair, create the bright Chekhovian gaiety. "Laughter through tears" is the cliché by which actors know Chekhov's demand, but the cliché is also a fundamental truth: Chekhov's characters are trying, often desperately, to seize their share of happiness. They may fail, by play's end, but the struggle goes on right up to the final curtain—and beyond. It is, finally, the laughter that should be played by Chekhov's actors, for the tears will take care of themselves.

16

Contemporary Styles

It is hard to see the styles of one's own era, perhaps because they seem so normal.

No one in the 1950s, for example, was particularly conscious of dressing in a 1950s style. It was only decades later, when invited to a "'50s party," that such people would have seriously reflected on what 1950s style might actually have been.

Likewise, neither Aeschylus, Sophocles, nor Euripides would have been consciously trying to write a "classical Greek tragedy." They were simply writing plays as they knew them; the term "classical Greek tragedy" was defined much later. And the same is true for medieval mystery plays, Italian *commedia erudita,* French neoclassic tragedy, and even twentieth-century theatre of the absurd. In each case, the works came first and the categorization of style later—sometimes much later.

A case may be made, however, that even beyond this fact, contemporary theatrical "style" is more varied and less reducible to categorization than dramas of the past. One reason is that today's playwrights gleefully process and amalgamate styles developed all over the world, and from every era, so that various combinations of many styles—Greek myth, Victorian melodrama, Shakespearean comedy, *kabuki* dance, African chant, Chinese opera, circus trapeze, official court transcripts, scientific debate—now find their way into contemporary dramas; while theories of alienation, absurdity, deconstruction, nonlinearity, interculturalism, interextualism, and metadrama (drama about drama) directly inform dramaturgical approaches.

Moreover, our age's premium is on novelty and originality in the arts; thus the artist gains fame by violating conventions rather than perfecting them. It is always a surprise for students to learn that, in the nineteenth century, the term "unexceptional" was used as a mark of praise in a theatrical review. Today it would be the gravest condemnation.

It is fair to say, then, that contemporary theatre artists are free—and encouraged—to create their own styles and are not absolutely tied to any single historical or geographical base. And actors are certainly asked to dig in to this smorgasbord of styles from all eras and mind-sets.

In this chapter, therefore, we will look at three contemporary dramatic styles, exemplified by widely differing—but Pulitzer Prize–winning—American plays from the 1990s. Playing these styles does not require the same intensity of historical research, for these plays are set in the present, or in the recent past, and the purely historical aspects of character deportment, behavior, and dress are abundantly around us still. But this familiarity only increases the complexity and subtlety of the actors' challenges as they extend themselves into the specific styles and characters portrayed in these interactions between a gay man and a Mormon wife, a rural black man and an urban black woman, a dying female professor and an ambitious young male doctor. Each of these characters comes from his or her own world, and with his or her own personal appeal and limitations, and moves out into a world that proves quite different, problematical, and filled with challenges. You will have something in common with all of these characters, I hope; with none of them, however, or one at most, will you have everything in common.

Clashing Cultures

Tony Kushner's two-part *Angels in America* is the most honored American play since 1950, having won not only the 1993 Pulitzer Prize for drama but no less than *two* Tony Awards for best play (its two parts premiering on Broadway in consecutive seasons).

Kushner, born in 1956, creates a new category for his play, spelled out in its subtitle: "A Gay Fantasia on National Themes." And indeed, everyone in the play operates within the unique "fantasia" of Kushner's imagination: Actors play many roles (living and dead, natural and supernatural, often of differing genders and ages), scenes overlap each other and take place simultaneously on different areas of the stage, and characters talk to the audience, appear in each other's dreams, climb up to heaven, and return from the dead. And, while the issues addressed by the play are extremely powerful (sexual betrayal, the spread of AIDS, homophobia and religious persecution, death and transfiguration), the duration exhausting (about eight hours), and the tone often savage, the play is, at many times, enormously funny. Kushner's language is often as wickedly clever as Shaw's and often, too, as brilliantly elliptical, and awkwardly stammered, as Chekhov's. There is good reason, in other words, to consider this the one true dramatic masterpiece of the 1990s.

Two different American subcultures come together in this work: gay males in New York City, and Mormons (members of the Church of Jesus Christ of Latter-Day Saints) from Utah. While none of the play's characters should be considered precisely typical, virtually all of them show the influence of prevailing—and conflicting—cultural attitudes. Indeed, that is the axis on which almost all of the play's scenes turn.

This scene, from *Angels in America, Part One: Millennium Approaches*, Act 1, Scene 7, is a fantasy conversation between Prior Walter and Harper Pitt. Prior, Kushner tells us, "occasionally works as a club designer or caterer, otherwise lives very modestly but with great style off a small trust fund." He has also recently discovered himself to be HIV positive. In his dream he is dressed in women's clothing, presumably preparing for a drag performance. Harper is a young woman from Utah, a member of the Mormon church, who has followed her husband, Joe, to New York; she is described by Kushner as "an agoraphobic with a mild Valium addiction."

[Prior is at a fantastic makeup table, having a dream, applying the face. Harper is having a pill-induced hallucination. [. . .] For some reason, Prior has appeared in this one. Or Harper has appeared in Prior's dream. It is bewildering.]

PRIOR: *[alone, putting on makeup, then examining the results in the mirror; to the audience]* "I'm ready for my closeup, Mr. DeMille."
    One wants to move through life with elegance and grace, blossoming infrequently but with exquisite taste, and perfect timing, like a rare bloom, a zebra orchid. . . . One wants . . . But one so seldom gets what one wants, does one? No. One does not. One gets fucked. Over. One . . . dies at thirty, robbed of . . . decades of majesty. Fuck this shit. Fuck this shit.

[He almost crumbles; he pulls himself together; he studies his handiwork in the mirror]

I look like a corpse. A corpsette. Oh my queen; you know you've hit rock-bottom when even drag is a drag.

[Harper appears.]

HARPER: Are you . . . Who are you?

PRIOR: Who are you?

HARPER: What are you doing in my hallucination?

PRIOR: I'm not in your hallucination. You're in my dream.

HARPER: You're wearing makeup.

PRIOR: So are you.

HARPER: But you're a man.

PRIOR: *[Feigning dismay, shock, he mimes slashing his throat with his lip-stick and dies, fabulously tragic. Then]*   The hands and feet give it away.

HARPER: There must be some mistake here. I don't recognize you. You're not . . . Are you my . . . some sort of imaginary friend?

PRIOR: No. Aren't you too old to have imaginary friends?

HARPER: I have emotional problems. I took too many pills. Why are you wearing makeup?

PRIOR: I was in the process of applying the face, trying to make myself feel better—I swiped the new fall colors at the Clinique counter at Macy's. *[showing her]*

HARPER: You stole these?

PRIOR: I was out of cash; it was an emotional emergency!

HARPER: Joe will be so angry. I promised him. No more pills.

PRIOR: These pills you keep alluding to?

HARPER: Valium. I take Valium. Lots of Valium.

PRIOR: And you're dancing as fast as you can.*

HARPER: I'm not *addicted*. I don't believe in addiction, and I never . . . well, I *never* drink. And I *never* take drugs.

PRIOR: Well, smell *you,* Nancy Drew.†

HARPER: Except Valium.

PRIOR: Except Valium; in wee fistfuls.

HARPER: It's terrible. Mormons are not supposed to be addicted to any-thing. I'm a Mormon.

PRIOR: I'm a homosexual.

HARPER: Oh! In my church we don't believe in homosexuals.

PRIOR: In my church we don't believe in Mormons.

HARPER: What church do . . . oh!   *[She laughs]*   I get it.
        I don't understand this. If I didn't ever see you before and I don't think I did then I don't think you should be here, in this hallucination,

---

*   An allusion to a 1979 book by Barbara Gordon about Valium addiction. It was made into a 1981 movie.

†   The wholesome young heroine of a series of children's mystery novels.

because in my experience the mind, which is where hallucinations come from, shouldn't be able to make up anything that wasn't there to start with, that didn't enter it from experience, from the real world. Imagination can't create anything new, can it? It only recycles bits and pieces from the world and reassembles them into visions. . . . Am I making sense right now?

PRIOR: Given the circumstances, yes.

HARPER: So when we think we've escaped the unbearable ordinariness and, well, untruthfulness of our lives, it's really only the same old ordinariness and falseness rearranged into the appearance of novelty and truth. Nothing unknown is knowable. Don't you think it's depressing?

PRIOR: The limitations of the imagination?

HARPER: Yes.

PRIOR: It's something you learn after your second theme party: It's All Been Done Before.

HARPER: The world. Finite. Terribly, terribly . . . Well . . . This is the most depressing hallucination I've ever had.

PRIOR: Apologies. I do try to be amusing.

HARPER: Oh, well, don't apologize, you . . . I can't expect someone who's really sick to entertain me.

PRIOR: How on earth did you know . . .

HARPER: Oh that happens. This is the very threshold of revelation sometimes. You can see things . . . how sick you are. Do you see anything about me?

PRIOR: Yes.

HARPER: What?

PRIOR: You are amazingly unhappy.

HARPER: Oh big deal. You meet a Valium addict and you figure out she's unhappy. That doesn't count. Of course I . . . Something else. Something surprising.

PRIOR: Something surprising.

HARPER: Yes.

PRIOR: Your husband's a homo.

[pause]

HARPER: Oh, ridiculous.   [pause, then very quietly]   Really?

PRIOR: [shrugs]   Threshold of revelation.

In Kushner's "gay fantasia," hallucinations and dreams are as real and vibrant as earthly dialog, and direct address makes the audience a participant in the struggles as well as the "performances" of the characters. He even calls this "bewildering" in his stage direction, but it needn't bewilder us: It is what we accept as the reality—the world—of his play.

And the play, while considered "contemporary," is in fact set in 1985–86, during the Reagan era, which makes it increasingly subject to historical evaluation as the years go by.

Within this overall style, Kushner creates separate subcultural styles: here the drag queen and the Mormon wife. Not all (or even most!) gay American males are drag queens, of course, and not all drag queens adore diva actresses, catty profanity, florid imagery, or quoting from old movies like *Sunset Boulevard*. But there is a distinct drag queen subculture nonetheless (it was first portrayed theatrically in Lanford Wilson's brilliant *Madness of Lady Bright* in 1964), and any actor playing Prior Walter should understand the common practices and attitudes of that subculture. Reading Wilson's play, seeing drag performances live or on film, and experiencing or reading in the literature of the subculture are all useful in understanding the goals, motivations, and favored tactics of a character such as Prior.

Cultural—and subcultural—behaviors are learned, of course. In life, they are learned by observation and emulation; this is how a group of relatively generic fifth-grade boys can become, six years later, diversely identified as, for instance, jocks, nerds, stoners, preppies, or skinheads. Whatever genetic predisposition may have led to these identifications, the practical cause was each boy's increased association with a particular group, leading to emulation of group dress, behavior, and attitudes and their increasing desire to fit in to—and be defined by—the chosen group. This would be how a "real" Prior Walter would become what we see in the play; the actor must undergo a similar process, though usually in imagination and rehearsal.

But of course Prior's chosen style doesn't fully, or even principally, define him. He is also a member of other subcultures: descendants of *Mayflower* Americans and AIDS patients among them. And he rebels against his drag queen subculture, finds it a drag, and transcends it in supernatural ways. Prior is an individual, whose brilliant wit and deep (though often disguised) compassion make him unlike not only any other drag queen but any other human being in the world.

Similarly, not all Mormon wives—nor even most of them—are unhappy, or in denial about their husband's sexuality, or addicted to drugs, as Harper appears to be. But the Mormon church is an association of men and women who regularly express, and who seek to teach their children, spiritual values that promote heterosexual life and that forbid homosexuality, alcohol, drugs, and profanity. Clearly the character of Harper, seen as a real person (even in a "fantasia"), would have been affected by her Mormon upbringing and her continuing Mormon beliefs and attitudes. An actor playing Harper would therefore wish to study Mormon society, either through direct experience or through literature, films, conversations with members of that faith, and other sources, in order to understand and truthfully perform the mind-set of her complex character.

But of course Harper, too, is not defined just by her Mormon beliefs and heritage. She has made the move to New York with her husband, she has accepted this conversation (and the jokey byplay) with the admitted homosexual whom her church would shun, and she has confessed to him her violations of her church's rules against drugs. Like Prior, she is a combination of her individual mind-set, goals and desires (her "character"), and her culturally derived channels of dress, deportment, language, and attitudes (her "style").

Let's look at key moments in the scene itself, seeing how the characters employ many of the devices we have explored in the historical sections of this book—language styles, rhetorical ploys, rhyme, assonance, voices of the supernatural, a *tirade,* and performative behaviors—in order to achieve their goals. In this, we will be doing as much a literary as an acting analysis, but these will provide guidelines for creating your own performance in the scene.

> *[Prior is at a fantastic makeup table, having a dream, applying the face. . . .]* "I'm ready for my closeup, Mr. DeMille."

Prior begins the scene not just dressed as a woman, but speaking the words of the character Norma Desmond, a delusional old silent-film actress played by Gloria Swanson in the celebrated 1950 film *Sunset Boulevard.* The actor's research, here, clearly requires viewing this film. Prior is, according to Kushner, speaking to the "audience," but which audience? Certainly through the imaginary mirror, the actor playing Prior is speaking to the theatre audience that is watching him in real time. But in his imagination, Prior might also be addressing the drag show nightclub audience—in the role of Desmond. Perhaps Prior is rehearsing a line from an actual drag act. It is at moments like these that performative behavior becomes a crucial part of the play's style: not just Prior performing in drag* but performing a specific character in another dramatic work. Such expropriation of another's performance can permit—indeed, often demands—"overacting," but this is no artistic sin, since it is your *character* doing the overacting, not you. You are only acting the overacting of Prior Walter—who is satirizing Norma Desmond's acting!

Some of this performative behavior spills over, though not in quotation marks (as with the Desmond line), as Prior continues—now directly to the

---

* Drag, and even gender itself, can persuasively be seen as performative behavior; see Judith Butler, "Imitation and Gender Insubordination," in *Inside/Out,* Diana Fuss, ed. (Routledge, 1991), pp. 13–31.

theatre audience—his speech—during which he oscillates between being Prior and being Desmond:

> One wants to move through life with elegance and grace, blossoming infrequently but with exquisite taste, and perfect timing, like a rare bloom, a zebra orchid . . . One wants . . . But one so seldom gets what one wants, does one? No. One does not. One gets fucked. Over. One . . . dies at thirty, robbed of . . . decades of majesty. Fuck this shit. Fuck this shit.
>
> *[He almost crumbles; he pulls himself together; he studies his handiwork in the mirror]*
>
> I look like a corpse. A corpsette. Oh my queen; you know you've hit rock-bottom when even drag is a drag.

This speech, filled with Chekhovian repetitions and trail-offs ("One wants . . ."), rhetorical questions ("does one?"), abstract philosophical musings (identified by the impersonal "one") quickly brought to earth by savage profanity ("One gets fucked"), whimsical wordplay ("corpsette"; "even drag is a drag"), is a deliberate and dazzling literary display: Prior bravely showing off his brilliant mind in order to hide (from us? from himself?) his deteriorating body. The performative speech—delivered before a mirror—may make us think perhaps, of the mirror-inspired monologue in Act 4, Scene 1 of Shakespeare's *Richard II*: "Give me that glass, and therein will I read. / No deeper wrinkles yet? Hath sorrow struck / So many blows upon this face of mine, / And made no deeper wounds?", or Mimi's glorious aria in the death-throes of tuberculosis in Puccini's *La Bohème*.

With Harper's entrance, Kushner moves to an exchange of single lines, each rhetorically linked with its predecessor by one or more words:

HARPER: Are you . . . Who are you?

PRIOR: Who are you?

HARPER: What are you doing in my hallucination?

PRIOR: I'm not in your hallucination. You're in my dream.

HARPER: You're wearing makeup.

PRIOR: So are you.

HARPER: But you're a man.

PRIOR: *[Feigning dismay, shock, he mimes slashing his throat with his lipstick and dies, fabulously tragic. Then]*   The hands and feet give it away.

Each plays on the other's speech, partly copying, partly mocking, and partly restating it, thereby trying to seize control not only of the topic but of the tone. Prior caps the exchange, however, by a *physical* response to Harper's last provocation: a gesture, and it is also a *performative* gesture, bringing into play his cross-gendered attire and a Grand Guignol (or slasher film, if you prefer) theatricalized bloodletting, which he then immediately deflates with a cliché. He is not really dead, he is not really female, and the most obvious things about him ("hands and feet," the well-known giveaways of transvestites) have betrayed him.

Prior and Harper subsequently play off their problems and genders. To Harper's girlish fantasy ("imaginary friend"), Prior poses his familiarity with girls' fiction ("Nancy Drew"); to her "emotional problems," he responds with his "emotional emergency"; she matches his brand-name makeup (Clinique) with a brand-name medication (Valium); he counters her church with his sexual orientation. And as they trade what superficially seem like catty insults, they grow inevitably closer: Their dialog, their repetition of each other's words and phrases, their mutual performative act, become a strong dramatic bond, blending their larger subcultures into a new, shared one—which consists, at the moment, of just the two of them.

Emboldened by their increasingly parallel discourse, Harper confesses with a rhetorical flourish (a bit of epistrophe—phrases ending with the same word), her drug problem to this strange new person who somehow, unlikely as it may first have appeared, increasingly seems to be her friend:

HARPER: Valium. I take Valium. Lots of Valium.   *[. . .]*   I'm not *addicted*. I don't believe in addiction, and I never . . . well, I *never* drink. And I *never* take drugs.

PRIOR: Well, smell *you*, Nancy Drew.

The euphemistic attack line, abjuring the f-word and sweetened with a rhyme *[you/Drew]* leaves Harper more amused than insulted—she *did* read Nancy Drew books as a child and has never met a *man* who ever did. She's emboldened further toward confession: "Except Valium."

Prior repeats her phrase, then ironically both amplifies and takes the edge off it with an adjective that has baby-talk overtones (as in Lesson 1), creating an even deeper trust and leading to their paired revelations:

PRIOR: Except Valium; in wee fistfuls.

HARPER: It's terrible. Mormons are not supposed to be addicted to anything. I'm a Mormon.

PRIOR: I'm a homosexual.

The paired revelations are followed by their subcultures' paired objections:

HARPER: Oh! In my church we don't believe in homosexuals.

PRIOR: In my church we don't believe in Mormons.

HARPER: What church do . . . oh!   *[She laughs]*   I get it.

The laughter is of recognition and admission: the recognition that the two of them aren't as different as she had thought and the admission that reliance on their individual subcultures won't be enough to sustain them through their present crises. None of this, of course, is said directly through the *meaning* of the lines; rather, it is expressed, and unambiguously expressed (as meaning alone can rarely if ever be), in the *style* of the language and actions the actors employ.

Harper continues with a *tirade* (see Lesson 13) in which she tries to come to terms with the fantasia Kushner has placed her in:

> I don't understand this. If I didn't ever see you before and I don't think I did then I don't think you should be here, in this hallucination, because in my experience the mind, which is where hallucinations come from, shouldn't be able to make up anything that wasn't there to start with, that didn't enter it from experience, from the real world. Imagination can't create anything new, can it? It only recycles bits and pieces from the world and reassembles them into visions . . . Am I making sense right now?

And Prior, fascinated, hoping to find some answer himself, keeps her going: "Given the circumstances, yes."
Which she does:

> So when we think we've escaped the unbearable ordinariness and, well, untruthfulness of our lives, it's really only the same old ordinariness and falseness rearranged into the appearance of novelty and truth. Nothing unknown is knowable.

The *tirade* is complete, but it is unfulfilling. Imagination—which includes transvestite performance and drug-induced hallucination—can only recycle the world; it can't remake it, and it certainly can't cure AIDS. Harper is left only to see whether Prior shares her conclusion, which he does. And, true to his performative nature (he's a pro at being funny), he tries to lighten her mood; it's probably the sort of line that suggested to homosexual men, around the 1940s, the appellation "gay": "It's something you learn after your second theme party: It's All Been Done Before."

But Harper, still brooding about her addiction and how it violently conflicts with her religious beliefs, will not be cheered up: "The world. Finite. Terribly, terribly . . . Well . . . This is the most depressing hallucination I've ever had."

Prior responds, "Apologies. I do try to be amusing"—a distant allusion, perhaps, to a self-deprecating line from a song by playwright Noel Coward: "The most I've had is just / A talent to amuse."

Prior and Harper share the insights that their emotional and, now, psychological proximity have gained them. For both are, at bottom, spiritual creatures: This is, after all, a play about angels.

HARPER: Oh, well, don't apologize, you . . . I can't expect someone who's really sick to entertain me.

PRIOR: How on earth did you know . . .

HARPER: Oh that happens. This is the very threshold of revelation sometimes. You can see things . . . how sick you are. Do you see anything about me?

PRIOR: Yes.

HARPER: What?

PRIOR: You are amazingly unhappy.

Now it's Harper's turn to make the jest, lighten the mood, show a little just-learned New York sarcasm: "Oh big deal. You meet a Valium addict and you figure out she's unhappy. That doesn't count."

The bonding is nearly complete. Harper has bought in to Prior's subculture; she shares his language and attitude. And she can trust him with the worst: She asks him to tell her something about herself that's surprising.

PRIOR: Something surprising.

HARPER: Yes.

PRIOR: Your husband's a homo.

[pause]

HARPER: Oh, ridiculous.   *[pause, then very quietly]*   Really?

And, with a studied-casual acknowledgment *("shrugs")* to the profound tie that now binds them, he repeats her phrase: "Threshold of revelation."

Angels in America is a play of extraordinary sensitivity, conveyed through far more than just cleverness and open-heartedness; it is a masterpiece of intricately blended styles and characters who communicate through every act of performance: speaking, sighing, crying, laughing, quoting, miming, pretending, revealing, hiding, loving, and suffering.

The discussion in the preceding pages, which in several ways is an analysis of Kushner's art, provides cues for the actors' performance on virtually every line, by showing how you can use not merely the meanings of the words but their shapes and forms as well to seek to achieve your character's goal. How do you shape your words, and your body, to express your opinions and contradict your opponent's, but still get the help you need (and the love you want) from other human beings? These are the issues for both Prior and Harper, coming from very different backgrounds but seeking the shared experience—and revelation—they both desire.

◆ SCENE 16-1

Prior and Harper

Prepare and perform the scene between Prior and Harper. Get yourselves a dressing table with a mirror frame. Dress the roles—not to "explain" your characters to the classroom audience but to get the feel of your characters: Prior in a satin bathrobe and barefoot, and Harper in what you consider to be a prim, country-wifely outfit—with shoes to match. Perform your characters' actions as though your own subculture were watching you from afar (Harper's mother and minister; Prior's lover and former lovers). Imagine the theatre audience (with or without looking at them) as members of your subculture—until your acting partner becomes more dominant in your life at this particular moment.

Luxuriate in the wonderful, if different, world of your character, and relish any area in which your character's world may be preferable to your own.

Use the rhetoric and poetry of your part to better your character's lot and to create a new friend in your acting partner.

Clashing Subcultures

August Wilson, born in 1945, is, in my opinion, America's finest active playwright; he's already won one Tony Award and two Pulitzer Prizes, and his series of ten plays, which when complete (he has two to go) will cover every decade of African American life in the twentieth century, is already a towering, unprecedented dramatic achievement.

Surely no one—black or white—can perform Wilson's plays without a profound understanding of American black culture and its complex roots. As Wilson says,

> Black Americans have their own culture. While we all do the same things, we all do them differently. We decorate our houses differently, bury our dead differently. Sometimes the differences aren't all that great, but if you ever went to a Black funeral and then to a white funeral, you'll definitely know that there are two distinct, separate cultures at work. Neither is better than the other one. They're just two different ways of approaching life.

Describing this difference as it appears in the dialog of his plays, Wilson adds an illuminating anecdote:

I once had some problems with some producers of *Fences* because of repetition. For instance, Troy says to Rose, "What're you cookin' there?" [She replies] "I got some chicken. I'm cookin' up some chicken with collard greens." "You already said that," the producers said. "Why are you repeating that?" But that's the way Black folks say it. The language is the language of the people, and you can't deny them that. To deny them that is . . . denying them their humanity, trying to make them into somebody else. . . . We can say exactly the same things as others, but we say them differently because we're a different people."*

We will see repetition masterfully used in the scene that follows.

But the difference is hardly limited to speech. Wilson's plays—and indeed most plays in the African American repertory—are more often driven by character than plot, and emotional exchange rather than dispassionate debate. And while Wilson's reproduction of black American speech is superb, his is not a mere stenographic transcription of black conversation: Wilson began his career as a poet, and even though his theatre is often naturalistic like Chekhov's, it is not rigidly so. There is often a level of spirituality in his work (there's a ghost in *The Piano Lesson,* for example) and always a profound musicality.

In *The Piano Lesson,* set in the 1930s, Boy Willie, from rural Mississippi, comes up to his sister Berniece's house in Pittsburgh (the city where most of Wilson's plays are set) to sell watermelons; he's also trying to talk Berniece into selling the family's heirloom piano so he can buy the Mississippi property where their family had worked. Boy Willie is described by Wilson as "thirty years old. He has an infectious grin and a boyishness that is apt for his name. He is brash and impulsive, talkative and somewhat crude in speech and manner." In this scene, from Act 2, Scene 3, having gone out with a buddy, Lymon, to "find some women" at a local bar, Boy Willie has met Grace and is bringing her back to Berniece's house.

Both characters are African American. Both have been drinking prior to this scene, but neither should be considered intoxicated.

Read through the scene.

[Boy Willie enters the darkened house with Grace]

BOY WILLIE: Come on in. This my sister's house. My sister live here. Come on, I ain't gonna bite you.

GRACE: Put some light on. I can't see.

---

* Both quotes are from "Men, Women, and Culture: A Conversation with August Wilson," an interview conducted by Nathan L. Grant, 1993. Published at http://blues.fdl.uc.edu/www/amdrama/wilsonint.html.

Victor Mack is Boy Willie and Kim Staunton his sister Berniece in a South Coast Repertory production of August Wilson's *The Piano Lesson.* (Courtesy South Coast Repertory; photo by Cris Gross)

BOY WILLIE: You don't need to see nothing, baby. This here is all you need to see. All you need to do is see me. If you can't see me you can feel me in the dark. How's that, sugar?   *[He attempts to kiss her.]*

GRACE: Go on now . . . wait!

BOY WILLIE: Just give me one little old kiss.

GRACE: *[pushing him away]*   Come on, now. Where I'm gonna sleep at?

BOY WILLIE: We got to sleep out here on the couch. Come on, my sister don't mind. Lymon come back he just got to sleep on the floor. He run off with Dolly somewhere he better stay there. Come on, sugar.

GRACE: Wait now . . . you ain't told me nothing about no couch. I thought you had a bed. Both of us can't sleep on that little old couch.

BOY WILLIE: It don't make no difference. We can sleep on the floor. Let Lymon sleep on the couch.

GRACE: You ain't told me nothing about no couch.

BOY WILLIE: What difference it make? You just wanna be with me.

GRACE: I don't want to be with you on no couch. Ain't you got no bed?

BOY WILLIE: You don't need no bed, woman. My granddaddy used to take women on the backs of horses. What you need a bed for? You just want to be with me.

GRACE: You sure is country. I didn't know you was this country.

BOY WILLIE: There's a lot of things you don't know about me. Come on, let me show you what this country boy can do.

GRACE: Let's go back to my place. I got a room with a bed if Leroy don't come back there.

BOY WILLIE: Who's Leroy? You ain't said nothing about no Leroy.

GRACE: He used to be my man. He ain't coming back. He gone off with some other gal.

BOY WILLIE: You let him have your key?

GRACE: He ain't coming back.

BOY WILLIE: Did you let him have your key?

GRACE: He got a key but he ain't coming back. He took off with some other gal.

BOY WLLIE: I don't wanna go nowhere he might come. Let's stay here. Come on, sugar.   *[He pulls her over to the couch]*   Let me heist your hood and check your oil. See if your battery needs charged.   *[He pulls her to him. They kiss and tug at each other's clothing.]*

This scene is about young people quarreling about sex: whether to have it, where to have it, how to have it, and when to have it. In this it is not unlike any of hundreds of American plays, such as Tennessee Williams's *Streetcar Named Desire,* Sam Shepard's *Fool for Love,* Eric Bogosian's *subUrbia,* Wendy Wasserstein's *Heidi Chronicles,* and Lanford Wilson's *Burn This.* But August Wilson, naturally, layers this situation with a particularly African American style, both in language and tone. Wilson's commitment to explore black culture is both political and aesthetic; he is a playwright who refuses to synthesize races, gloss over cultural differences, or minimize cultural glories. "I find in black life a very elegant kind of logical language, based on the logical order of things," he says.

But logical language does not mean factually logical. As it turns out, Boy Willie's sister *does* mind, and, when they end up at Grace's home, her boyfriend Leroy *does* show up. "There's the idea of metaphor," Wilson continues. "When you ask a question, instead of getting an answer to the question, you get . . . ideas . . . opinions about everything, a little explanation. You get all these kinds of things just from one question."

And under the umbrella of African American culture, Wilson portrays, in this scene, two of its idealized subcultures: Willie's Southern, rural (or, as

Grace calls it, "country") style and Grace's Northern, big-city attitude. And of course he portrays two idealized genders as well, with men (in this case) primarily interested in sex, and women primarily in material comfort. Neither Grace nor Boy Willie should be reduced to mere stereotypes, however, as both are complex characters trying to escape such typing. In the very act of having their conversation, each character is trying to shed the idealized role of his or her upbringing or environment: Though they dare not show it openly, Willie is fascinated by Grace's urban sophistication, and Grace is enchanted by Willie's countrified brashness and naïveté. Thus this scene is not merely an argument about sex, it is a negotiation, within the framework of an overarching culture, of differing substyles and language codes.

Their opening exchange is not simply an argument about lights or furniture; it's about "How are you going to treat me?" And the questions are posed not in the content but in the style of the language: Boy Willie calling Grace by pet names ("baby," "sugar") and Grace complaining that she's not being *treated* as the "baby" or "sugar" he's calling her.

Boy Willie makes a macho move, showing how he controls his older sister and can easily order his buddy Lymon around: "We got to sleep out here on the couch. Come on, my sister don't mind. Lymon come back he just got to sleep on the floor. He run off with Dolly somewhere he better stay there."

He concludes by repeating his order ("Come on") and softening it by repeating an endearment: "Come on, sugar."

Grace is all big-city legalisms and facts: "Wait now . . . you ain't told me nothing about no couch. I thought you had a bed. Both of us can't sleep on that little old couch."

Willie tries his best to get around her argument, but he fails miserably: "It don't make no difference. We can sleep on the floor. Let Lymon sleep on the couch." He's humiliated. He's blown it.

But this is not about a couch! Grace doesn't really care about the furniture arrangements; she just doesn't want to spend the night with a man who can't provide a proper setting. It's bad enough he's called "Boy" Willie: If she's going to sleep with him, she at least needs him to show some resourcefulness and authority. She wants him to be a man! Grace persists, amplifying her demand with a triple negative for emphasis: "You ain't told me nothing about no couch."

Willie realizes there's no arguing with her. Where is the delightful young woman who responded to him earlier in the saloon? ("She real nice. Laugh a lot. Lot of fun to be with" is how Lymon later describes Grace on that occasion.) Willie tries valiantly—but rather foolishly—to call on the promise of that earlier encounter: "What difference it make? You just wanna be with me."

It's loggerheads: How can Boy Willie tell Grace what *she* wants? And Willie knows it. But Grace has run out of tactics now. She can't simply acquiesce to a childish plea, and she still wants to be treated right by a man she can admire. All she can do is repeat her demand: "I don't want to be with you on no couch. Ain't you got no bed?"

And so Boy Willie summons his nerve to become the man he realizes she's looking for: "You don't need no bed, woman. My granddaddy used to take women on the backs of horses. What you need a bed for? You just want to be with me." A man like his grandfather. A man from Mississippi. A man on horseback! These Pittsburgh girls have never made love to a real man like this.

Grace is stunned: confused, excited, revolted, overwhelmed. How does a city girl deal with such rural hyperbole? Boy Willie is just kidding, isn't he? Or do they really do it on horseback in Mississippi? Graphic images fly through her mind—she can't stop them. But she's no fool. Or is she? Grace temporizes, testing the waters further before making a commitment: "You sure is country. I didn't know you was this country."

Now sure of success, Willie gallops ahead. He finds the biggest, sexiest, movie-star voice he can come up with, exaggerating his down-home Southern accent and plunging to his lowest, most resonant vocal register: "There's a lot of things you don't know about me. Come on, let me show you what this country boy can do."

Grace is hooked. But she needs to save face too. She's no doormat. In two brief lines she makes clear: OK, but in my place and in my bed and, in case things get out of hand, I've got a boyfriend who'll beat you to a pulp: "Let's go back to my place. I got a room with a bed if Leroy don't come back there."

Uh-oh! The horse has disappeared. Boy Willie has another obstacle to overcome. "Who's Leroy? You ain't said nothing about no Leroy."

Leroy, Grace makes clear, is no Boy Leroy: "He used to be my man. He ain't coming back. He gone off with some other gal."

Boy Willie fences with her about the logistics of this potential problem, with each rephrasing and repeating the other's words in a mini-fugue of keys and comings, *k* and *g* consonants:

BOY WILLIE: You let him have your key?

GRACE: He ain't coming back.

BOY WILLIE: Did you let him have your key?

GRACE: He got a key but he ain't coming back. He took off with some other gal.

Relieved that she's been dumped by Leroy, Boy Willie now feels strong enough to reassert his authority, even in retreat. He explains, then orders, then seduces, employing the pet name with which he began the scene: "I don't wanna go nowhere he might come. Let's stay here. Come on, sugar." He concludes with a peroration: a line of wonderful bravado and creative sexual imagery ("the idea of metaphor," Wilson has said) that locks in his victory: "Let me heist your hood and check your oil. See if your battery needs charged."

Only this grand speech *doesn't* lock in a victory! In the very next moment, Willie's sister comes down and kicks them out of the house, whereupon they go to Grace's home and Leroy interrupts them, forcing Willie to flee the premises.

August Wilson is America's living Chekhov, revealing both the awkwardness and loveliness of human imperfection. His characters are sensually detailed, made so by the rich texture and style of the language, by which they imply (and we infer) an almost infinite subtext.

♦ S C E N E   16-2

Boy Willie and Grace

With a partner, prepare and present the scene between Boy Willie and Grace.

Play your character's background, era, and goals, not your own. Look at old magazines to find what African Americans might have worn for a night out in the city during the depression years—with particular attention to Boy Willie's rural roots. Find a couch in your prop room, if possible, for use in rehearsing and presenting the scene—and use it in your staging.

Clashing Professions

Margaret Edson, born in 1961, won the Pulitzer Prize for *Wit*, her first and still only play, in 1999; it is a powerful drama concerning a brilliant and somewhat authoritarian professor of English literature, Vivian Bearing, who is dying of ovarian cancer in a research hospital. The play jumps back and forth in time and alternates between starkly realistic portrayals of her suffering to her reflections—often whimsical—largely given directly to the audience; these concern not only her current medical plight but her life, her academic career, and, more surprisingly, the strange play she finds herself in.

In the following scene, Vivian is being attended by Jason Posner, a young research physician who was once a student in her literature class, which was on the poetry of John Donne, her specialty.

Note: While Vivian is described as being fifty years old at the point this scene takes place, over the course of the play she plays herself at various ages

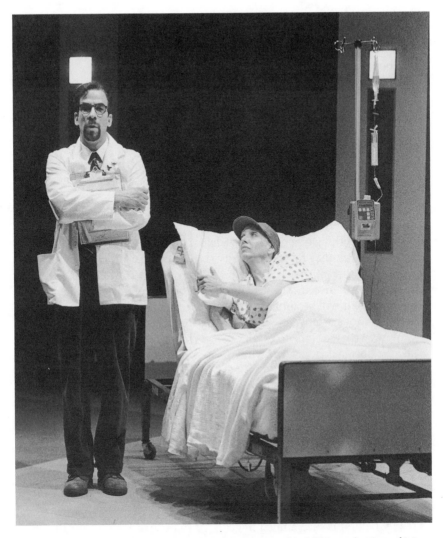

Linda Alper is Vivian and Jonathan Toppo is Jason in this 2000 production of Margaret Edson's *Wit* by the Oregon Shakespeare Festival. (Courtesy Oregon Shakespeare Festival; photo by David Cooper)

from five onward, so it is does not inordinately strain credulity for her to be played by a college-age actor.

With a partner, read the scene aloud, for familiarity, before moving on.

VIVIAN: *[sits weakly in a wheelchair; to the audience]*
   This is my playes last scene, here heavens appoint
   My pilgrimages last mile; and my race

Idly, yet quickly runne, hath this last pace,
My spans last inch, my minutes last point,
And gluttonous death will instantly unjoynt
My body, and soule
John Donne. 1609.

I have always particularly liked that poem. In the abstract. Now I find
the image of "my minutes last point" a little too, shall we say, *pointed.*

I don't mean to complain, but I am becoming very sick. Very, very
sick. Ultimately sick, as it were.

In everything I have done, I have been steadfast, resolute—some
would say in the extreme. Now, as you can see, I am distinguishing myself in illness.

I have survived eight treatments of Hexamethophosphacil and Vinplatin at the *full* dose, ladies and gentlemen. I have broken the record. I have
become something of a celebrity. Kelekian* and Jason are simply delighted. I think they foresee celebrity status for themselves upon the appearance of the journal article they will no doubt write about me.

But I flatter myself. The article will not be about *me,* it will be about
my ovaries. It will be about my peritoneal cavity, which, despite their
best intentions, is now crawling with cancer.

What we have come to think of as *me* is, in fact, just the specimen jar,
just the dust jacket, just the white piece of paper that bears the little
black marks.

My next line is supposed to be something like this:
"It is such a *relief* to get back to my room after those infernal tests."
This is hardly true.

It would be a relief to be a cheerleader on her way to Daytona Beach
for Spring Break.

To get back to my room after those infernal tests is just the next thing
that happens.

[She returns to her bed.]

Oh, God. It is such a relief to get back to my goddamn room after
those goddamn tests.

[Jason enters.]

JASON: Professor Bearing. Just want to check the I&O.°   °*intake and outgo
of fluids*

Four-fifty, six, five. Okay. How are you feeling today?   *[He makes notations on his clipboard throughout the scene.]*

VIVIAN: Fine.

---

*   her doctor

JASON: That's great. Just great.

VIVIAN: How are my fluids?

JASON: Pretty good. No kidney involvement yet. That's pretty amazing, with Hex and Vin.

VIVIAN: How will you know when the kidneys are involved?

JASON: Lots of in, not much out.

VIVIAN: That simple.

JASON: Oh, no way. Compromised kidney function is a highly complex reaction. I'm simplifying for you.

VIVIAN: Thank you.

JASON: We're supposed to.

VIVIAN: Bedside manner.

JASON: Yeah, there's a whole course on it in med school. It's required. Colossal waste of time for researchers.   *[He turns to go.]*

VIVIAN: I can imagine.   *[Trying to ask something important]*   Jason?

JASON: Huh?

VIVIAN: *[Not sure of herself]*   Ah, what . . .   *[Quickly]*   What were you just saying?

JASON: When?

VIVIAN: Never mind.

JASON: Professor Bearing?

VIVIAN: Yes.

JASON: Are you experiencing confusion? Short-term memory loss?

VIVIAN: No.

JASON: Sure?

VIVIAN: Yes.   *[Pause]*   I was just wondering: why cancer?

JASON: Why cancer?

VIVIAN: Why not open-heart surgery?

JASON: Oh, yeah, why not *plumbing*. Why not run a *lube rack,* for all the surgeons know about *Homo sapiens sapiens.* No way. Cancer's the only thing I ever wanted.

VIVIAN: *[Intrigued]*   Huh.

JASON: No, really. Cancer is . . .   *[searching]*

VIVIAN: *[Helping]*   Awesome.

JASON: *[Pause]*   Yeah. Yeah, that's right. It is. It is awesome. How does it do it? The intercellular regulatory mechanisms—especially for proliferation and differentiation—the malignant neoplasia just don't get it. You grow normal cells in tissue culture in the lab, and they replicate just enough to make a nice, confluent monolayer. They divide twenty times, or fifty times, but eventually they conk out. You grow cancer cells, and they never stop. No contact inhibition whatsoever. They just pile up, just keep replicating forever.   *[Pause]*   That's got a funny name. Know what it is?

VIVIAN: No. What?

JASON: Immortality in culture.

VIVIAN: Sounds like a symposium.

JASON: It's an error in judgment, in a molecular way. But *why?* Even on the protistic level the normal cell–cell interactions are so subtle they'll take your breath away. Golden-brown algae, for instance, the lowest multicellular life form on earth—they're *idiots*—and it's incredible. It's perfect. So what's up with the cancer cells? Smartest guys in the world, with the best labs, funding—they don't know what to make of it.

VIVIAN: What about you?

JASON: Me? Oh, I've got a couple of ideas, things I'm kicking around. Wait till I get a lab of my own. If I can survive this . . . *fellowship.*

VIVIAN: The part with the human beings.

JASON: Everybody's got to go through it. All the great researchers. They want us to be able to converse intelligently with the clinicians. As though *researchers* were the impediments. The clinicians are such troglodytes. So smarmy. Like we have to hold hands to discuss creatinine clearance. Just cut the crap, I say.

VIVIAN: Are you going to be sorry when I— Do you ever miss people?

JASON: Everybody asks that. Especially girls.

VIVIAN: What do you tell them?

JASON: I tell them yes.

VIVIAN: Are they persuaded?

JASON: Some.

VIVIAN: Some. I see.   *[With great difficulty]*   And what do you say when a patient is . . . apprehensive . . . frightened?

JASON: Of who?

VIVIAN: I just . . . Never mind.

JASON: Professor Bearing, who is the President of the United States?

VIVIAN: I'm fine, really. It's all right.

JASON: You sure? I could order a test—

VIVIAN: No! No, I'm fine. Just a little tired.

JASON: Okay. Look. Gotta go. Keep pushing the fluids. Try for 2,000 a day, okay?

VIVIAN: Okay. To use your word. Okay.

Now study the scene in more detail.

In addition to the metatheatrical stylization of the dramaturgy (Vivian speaking to the audience, specifically about the play she is in), this scene also carries the weight of professional jargon, as both characters see the world in terms of their professional training and experience (in literary criticism and medical research). Actors in these roles, therefore, must master not only the vocabulary of each part (which is at minimum the meaning, pronunciation, and importance of each term) but the *professional mind-set* of their characters. The actor playing Vivian must be able to read the John Donne poem as a professor of English poetry would; the actor playing Jason must be able to rattle casually on, with seemingly absolute assurance, about intercellular regulatory mechanisms. No one could play either of these roles without doing research on the professions involved and practicing the jargon in the lines until they could speak it with both fluidity and apparent conviction.

Indeed, playing roles of this nature virtually requires that the actor take an accelerated "training course" in the profession portrayed, a course which, however short (and rehearsal time often allows little beyond a few days or even hours), nonetheless explores not just what persons in the profession actually do but what they seek, what they worry about, and what they pride themselves on. The actors playing Vivian and Jason must, above all, allow us to accept them as authentic and fully dimensional professionals in their fields: Without this, the life-and-death and moral issues of the play will not be very convincing.

Read through the scene aloud a second time, stopping at each of the discussion points to read and discuss each fragment. Then read it aloud again. And again—until you feel reasonably comfortable with the professional language and the points raised in this text, and in your own discussion.

This is my playes last scene, here heavens appoint
My pilgrimages last mile; and my race
Idly, yet quickly runne, hath this last pace,
My spans last inch, my minutes last point,
And gluttonous death will instantly unjoynt
My body, and soule
John Donne. 1609.

Spoken by a dying woman, the Donne poem excerpt is doubly sad; but that it is a speech in a play about the last scene of another "play" (one we already know will end with the speaker's death) gives it a certain wittiness (befitting the play's title) which beautifully balances the pathos, making Vivian an ironic commentator on her own despair. Author Edson immeasurably helps the actor in this role by beginning the speech without introduction; unless we (the audience) are ourselves Donne fanciers, we have no idea Vivian is reciting a Donne poem, or indeed any poem at all, until the first rhyme is completed at the end of the third line. So we are momentarily confused, not knowing exactly what to think or how to feel until the poem concludes, with its sadness and ironic commentary intermixed.

The actor exploits this confusion, as does the character; both are performing for us, and our ease at sympathizing with Vivian's plight comes, in part, from knowing that the actor playing the part is presumably not, herself, dying of ovarian cancer. So when Vivian identifies the author and date of the poem at the end, we all relax, knowing both that the character will die today but the actor (and we) will not and that these lines were written a long time ago and will not apply to us until a long time from now.

Vivian continues with her ironic commentary on her self-mourning, showing, in her very verbosity (punning *point* and *pointed*; emending *very, very* to *ultimately*; insisting on her dispassionate objectivity with the distancing "as it were"; unnecessarily pairing a synonym, *resolute*, to *steadfast*), an attempt to conquer the fear of death through rhetoric: an effort to talk her way out of the grave:

> I have always particularly liked that poem. In the abstract. Now I find the image of "my minutes last point" a little too, shall we say, *pointed*.
>
> I don't mean to complain, but I am becoming very sick. Very, very sick. Ultimately sick, as it were.
>
> In everything I have done, I have been steadfast, resolute—some would say in the extreme. Now, as you can see, I am distinguishing myself in illness.

She will conquer her fear of cancer by acquiring medical expertise, particularly the ability to pronounce the complicated names of chemical compounds so effortlessly as to follow them with "ladies and gentlemen," as though they were part of a Mistress of Ceremonies cabaret routine: "I have survived eight treatments of Hexamethophosphacil and Vinplatin at the *full* dose, ladies and gentlemen. I have broken the record." Boldly, she rises to the top of her ironic form: "I have become something of a celebrity. Kelekian and Jason are simply delighted. I think they foresee celebrity status for themselves upon the appearance of the journal article they will no doubt write about me."

And then, just as boldly, she falls; her medical expertise can only describe, not reverse, her physical affliction:

But I flatter myself. The article will not be about *me*, it will be about my ovaries. It will be about my peritoneal cavity, which, despite their best intentions, is now crawling with cancer. What we have come to think of as *me* is, in fact, just the specimen jar, just the dust jacket, just the white piece of paper that bears the little black marks.

Vivian can no longer maintain her performative, professorial lecture mode, and, quite brilliantly, Edson now has her step outside the play she's in:

My next line is supposed to be something like this:
"It is such a *relief* to get back to my room after those infernal tests."
This is hardly true.
It would be a *relief* to be a cheerleader on her way to Daytona Beach for Spring Break.
To get back to my room after those infernal tests is just the next thing that happens.

And we're back to the hospital bed, where she is once again a victim, away from her professorial pulpit. And her language suffers. Her despair even mangles the line she was "supposed" to deliver, which now has a pair of "ad libbed" *goddamn*s. *Infernal* is too professorial a word to issue from her lips once the physical torment returns; only a vulgarity (though a relatively sedate one) can suffice: "Oh, God. It is such a relief to get back to my goddamn room after those goddamn tests."

Jason at first makes light of his learning, using abbreviations ("I&O"; "Hex and Vin") and repeated euphemisms ("Okay"; "Great. Just great") in an effort to simplify and to improve his bedside manner. Vivian calls him on it; she doesn't want to be treated like a child:

JASON: Professor Bearing. Just want to check the I&O. Four-fifty, six, five. Okay. How are you feeling today?   *[He makes notations on his clipboard throughout the scene.]*

VIVIAN: Fine.

JASON: That's great. Just great.

VIVIAN: How are my fluids?

JASON: Pretty good. No kidney involvement yet. That's pretty amazing, with Hex and Vin.

VIVIAN: How will you know when the kidneys are involved?

JASON: Lots of in, not much out.

VIVIAN: That simple.

JASON: Oh, no way. Compromised kidney function is a highly complex reaction. I'm simplifying for you.

VIVIAN: Thank you.

Jason can't let it go at that. Though it's his job to minister to the patient, he needs some ministering himself. He proceeds to gratuitously tell the dying Vivian *his* problems, seeking her sympathy as a fellow intellectual with an implicit shrug: "We're supposed to."

Her response is deliberately brief: just the term, not her feeling about it, letting Jason do all the interpreting.

VIVIAN: Bedside manner.

JASON: Yeah, there's a whole course on it in med school. It's required. Colossal waste of time for researchers.   *[He turns to go.]*

Jason's "Yeah" (in lieu of "Yes") begins a subtle relaxation of his official style, as he begins to treat Vivian not as a patient but more as a fellow intellectual, an honorary colleague, conspiratorially indicating his contempt for the caregiving role he's required to play and begging for sympathy: Vivian, he is saying, should be sorry for *him* for having to waste his time being sympathetic toward *her*. A transition occurs between them as they now jostle for control of the dialog. Chekhovian hesitations, questions unanswered, or answered by other questions ("Huh?" "When?"), proliferate:

VIVIAN: I can imagine.   *[Trying to ask something important]*   Jason?

JASON: Huh?

VIVIAN: *[Not sure of herself]*   Ah, what . . .   *[Quickly]*   What were you just saying?

JASON: When?

VIVIAN: Never mind.

Alarmed at what he might have opened himself up to, Jason tries to seize the high ground by becoming doctorlike, probing her, asking medical questions to reestablish his authority.

JASON: Professor Bearing?

VIVIAN: Yes.

JASON: Are you experiencing confusion? Short-term memory loss?

VIVIAN: No.

JASON: Sure?

VIVIAN: Yes.   *[Pause]*

And Vivian comes to the point: Let's talk about *you* instead of me: "I was just wondering: why cancer?   [. . .]   Why not open-heart surgery?" And

Jason, thrilled to be the subject of her inquiry (something that would have been impossible when he was her undistinguished undergraduate student), reveals his intellectual brilliance—and emotional tone-deafness—through adolescent sarcasm: "Oh, yeah, why not *plumbing*. Why not run a *lube rack,* for all the surgeons know about *Homo sapiens sapiens.* No way. Cancer's the only thing I ever wanted." The paradox—lost on Jason—is overwhelming: What he *wants* is precisely what's killing her.

VIVIAN: *[Intrigued]* Huh.

JASON: No, really. Cancer is . . .   *[searching]*

Vivian finds the perfect teenage adjective for the era: "Awesome." And he finds the perfect affirmative: "Yeah." Now Jason, still not catching her sarcasm (indeed, he proudly repeats the supplied adjective), is in high gear, showing off, along with his unlettered slang ("Yeah"; "conk out"), all the scientific language he has picked up since he left her English class; there will be no more simplifying, nor no gentle easing of the horror to a woman who is dying of the very process he's giddily boasting about:

> Yeah, that's right. It is. It is awesome. How does it do it? The intercellular regulatory mechanisms—especially for proliferation and differentiation—the malignant neoplasia just don't get it. You grow normal cells in tissue culture in the lab, and they replicate just enough to make a nice, confluent monolayer. They divide twenty times, or fifty times, but eventually they conk out. You grow cancer cells, and they never stop. No contact inhibition whatsoever. They just pile up, just keep replicating forever.

And now he feels bold enough to enter her world: a world of words, images, poetry. The English student is becoming the English teacher:

JASON: [. . .]   *[Pause]*   That's got a funny name. Know what it is?

VIVIAN: No. What?

JASON: Immortality in culture.

VIVIAN: Sounds like a symposium.

Nailing his point with medical terminology that he knows she cannot contest (who besides medical researchers knows what *protistic* means?), Jason flies: He is now an expert on errors in judgment, on subtlety, on perfection; and he can now show his contempt for "idiots" with ferocity (Edson has italicized the word to indicate this). Can we not see, in this italicized *idiots*, that this is how Jason himself once felt—as one of Vivian's literature students? Like the lowest life form on earth:

> It's an error in judgment, in a molecular way. But *why*? Even on the protistic level the normal cell–cell interactions are so subtle they'll take

your breath away. Golden-brown algae, for instance, the lowest multi-cellular life form on earth—they're *idiots*—and it's incredible. It's perfect. So what's up with the cancer cells? Smartest guys in the world, with the best labs, funding—they don't know what to make of it.

No sentimentalist herself (remember the irony of her comments on the Donne poem), Vivian sees something of herself in this cocky young intellectual. Still a teacher, she wants to teach him something she never got to in her class.

VIVIAN: What about you?

JASON: Me? Oh, I've got a couple of ideas, things I'm kicking around. Wait till I get a lab of my own. If I can survive this . . . *fellowship*.

He is again unaware of his insensitivity: He's complaining about the difficulty of (figuratively) surviving his fellowship—to a person who cannot (literally!) survive cancer. She finally makes him aware of it: "The part with the human beings."

She has succeeded, and Jason's tone changes. But he's not going to retreat. Perhaps he knows she enjoys this discourse. Perhaps he knows she admires his tactless honesty. Once the "bedside manner" game has been discarded, there's no sense pretending it's anything other than fiction.

JASON: Everybody's got to go through it. All the great researchers. They want us to be able to converse intelligently with the clinicians. As though *researchers* were the impediments. The clinicians are such troglodytes. So smarmy. Like we have to hold hands to discuss creatinine clearance. Just cut the crap, I say.

The "cut the crap" was to her. In other words, empathy is worthless; clinicians are phonies; we both know it; you didn't hold my hand in the Donne class, and I'm not going to hold yours now; let's at least respect each other's intelligence—and honesty.

The scene finally plays out as a simple and frank discussion, with a subtext—of impending death and the limits of professional expertise (literary or medical) to ameliorate death—shared fully between them.

VIVIAN: Are you going to be sorry when I—Do you ever miss people?

JASON: Everybody asks that. Especially girls.

VIVIAN: What do you tell them?

JASON: I tell them yes.

VIVIAN: Are they persuaded?

No false bravado here, but no self-effacement either.

JASON: Some.

VIVIAN: Some. I see.   *[With great difficulty]*   And what do you say when a patient is . . . apprehensive . . . frightened?

JASON: Of who?

VIVIAN: I just . . . Never mind.

It's too much for him. He becomes doctorly again; this time, however, mainly to end the dialog before it gets too deep (for him, not for her):

JASON: Professor Bearing, who is the President of the United States?

VIVIAN: I'm fine, really. It's all right.

JASON: You sure? I could order a test—

VIVIAN: No! No, I'm fine. Just a little tired.

This is just the answer he was hoping for.

JASON: Okay. Look. Gotta go. Keep pushing the fluids. Try for 2,000 a day, okay?

VIVIAN: Okay. To use your word. Okay.

◆ S C E N E   16-3

Vivian and Jason

Now memorize, prepare, and rehearse the scene between Vivian and Jason for presentation in line with your work to this point.

Take time on your own to research the medical and scholarly language so that you can feel these words are truly coming out of your *brain*, not just your mouth. Say the difficult words in different contexts: Make up five sentences using the words *protistic* and *peritoneal cavity*, for example, and practice using them in a mock conversation (or drop them into a *real* conversation) until you can feel that it is *you* choosing to speak this way. Study and discuss with others (including your partner, if you wish) the poetry of John Donne, so you feel you can speak about Donne's work from the background of your own perspective, not just Edson's or her character's.

Dress and stage the scene: A bed would help the actor playing Vivian to feel the awkward vulnerability of a flat-on-her-back patient towered over by a standing doctor (who was once her student). And wearing a hospital gown would also help induce, in that actor, the reality of the social discomfort into which Vivian has now been thrown; as would a buttoned-to-the-neck white coat, or some equivalent, help the actor playing Jason assume the clinical air that for him is a struggle to maintain.

And if the actor playing Vivian were wearing no underwear beneath the hospital gown, which would of course be the case in a real situation, her feeling of vulnerability (to exposure, or to a doctor's sudden and casual probing) would be powerfully intensified.

All of these dressings—the bed, the gown, the lack of underwear—can be simply imagined, of course, and acting always involves imagination; as a practical matter, the no-underwear suggestion is probably better imagined (at least in a classroom setting) than actually employed.* But the support of key furniture and costume elements, particularly when they determine the physical relationships (standing, sitting, lying) and power relationships (relatively dressed and undressed) of the characters, is not mere storytelling for the audience, nor is it an acting gimmick: It conjures key elements of the situation's reality and the obstacles against which the actors must forcefully struggle, all of which will greatly intensify the acting.

Imagining the ovarian tumor destroying you, or the tasks that stand between you and a career as a brilliant medical researcher, will be a sufficient challenge in any case.

Play the scene with your partner and seek to achieve your character's goals in the context of the professional language, hospital staging, and character subtext that you and your partner have derived from these and your own discussions.

---

* In the play as performed, Vivian is wearing no underwear, as is revealed in a momentary vignette when she lets her gown fall to the floor as the play ends. "[S]he is naked and beautiful, reaching for the light," Edson writes in the stage direction.

L'Envoi

As both acting teacher and author, I have a single overriding goal, which is to have the actor not only say the playwright's lines but appear to think them up as well. This is, to me, what great acting is: to get the audience to believe that you are not only speaking Hamlet's lines but making all of his decisions: where to go, what to wear, and how to dress your hair, tie your shoelaces, and greet your friends—even though in reality these decisions have been made ahead of time by the playwright, the director, the costume designer, and a whole host of people, including you in your earlier research and rehearsals.

The goal of acting is to look like you're doing all of this right now, right before us, and in fact most great actors feel that they *are* doing it right now, right before us, even in plays written hundreds or even thousands of years ago. But this is not as easy as it sounds, as you surely have found out by now.

This immediacy of action is probably even more important in a classic play, or in a musical comedy or farce, than in the gritty realistic contemporary dramas that are written out of our own immediate experience. For while you might actually *be* the sort of contemporary college student portrayed in the current new play, you're obviously not an ancient Athenian *tyrannus*, nor a royal widow, nor, I hope, a cancer-ridden English professor specializing in John Donne. So you've got to think the part as well as do the part, and that's the long-range purpose behind the exercises, discussions, and scenes in this book.

I don't presume, of course, that addressing this single goal answers all the questions and problems of acting, or even most of them, but it does focus the dialog that goes on in the classroom and rehearsal hall. It is by thinking the characters' thoughts that you integrate your real emotional impulses with the structured dramaturgy of the play, no matter how seemingly artificial or stylized it may appear at first glance. This will help you find the level of emotional improvisation, and even the confusion, that remains at the heart of the dramatic text, no matter how sharply configured its externals may be. Ultimately, I hope you will learn how to work at the precise point where unconscious emotion flows into structured language and dramaturgy—for that's where the greatest acting lies.

Playing style and character is learned only by a great deal of practice. After all, characters are presumed to have grown up in their roles: Play a fifty-year-old Renaissance Italian, and you are playing someone who has had fifty years of daily learning to be that person. Such tasks as convincing your *tyrannus* that you speak with the authority of the gods, or negotiating your way to the crown of England, or bedding the most interesting Englishman in Naples without losing your self-respect, or speaking medical jargon with authority—these take people years to master, if they ever do. And performing these roles with passion, acuity, brio, and complete unselfconsciousness takes the confidence that only experience can bring.

The work in this book is therefore inexhaustible: Let me assure you that you can get better at every speech and scene herein for at least the next twenty years. Some roles are easily worth a lifetime of preparation; they are mountains that—to paraphrase Charles Laughton on the role of Lear—can be scaled only by stepping over the corpses of those who have so far failed to reach the summits. But do not be dissuaded, for the greatness is in the effort.

I have led you on different paths in approaching the different scenes, suggesting ways, for example, to find different-than-ordinary voices for Teiresias and Oedipus, comic physical business (OK, "shtick") for Nicomaco and Sofronia, versified dueling for Richard and Anne, a performative mini-dance for Willmore and Hellena, rhetorical tropes for Barbara and Undershaft, subtext for Masha and Vershinin, professional jargon for Jason and Vivian. We've dealt with medieval, Elizabethan, and French neoclassic verse, well-turned and halting prose, Kushner's and the Bible's angels, age and youth, city and country, tragic and farcical—all coming together, and coming into conflict, in the diversity of theatre.

And all different. There is no one way to play style because style comes from many sources: the historical period, the specific environment, the author's literary proclivities, the world of the characters, and the subcultures within that world.

And there is no single approach to character. You can quickly see that some playwrights create characters of psychological complexity and depth: Chekhov, Shakespeare, and August Wilson are clearly examples. Other dramatists who can be equally championed—Machiavelli, Moliére, and Shaw, for example—draw more on their character's theatrical, behavioral, or social positions. An understanding of the variety of theatrical construction—the way roles are created by their authors—can be immensely useful in helping you find where to look first and how to build a role that blends your appropriate features with those of the part as the dramatist conceived it.

There is no single key to performing on the stage. It is all of these things, and it is all of you.

Nothing in this book—nor nothing in style, character, and performance—contradicts any principle of basic acting, or in my own *Acting One* text. The words of George Bernard Shaw might serve to illustrate this and put a damper on the idea that plays of earlier periods, or earlier styles, can somehow be performed without the fundamental acting passion and authentic communication that are the basic acting goals of theatre professionals everywhere. Regarding Shakespearean blank verse, Shaw wrote back in 1895 (a long time before anyone outside of Russia had heard of Stanislavsky):

> To our young people studying for the stage I say . . . leave blank verse patiently alone until you have experienced emotion deep enough to crave for poetic expression, at which point verse will seem an absolutely natural and real form of speech to you. Meanwhile, if any pedant, with an uncultivated heart and a theoretic ear, proposes to teach you to recite, send instantly for the police.

Neither pedantry, nor an uncultivated heart, nor a theoretic ear, informs the discussions in this book; nor should they—or will they—in your work.

Index